# Microsoft Azure Fundamentals Certification and Beyond

## *Second Edition*

A complete AZ-900 exam guide with online mock exams, flashcards, and hands-on activities

**Steve Miles**

# Microsoft Azure Fundamentals Certification and Beyond
## *Second Edition*

Copyright © 2024 Packt Publishing

**Author**: Steve Miles

**Technical Reviewer**: Peter De Tender

**Publishing Product Manager**: Anindya Sil

**Development Editor**: M Keerthi Nair

**Senior-Development Editor**: Ketan Giri

**Production Editor**: Shantanu Zagade

**Editorial Board**: Vijin Boricha, Megan Carlisle, Ketan Giri, Saurabh Kadave, Alex Mazonowicz, Aaron Nash, Abhishek Rane, Gandhali Raut, and Ankita Thakur


First Published: January 2022

Second Edition: January 2024

Production Reference: 2060624

Published by Packt Publishing Ltd.

Grosvenor House

11 St Paul's Square

Birmingham

B3 1RB

ISBN: 978-1-83763-059-2

www.packtpub.com

# Foreword

Welcome to this Second Edition of Steve Miles' Microsoft Azure Fundamentals Certification and Beyond. Today is the first day of a life-changing event, where you will become certified in Azure.

My own career started in 1996 as a physical data center technician, messing around with power, cooling, network cables, and deploying server, storage, and network appliances for customers. The Internet was unknown, email was in its infancy, and most businesses were still using Mainframes and terminals (black screens with green- or orange-colored fonts). I had the opportunity to learn about Microsoft Windows NT4 Server in its early days and became quite proficient in deploying, managing, and troubleshooting Microsoft Server products (Exchange Server, SQL Server, Internet Information Server, and alike). I've seen the shift from physical servers to virtualization with VMware and Microsoft Hyper-V. I migrated all sorts of customer environments to Office 365 when it was a hard sell to even convince customers to move their corporate data to a cloud environment. I tasted the early bits of Project Red Dog in 2009, what eventually would become Windows Azure, and later/ now Microsoft Azure.

I'm no longer touching physical components, but I am still helping customers migrate and deploy their business-critical workloads to the cloud. Because even in the cloud, a lot of the traditional IT concepts are still valid. When deploying Azure Virtual Machines, you need to integrate storage and network. When deploying Web Apps, Identity, and Databases, while no longer managing the actual Virtual Machines, your organization still needs your knowledge and expertise on how to monitor your environment, how to troubleshoot, how to make it more reliable and highly available, etc.

All of that – and much more actually – is what you will learn from going through this book. Starting from cloud fundamental concepts, Steve takes you on a journey to learn a lot about different common Azure services. You will learn how to set up your Azure environments with governance and security in mind, how to keep costs in control, as well as how to optimize your deployments using Infrastructure as code. While the book title says it's Azure Fundamentals, allow me to say it covers substantially more than that. The good thing is, and I'm talking about my own experience, once you start understanding Azure better, you won't let go. This book will help you along the way, not only by reading through the chapters but validating your knowledge with actual exercises and skills validation questions as bonus material.

So get on that bandwagon of studying for the AZ-900 exam, but be aware, it won't be your last Azure exam to take. You will get excited, you will discover new services and capabilities while traveling to the amazing new world called Azure, and you will become a trusted cloud advisor to your organization and your customers.

Getting certified truly can be a life-changer (hey, it landed me a job at Microsoft in Redmond!). You put time and effort into learning, deploying, building, and working toward understanding more about technology. It makes you proud to be part of a worldwide club of Microsoft technology adepts like yourself. It can be a ticket for a pay rise, for a promotion, for moving to a new role… but, most of all, it's a statement to yourself that "I know this stuff…!!"

If, after reading this book, you have an appetite for more Azure learning content and are thinking of taking more Microsoft exams, make sure you bookmark the Microsoft Learn website (`https://aka.ms/learn`), with more than 3,000 modules for you to read, watch, or follow along. Azure is a dynamic platform, and so is the certification path. You will love it.

Good luck with your studying journey, and welcome to the club of Microsoft Certified Professionals and Azure enthusiast. Let me know when you have passed that exam!

**Peter De Tender**
*Microsoft Azure Technical Trainer*
*Enterprise Skills Initiative (ESI) – Microsoft World Wide Learning (WWL)*

# Contributors

## About the Author

**Steve Miles**, aka *smiles* or *Mr. Analogy*, is a **Microsoft Azure MVP, Microsoft Certified Trainer** (**MCT**), multi-cloud, and hybrid technologies author, and technical reviewer with over 25 years of experience in data center infrastructure, managed hosting, and cloud solutions. His experience comes from working in end user, reseller channel, and vendor spaces, with global networks, data and app security vendors, global telco hosters, and colocation and data center services providers, as well as in managed hosting and hardware, software, and services distribution. His roles have been varied and have included many engineering and architecture roles, as well as technical project management and most recently as Azure practice technical lead and senior technology leadership function for a multi-billion cloud distributor based in the UK and Dublin.

Most happy in front of a whiteboard, he prefers to speak using illustrations. He is renowned for his analogies for breaking down complex technologies and concepts into everyday, real-world scenarios.

His first Microsoft certifications were MCSE on Windows NT and CCNA. He has over 20 Microsoft certifications—14 of those being Azure, including Microsoft Certified Azure Expert—in addition to many other vendor certifications. He also holds PRINCE2 and ITIL. Finally, as part of the multi-cloud aspect, he has experience with GCP and AWS, is Alibaba-Cloud-certified, and is an Alibaba Cloud MVP.

I want to thank the people who have been close to me and supported me, professionally and at home; especially my wife, Pippa, aka Mrs. Smiles, and my family.

# About the Reviewer

**Peter De Tender** has an extensive background in architecting, deploying, managing, and training Microsoft technologies, dating back to Windows NT4 Server in 1996, all the way to the latest and modern cloud solutions available in Azure today. With a passion for cloud Architecture, Devops and App Migration, Peter always has a story to share on how to optimize your Enterprise-ready cloud workloads. When he's not providing a technical Azure workshop out of his role as Azure Technical Trainer at Microsoft Corp, for which he relocated from Belgium to Seattle early 2022, he's developing web apps on .NET Blazor as a new hobby. Peter was an Azure MVP for 5 years, is a Microsoft Certified Trainer (MCT) for over 13 years, and still actively involved in the community as public speaker, technical writer, book author and publisher.

You can follow Peter on X (formerly Twitter) @pdtit and read his technical blog adventures on `http://www.007ffflearning.com`.

# Table of Contents

# 4

## Azure Core Resources                                                        87

# 5

## Azure Identity and Access                                                   139

# Preface

The biggest change to the technology landscape in recent times has been triggered by the COVID-19 global pandemic; it has changed so much of what you do and how you do it forever. This has led to redefining the attitudes and approaches to hybrid working and the technology systems you use to adopt and embrace it. Azure is Microsoft's cloud computing platform and provides organizations with on-demand access to computing, storage, networking, and many other resources to meet their needs.

The content of this book, *Microsoft Azure Fundamentals Certification and Beyond, Second Edition*, is intended to provide complete coverage of the skills measured in the exam to prepare you for the Microsoft certification Exam AZ-900: Microsoft Azure Fundamentals.

This book will focus on the following key areas for the exam:

- Describing cloud concepts

- Describing Azure architecture and services

- Describing Azure management and governance

This book also aims to go beyond exam objectives. By the end of the book, you will have gained an extra depth of knowledge that will be of value in a day-to-day Azure-focused role.

## Second Edition

More than two years have passed since the first edition of this book. There have been a lot of changes to Microsoft's Azure cloud platform and the Microsoft cloud ecosystem in that time. The second edition offers updated exam "skills measured" materials to you and provides additional notes, hints, tips, and tricks to help you navigate the exam and certification process, as well as the ever-evolving world of cloud computing. The new edition now gives you unlimited access to our online practice resources platform, letting you practice what you learned in the book from any device. There, you can get access to flashcards and exam tips specially designed to help you memorize key topics and be fully prepared to ace the exam. Furthermore, in the new edition, information is organized in a way that makes it easier to test your knowledge. Some topics have also been updated to align with the revised "skills measured" for the exam and incorporate the latest innovations and advancements in the Microsoft cloud ecosystem.

# Online Practice Resources

With this book, you will unlock unlimited access to our online exam-prep platform (*Figure 0.1*). This is your place to practice everything you learn in the book.

> **How to access the resources**
>
> To learn how to access the online resources, refer *to Chapter 11, Accessing the Online Resources* at the end of this book.

Figure 0.1 – Online exam-prep platform on a desktop device

Sharpen your knowledge of AZ-900 concepts with multiple sets of mock exams, interactive flashcards, and hands-on activities accessible from all modern web browsers. If you get stuck, you can raise your concerns with the author directly through the website. Before doing that, go through the list of resolved questions as well. These are based on questions asked by other users. Finally, review the exam tips on the website to ensure you are well prepared.

# Who Is This Book For

This book is for those in commercial, operational, or technical roles looking to pass the Microsoft certification Exam AZ-900: Microsoft Azure Fundamentals. The exam is intended for candidates who are just beginning to work with cloud-based solutions and services or are new to Azure. You can learn more about the certification and exam at `https://packt.link/arKva`.

# What This Book Covers

This book is aligned with the revised syllabus of Exam AZ-900: Microsoft Azure Fundamentals and comprises the following chapters.

*Chapter 1, Introduction to Cloud Computing*, introduces cloud computing, where it has evolved from, why cloud computing is used, and the target audience. It also takes a look at the delivery and service models of cloud computing, how they compare, and the shared responsibility model.

*Chapter 2, Benefits of Using Cloud Services*, discusses cloud computing as a digital transformation enabler and the cloud computing mindset, as well as the cloud computing operations model and the economics of cloud computing.

*Chapter 3, Azure Core Architectural Components*, outlines the Azure global infrastructure that comprises the Azure regions, geographies, and availability components. In addition, this chapter explores Azure resource management topics.

*Chapter 4, Azure Core Resources*, focuses on the Azure platform's core building block resources of compute, network, and storage.

*Chapter 5, Azure Identity and Access*, explains the concepts of authentication and authorization and Identity and Access Management (IAM) and explores Microsoft Entra ID.

*Chapter 6, Azure Security*, discusses the threat landscape and explains the principles of security posture, zero trust, and Defense-in-Depth (DiD). In addition, the chapter explores cloud posture management and workload protection with Microsoft Defender for Cloud and Microsoft Sentinel security tooling.

*Chapter 7, Azure Cost Management*, explores cost management and the factors that influence costs, and it also explains the Azure pricing calculator and the Azure TCO calculator.

*Chapter 8, Azure Governance and Compliance*, explores Microsoft's Purview in Azure, Azure Policy, resources locks, and tags, as well as the Azure service lifecycle, core security, privacy and security tenets, and the Microsoft Trust Center.

*Chapter 9, Azure Resource Deployment and Management*, introduces the Azure portal, as well as Azure PowerShell, the Azure CLI, and Azure Cloud Shell. The chapter also explains Azure Resource Manager templates and Azure Arc.

*Chapter 10, Azure Monitoring and Tools,* explores actionable insights into Azure environments, using tooling such as Azure Advisor, Azure Monitor, and Azure Service Health.

*Appendix, Assessing AZ-900 Exam Skills,* focuses on the skills measured by the certification and the potential topics the exam may cover. As you become competent in each skill area, this can help in tracking progress.

## Requirements for Online Content

The online content includes interactive elements such as flashcards and exam tips. For an optimal experience, it is recommended that you use the latest version of a modern desktop (or mobile) web browser, such as Edge, Chrome, Safari, or Firefox.

## How to Get the Most Out of This Book

This book's content is intended for candidates who are just beginning to work with cloud-based solutions and services or are new to Azure; no specific knowledge is assumed or required.

To carry out any tasks to further your learning using the Microsoft Azure cloud platform, you will require the following:

- Access to an internet browser

- A Microsoft account; if you do not have one, you can create a free account at this URL: `https://packt.link/sRKgo`

- An Azure subscription that has access to create and delete resources in it; if you do not have an Azure subscription, you can create a free Azure account at this URL: `https://packt.link/hMtqw`

## Download the Color Images

We also provide a PDF file that has color images of the screenshots and diagrams used in this book. You can download it here: `https://packt.link/AZ900graphics`.

## Conventions Used

There are a number of text conventions used throughout this book:

`Code in text`: This indicates code words in text, database table names, folder names, filenames, file extensions, pathnames, dummy URLs, user input, and X (formerly Twitter) handles. Here is an example: "This is done within the shell of the OS you have installed the Azure CLI on – for example, `cmd.exe` for Windows or Bash for Linux and Mac."

**Bold**: This indicates a definition or an important word or words that you see on screen. For instance, words in menus or dialog boxes appear in bold. Here is an example: "You can also use **Cloud Shell** from a browser to have a shell environment anywhere, anytime."

Important or additional information is provided as **Note** or **Further knowledge**. They appear as follows:

> **Note**
>
> You can find the detailed AZ-900 Azure Fundamentals exam skills area in the *Appendix, Assessing AZ-900 Exam Skills* of this book.

> **Further knowledge**
>
> VMs also support nested virtualization, which allows you to run Hyper-V inside a VM. Not all VM sizes support nested virtualization; however, this is liable to change. You can find the latest information at `https://packt.link/Zkejf`.

## Get in Touch

Feedback from our readers is always welcome.

**General feedback**: If you have questions about any aspect of this book, email us at `customercare@packt.com` and mention the book title in the subject of your message.

**Errata**: Although we have taken every care to ensure the accuracy of our content, mistakes do happen. If you have found a mistake in this book, we would be grateful if you would report this to us. Please visit `https://packt.link/vFgzz` and fill in the form. We ensure that all valid errata are promptly updated in the GitHub repository, with the relevant information available in the Readme.md file. You can access the GitHub repository at `https://packt.link/YnLgV`.

**Piracy**: If you come across any illegal copies of our works in any form on the internet, we would be grateful if you would provide us with the location address or website name. Please contact us at `copyright@packt.com` with a link to the material.

**If you are interested in becoming an author**: If there is a topic that you have expertise in and you are interested in either writing or contributing to a book, please visit `authors.packtpub.com`.

## Share Your Thoughts

Once you've read *Microsoft Azure Fundamentals Certification and Beyond, Second Edition*, we'd love to hear your thoughts! Scan the QR code below to go straight to the Amazon review page for this book and share your feedback.

https://packt.link/r/1837630593

Your review is important to us and the tech community and will help us make sure we're delivering excellent quality content.

# Download a Free PDF Copy of This Book

Thanks for purchasing this book!

Do you like to read on the go but are unable to carry your print books everywhere?

Is your eBook purchase not compatible with the device of your choice?

Don't worry, now with every Packt book you get a DRM-free PDF version of that book at no cost.

Read anywhere, any place, on any device. Search, copy, and paste code from your favorite technical books directly into your application.

The perks don't stop there, you can get exclusive access to discounts, newsletters, and great free content in your inbox daily.

Follow these simple steps to get the benefits:

1. Scan the QR code or visit the link below:

https://packt.link/free-ebook/9781837630592

2. Submit your proof of purchase.

3. That's it! We'll send your free PDF and other benefits to your email directly.

# 1

# Introduction to Cloud Computing

This is the **digital** and **cloud** era, with one of the leading cloud computing platforms being **Microsoft Azure**. Now, more than ever, it is important to know how cloud computing platforms function and how the different services and resources they provide can be utilized by an organization to meet their needs.

This book provides a solid grip on the cloud concepts and the Microsoft Azure cloud computing platform. By the end of this book, you will have a thorough and complete knowledge of cloud concepts and Azure fundamentals, enabling you to pass the AZ-900 certification exam confidently and easily.

This chapter primarily focuses on the **Describe cloud concepts** module from the *Skills Measured* section of the AZ-900 Azure Fundamentals exam.

> **Note**
> You can find a detailed AZ-900 Azure Fundamentals exam skills area in the *Appendix, Assessing AZ-900 Exam Skills* of this book.

## Making the Most Out of this Book – Your Certification and Beyond

This book and its accompanying online resources are designed to be a complete preparation tool for your **AZ-900 exam**.

The book is written in a way that you can apply everything you've learned here even after your certification. The online practice resources that come with this book (*Figure 1.1*) are designed to improve your test-taking skills. They are loaded with timed mock exams, hands-on activities, interactive flashcards, and exam tips to help you work on your exam readiness from now till your test day.

**Before You Proceed**

To learn how to access these resources, head over to *Chapter 11, Accessing the Online Practice Resources*, at the end of the book.

Figure 1.1: Dashboard interface of the online practice resources

Here are some tips on how to make the most out of this book so that you can clear your certification and retain your knowledge beyond your exam:

1.  Read each section thoroughly.

2.  **Make ample notes**: You can use your favorite online note-taking tool or use a physical notebook. The free online resources also give you access to an online version of this book. Click the BACK TO THE BOOK link from the Dashboard to access the book in **Packt Reader**. You can highlight specific sections of the book there.

3.  **Chapter Review Questions**: At the end of this chapter, you'll find a link to review questions for this chapter. These are designed to test your knowledge of the chapter. Aim to score at least **75%** before moving on to the next chapter. You'll find detailed instructions on how to make the most of these questions at the end of this chapter in the *Exam Readiness Drill - Chapter Review Questions* section. That way, you're improving your exam-taking skills after each chapter, rather than at the end.

4.  **Flashcards**: After you've gone through the book and scored **75%** more in each of the chapter review questions, start reviewing the online flashcards. They will help you memorize key concepts.

5.  **Mock Exams**: Solve the mock exams that come with the book till your exam day. If you get some answers wrong, go back to the book and revisit the concepts you're weak in.

6.  **Hands-On Activities**: After completing this book, complete the hands-on activities online to improve your practical experience.

7.  **Exam Tips**: Review these from time to time to improve your exam readiness even further.

The main emphasis of this chapter is on the module that delves into cloud concepts described in the *Skills Measured* section of the **AZ-900 Azure Fundamentals exam**.

By the end of this chapter, you will be able to confidently answer questions on the following topics:

*   Cloud computing
*   The shared responsibility model
*   Cloud models, including public, private, and hybrid
*   **Infrastructure as a Service (IaaS)**
*   **Platform as a Service (PaaS)**
*   **Software as a Service (SaaS)**
*   Appropriate use cases for each cloud service model (IaaS, PaaS, and SaaS)
*   Appropriate use cases for each cloud delivery model (public, private, and hybrid)

This chapter will outline what cloud computing is, where the cloud computing model evolved from, and the evolution of cloud computing architectures, as well as look at adopting cloud computing and knowing its target audience. You will learn about the shared responsibility model, the cloud computing delivery and service models, and the characteristics and a comparison of each model.

In addition, this chapter's goal is to take your knowledge beyond the exam's content to prepare you for a real-world, day-to-day Azure-focused role.

# What is Cloud Computing?

**Cloud computing** is something of a misnomer; it is a marketing term for a technology model that may be adopted to consume computing resources and services.

As a technology platform, the **cloud** can benefit many audiences, addressing a need to access self-service, on-demand computing resources and services that are secure, governed, automated, elastic, and scalable, allowing the platform to cater to demand.

The value of a cloud provider platform is as an enabler of **digital transformation** and **innovation**. It provides quicker time to market and value and economies of scale, with an operating model that is governed, elastic, agile, and combined with a flexible cost model.

These abilities provide choices in how computing resources and services can be provided and consumed to suit an organization's needs and operating model most appropriately.

**Microsoft**, **Amazon**, **Alibaba**, and **Google** are the largest cloud platform providers. The public cloud operating model implements hardware and software at the cloud platform provider's facilities, from which they create **compute**, **storage**, **network**, and other **resources** and **services**. These are made available to all tenants on the platform, who use their portion of the shared resources and services and are billed only for what they use (or consume). The users of these **multi-tenant** (shared) computing platforms benefit through economies of scale, that is, cost reductions that can be passed on due to efficiencies in the scale of operation.

Many of these providers now offer hybrid cloud solutions, meaning the hardware, software, services, and resources can also now sit in the customer's locations, or even a third-party provider's locations, with a **control plane** that operates over a network from the cloud provider's platform locations. Microsoft's examples of this are **Azure Stack** and **Azure Arc**.

The following section will further help in learning more about Cloud Computing.

## The NIST Definition of Cloud Computing

The US government agency **National Institute of Standards and Technology** (**NIST**) defines "cloud computing" as the following:

> *Cloud computing is a model for enabling ubiquitous, convenient, on-demand network access to a shared pool of configurable computing resources (e.g., networks, servers, storage, applications, and services) that can be rapidly provisioned and released with minimal management effort or service provider interaction. This cloud model is composed of five essential characteristics, three service models, and four deployment models.*

The following are the essential characteristics of cloud model:

- On-demand self-service
- Broad network access
- Resource pooling
- Rapid elasticity
- Measured service

The service models are listed as follows:

- **SaaS**

- **PaaS**

- **IaaS**

The deployment models include the following:

- **Private Cloud**

- **Public Cloud**

- **Hybrid Cloud**

> **Note**
>
> You can find more information about NIST at `https://csrc.nist.gov/pubs/sp/800/145/final`, and `https://nvlpubs.nist.gov/nistpubs/Legacy/SP/nistspecialpublication800-145.pdf`.

Building upon this knowledge of cloud computing, the following section will delve into its evolution.

## Evolution of the Cloud Computing Model

**Cloud computing** is the evolution of the traditional computing platform and a significant shift in the IT industry; it is another model for delivering computing resources and services to an organization. *Figure 1.2* illustrates this evolution:

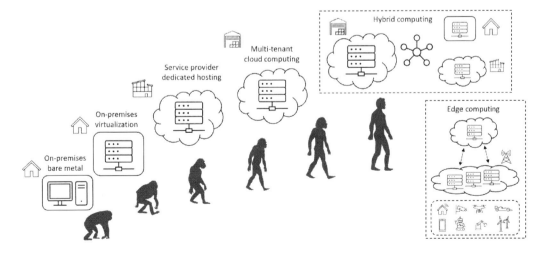

Figure 1.2 – Evolution of cloud computing

You may have evolved from physical hardware to virtualization that is run from your facilities or somebody else's to virtual machines to containers. The next stage in this evolution is the leap to **serverless**, where the **business logic layer** is the new scale unit.

Now, when dealing with various types of computing, you need to know the key difference between **public cloud computing** and **edge computing**.

The key difference between public cloud computing and edge computing is where the data processing happens. The **public cloud** is based on a "centralized" data collection, processing, and analysis approach. In contrast, **edge computing** uses a "distributed" computing model approach, where the data is collected, processed, and analyzed **locally**.

This model has benefits in terms of latency, but also for those organizations concerned with or mandated on data locality, where compliance may place strict controls on where data is stored and processed.

**Hybrid computing** aims to provide a balance of computing resources and services available anywhere, anytime. It gives businesses options and the power of choice as to the most suitable technology platform and data location for any given workload, business initiative, or scenario that needs to be supported.

Cloud computing is not only a "technical evolution" but also a "financial evolution." The expenditure model shifts from that of **Capital Expenditure** (**CapEx**) of hardware (buying upfront before you can use resources) to **Operating Expenditure** (**OpEx**) and paying as you use (consume) resources.

It should be noted that the private cloud model can contain an element of CapEx and OpEx; typically (and for the exam objectives), the primary cost expenditure model is CapEx. However, leased hardware and software are financially also considered OpEx, but that would mean building an on-premises infrastructure.

As computing platform environments have changed over time, so have the architectures.

The following section will look at the evolution of **cloud computing architectures**.

## Evolution of Cloud Computing Architectures

In this section, you will be introduced to the term **cloud-native** and the shift in mindset from the **monolith stacks** of **virtual machines** to **microservices** and **containers** and now to **serverless functions**.

This is a fundamental shift from **compute stack-centric** to **business logic-centric**, where the focus is only on the **outcomes** and not the **inputs**. Therefore, you no longer have to concern yourself with the lower layers, such as the languages, runtimes, and compute, as they are now provided as a service to consume. You provide the code, and the provider will decide how they will handle the execution of it.

The **serverless computing model** comes from another architectural shift in the compute layer and is an extension and evolution of **Platform as a Service** (**PaaS**). When you use PaaS resources to host a website or application or execute code, you still use servers, specify a set of underlying compute resources, and pay for them. In traditional hosting, this would be the server farm.

As the name suggests, you are not responsible for creating any compute resources (servers) in "serverless." Of course, there are servers involved, but the platform provider provides this compute layer; it is abstracted (removed) from your control or responsibility. Essentially, you provide your business logic layer, and they run it for you on their compute layer.

As discussed before, **serverless** is about abstracting the language runtime, **PaaS** is about abstracting the compute, and **IaaS** is about abstracting the hardware.

The term **abstract** means to remove; that is, you remove the requirement to provide the layer. You ascertain that layer as the cloud provider's responsibility to provide, scale, keep available, maintain, and so on. So, it is a layer you no longer need to know or care about.

*Figure 1.3* aims to illustrate this model of cloud computing architectures:

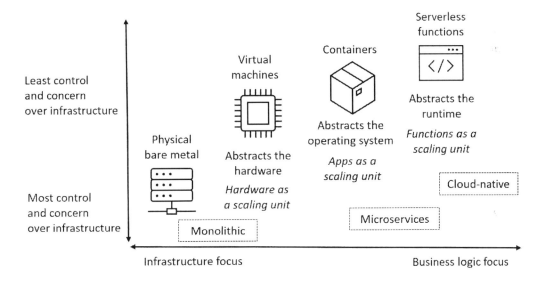

Figure 1.3 – Cloud computing architectures

*Figure 1.3* outlines where the architectures differ in their characteristics. It also outlines decision criteria to consider so that each architecture can be positioned to allow you to make the most appropriate choice for any given scenario.

This section looked at the evolution of computing platform environments and cloud computing architectures.

In the *Comparing the Cloud Computing Service Models* section, you will learn about the degrees of control each model offers.

Next you will learn why you need to adopt cloud computing.

## Why Cloud Computing?

**Cloud computing adoption** is often driven more by its **business** and **operational** model's advantages and benefits than its "technology" or "location" factors.

The benefit of the cloud computing model is that it gives another option and more choice in how computing resources can be provided and consumed by a business to suit its operating model most appropriately.

Cloud computing-based resources can be **hybrid**, so they can be located in the cloud platform provider's or customer's facilities. In the case of the **Azure Stack** portfolio (HCI, Edge, and Hub), the cloud provider platform can offer the control plane and operations platform elements.

Adopting cloud computing also does not have to be a **binary decision** between a fully public cloud or a more traditional on-premises computing model. Your compute resources and data may remain on-premises, and you may use the "cloud" for the control and operations plane. You may consider "Manage from" the cloud instead of "Move to" the cloud.

Adopting the hybrid model means having a mix of traditional on-premises and cloud computing resources; "cloud" does not always have to mean public compute resources in a provider's facility that are shared with others and accessible over a network.

The core benefits of the cloud computing model over the traditional computing model are outlined in *Figure 1.4*:

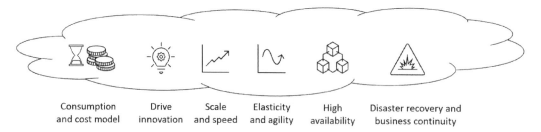

| Consumption and cost model | Drive innovation | Scale and speed | Elasticity and agility | High availability | Disaster recovery and business continuity |

Figure 1.4 – Benefits of cloud computing

Other operational advantages include no compulsion to replace failed hardware or address physical security for the public cloud, as the cloud provider manages the underlying hardware that hosts the resources. This means no CapEx to purchase hardware, although CapEx is still applicable in private cloud scenarios where hardware and facilities may be under your control. The hardware may be at a third-party hosting provider's facility that provides the hosting for your private cloud.

There is a requirement in public cloud computing environments to provide **control**, **security**, and **protection** for customer systems and data. You must ensure it is **redundant** and **available**, protect the identities that access the systems and data, govern access permissions, and manage updates.

This section outlined why you may consider adopting the cloud computing model. Cloud computing's target audience is looked at in the next section.

## Cloud Computing's Target Audience

Cloud computing can mean different things to different people depending on their perspective and their role or function. A business leader will have one idea of what cloud computing needs to deliver, which may be very different from a technology leader and may be very different from a developer, a database admin, or a data scientist. They all have specific wants and needs, so cloud computing as a model must almost be all things to everyone.

Azure typically provides the following high-level categorization of services to a business:

- Hosted infrastructure platform

- Application development platform

- Data, AI, and analytics platform

- Monitoring and management platform

- Hybrid and multi-cloud control plane platform

- Security operations platform

- Identity and compliance platform

In the context of Azure, Microsoft's cloud computing platform, these different functions are well catered for, making it relevant from all perspectives.

Azure is the only hybrid-consistent platform, combining Azure as the public cloud platform with Azure Stack as the private cloud platform while operating with other cloud platform providers and on-premises resources through **Azure Arc**.

You have now learned about the audience of cloud computing, and why it is important to consider not only the technology and process elements of adopting cloud computing but also the people element in terms of whose buy-in and sponsorship are required. You need to know who is being addressed as stakeholders of this technology model adoption, as well as learn the categorization of services available to a business, which outlines what capabilities and resources are in it for them.

The next section will discuss cloud computing's hierarchy of needs.

# Cloud Computing's Hierarchy of Needs

The IT services delivery model can draw parallels to **Maslow's hierarchy of needs**. This comes from a psychology theory, often represented in a hierarchical pyramid.

In this model, the "lower-level needs" add no value or benefit, but each lower-level need must be met before the "next-level needs" can be met, leading to "dependencies" on the lower levels.

The challenge is a delicate balance in that any change in the lower levels affects the chances of success or failure of the required outcome (higher levels); in this theory, the outcome to be achieved is "self-actualization."

This theory can be applied to the IT services delivery model. In this model, the typical technology stack provides the outcome that needs to be met, such as an app, code, or function…

- …must exist on a lower layer of **software**

- …needs to live on a lower layer of **compute**

- …needs to exist on a lower layer of **hardware**

- …needs to exist in a **physical facility**

- …needs power, cooling, **physical security**, facilities management, staffing, and so on

Just like Maslow's theory, the top-level needs "depend" on the lower levels being "fulfilled."

With the traditional computing approach, a large amount of the budget is not used to innovate but to maintain steady-state and business-as-usual operations. Resources and budget are trapped at the bottom, being used to procure hardware, and invest in data center facilities, not being utilized or benefiting from being invested in the higher-value-driver layers offering real value to the business.

It is a CapEx-constrained model; technology is seen as a "cost center" and not an "innovation center" for the business:

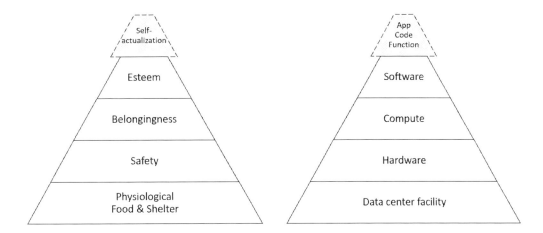

Figure 1.5 – Maslow's hierarchy versus the cloud computing hierarchy of needs

The cloud computing model aims to re-balance resource utilization and budget, allowing the cloud services provider to spend their budget and use their resources on the hardware and lower layers. This means a business can ensure its time is more effectively spent at the top, innovating, and not at the bottom, maintaining.

The goal is to move to a "flexible" and "agile" operations model, consuming only what is required from each layer down to deliver the **business need** and **value-driven outcome**.

You have now gained knowledge about the cloud computing hierarchy of needs in this section, and how the IT services delivery model can draw parallels with Maslow's hierarchy of needs.

The next section in this chapter brings to your awareness the concept of the **shared responsibility model**, one of the most misunderstood concepts of cloud computing but a critical one to know about. It underpins many decisions and their consequences for security and control measures.

## What Is the Shared Responsibility Model?

The **shared responsibility model** is a governance and control model that is critically important to grasp when operating resources and services within a public or hybrid cloud environment.

You should know when it is **your** responsibility to provide the appropriate level of control and where it is **not your** responsibility but that of the cloud service provider. This responsibility level may dictate what cloud computing service models you decide to deploy, such as IaaS, PaaS, or SaaS, to determine how much control and responsibility you must have or hand off to the cloud service provider.

There are three levels of responsibility to be considered. They are as follows:

- Responsibilities that the consumer of the cloud services **always retains**
- Responsibilities that vary by **resource type**
- Responsibilities that will **transfer** to the cloud service provider

*Figure 1.6* aims to visually set out the division or separation of responsibilities between the consumer of the cloud resources and the cloud service provider:

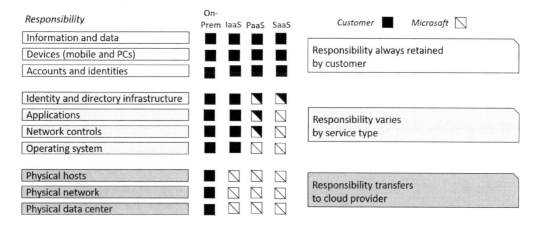

Figure 1.6 – Shared responsibility model

An important consideration in the hand off for the responsibility of the cloud platform components is that the responsibility changes depending on the cloud service model, such as IaaS, PaaS, and SaaS. The cloud service provider has "most responsibility" in the SaaS model, but "least responsibility" in the IaaS model.

For example, the cloud provider is "always responsible" for the **physical hosts**, **networks**, and **data centers** across IaaS, PaaS, and SaaS. While the cloud provider has a "shared responsibility" with the customer for the **applications** and **network controls** for the PaaS model resources, it has "no responsibility" for the **applications**, **network controls**, and **operating system** for the IaaS model resources.

By now you learned how critically important the shared responsibility model is within a public or hybrid cloud environment. The next section will focus on the delivery models in cloud computing.

# What Are the Cloud Computing Delivery Models?

Cloud computing generally has three **delivery models**: **public**, **private**, and **hybrid**. They are detailed as follows:

- **Public cloud**: This is a **shared entity** (multi-tenant) computing model. Hardware and resources, such as compute, storage, and networking, are owned by the cloud provider and shared with other tenants on the platform, in a system that is also known as multi-tenant or multi-tenancy; you may have a share in the control of the resources in the environment. Think of this as an apartment block, where you are a tenant who shares the building with other tenants and pays rent to a landlord for your apartment. In cloud computing, the landlord is the service provider.

- **Private cloud**: This is a **dedicated entity** (single-tenant) computing model. Hardware and resources, such as compute, storage, and networking, are dedicated to your organization's use only; you remain in complete control of the resources in the environment. Think of this as a house instead of an apartment block; you are a single tenant and do not share the building with any other tenants. You either own the building or rent the property and pay a landlord. A private cloud might be hardware that you own in your facility, a third-party hosting provider, or a colocation data center facilities provider. Alternatively, this could

- be the hardware they dedicate to you, such as traditional dedicated server hosting.

- **Hybrid cloud**: This is a combination of the **shared entity** (multi-tenant) and **dedicated entity** (single-tenant) computing models. Based on your requirements, you choose some computing resources to run in your private cloud environment and some to run in a public cloud environment; you may choose the location and therefore level of control of the resources. This model offers the most **agility** and **flexibility** to meet changes in demand and business requirements.

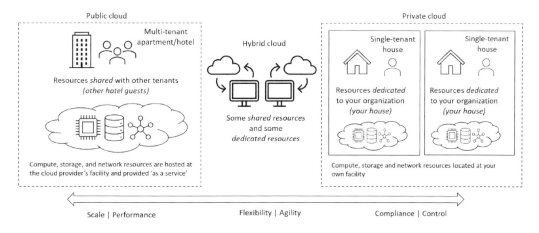

Figure 1.7 – Cloud computing delivery models

*Figure 1.7* outlines some key aspects of the public, private, and hybrid cloud delivery models.

In this section, you learned how to describe at a high level the three cloud delivery models: **public cloud**, **private cloud**, and **hybrid cloud**.

In the following section, you will compare each of these delivery models and look at the characteristics of each model in more detail.

## Comparing the Cloud Computing Delivery Models

From the last section, you can now define the cloud computing delivery models. This section looks at the characteristics of each model in more detail to help you when choosing one model over the other.

Each delivery model has several characteristics. The most appropriate model is defined by how much you want (or need) to **control**, **secure**, and **manage** your resources, for example, your apps, code, data, networks, and security. You need to consider what resources you share or need to have dedicated for your organization's use.

You can use the terms **multi-tenant** and **single-tenant** to differentiate between models that share resources and models that have dedicated resources.

You could use the analogy of a house compared to a hotel. With a house, you have a private and dedicated front door, stairs, kitchen, TV subscription service, and more. With a hotel, you have your private room dedicated to you for your sole use, but you share with other guests a front door, stairs, kitchen/restaurant, TV subscription service, and so on. *Figure 1.8* depicts an analogy:

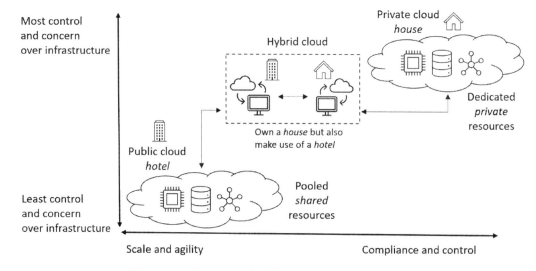

Figure 1.8 – Comparing cloud computing delivery models

Now that you have a basic knowledge of the delivery models, the next section will cover the characteristics of each delivery model in more depth.

## Characteristics of Public Cloud Computing Resources

To recap, a **public cloud** is a **shared entity** (multi-tenant) computing model. The following are the characteristics of public cloud computing resources:

- With metered pricing, consumption-based billing, and pay-as-you-go monthly usage costs, you only pay for the resources you use, allowing effective cost control.

- Almost unlimited resources are available.

- There is sound performance, scalability, and elasticity. You can enjoy the rapid, on-demand, and automated provisioning and de-provisioning of compute resources as required.

- You get availability, reliability, fault tolerance, and redundancy.

- Compute resource access is available anywhere, typically via the internet and a privately managed network, such as ExpressRoute.

- You get self-service management, typically through a web browser or a command-line interface.

- The model offers the least control over security, protection, and compliance. You do **not** have complete control over security and compliance with the public cloud model.

- Access to computing resources can be provided by **Microsoft Entra ID** (formerly named **Azure AD**) as the "cloud-native" identity and authentication layer and traditional **Windows Server Active Directory** when you synchronize the identity provider directories.

- Physical hardware is **not/cannot** be deployed to public cloud computing platforms; virtual servers are provided. However, some cloud providers allow physical hardware to be dedicated for an organization's use.

- The model may allow on-premises facilities hosting computing resources to be decommissioned.

- The expenditure model moves from a **CapEx** model to an **OpEx** model; there is no CapEx on hardware or compute resources.

The following are some examples of public cloud platforms:

- **Microsoft Azure**

- **Amazon Web Services**

- **Alibaba Cloud**

- **Google Cloud Platform**

## Characteristics of Private Cloud Computing Resources

To recap, a private cloud is a **dedicated entity** (single-tenant) computing model. The following are the characteristics of private cloud computing resources:

- Computing resources can be created on-premises at the organization's facility or can be provided at a third party's hosting facility; resources are only available within the capacity provisioned.

- A **CapEx** expenditure model is typically required for computing resources (leasing models may also be provided).

- Computing hardware (physical servers/virtualization platforms and so on) is implemented for the organization's sole use. The hardware/physical resources must be supported; failed hardware must be replaced.

- It is required to provide systems and data availability, fault tolerance, scalability, security, protection, update management, maintenance, and support.

- On-premises facilities hosting computing resources may be decommissioned in case the infrastructure resources are hosted by a third-party provider and the organization is no longer required to host its own resources.

- Computing resource access is available via a local/private network and typically will have an internet connection. However, the private cloud resources may be disconnected from the internet or have intermittent access in scenarios such as cruise ships, construction sites, Formula One teams on the trackside, and so on. In some other scenarios, such as regulated or high-security facilities such as medical, research, scientific, defense, and manufacturing, internet access may not be permitted and facilities may be disconnected from the internet. Being connected or disconnected from the internet is not a defining characteristic of private clouds.

- The same self-service management functionality and creation of resources are provided as with the public cloud computing model, but you remain in complete control of security and governance. You are also entirely responsible for purchasing, implementing, maintaining, and supporting the hardware and computing resources you provide from the private cloud platform.

- You **do** have complete control over hardware, physical resources, security, and compliance with the private cloud model.

- Traditional **Windows Server Active Directory** can provide access to computing resources as the identity and authentication layer, although **Microsoft Entra ID** (formerly named **Azure AD**) can also be utilized when connecting to public cloud computing resources.

- Physical servers **can** be deployed with the private cloud model.

The following are examples of private cloud platforms:

- **Azure Stack**
- **Red Hat OpenShift**
- **VMware vCloud Suite**

## Characteristics of Hybrid Cloud Computing Resources

To recap, a hybrid cloud combines the **shared entity** (multi-tenant) computing model and a **dedicated entity** (single-tenant) computing model. The following are the characteristics of hybrid cloud computing resources:

- You get the greatest flexibility in choosing the most appropriate location, and therefore control of computing resources and computing model.

- The hybrid cloud model allows you to create some computing resources on the service provider's public cloud computing platform, and other resources are created on your on-premises private cloud platform. These resources are connected via the internet or a private managed network such as Microsoft's **ExpressRoute** service.

- It allows bursting or extending computing resource capacity to a public cloud.

- Computing hardware (physical servers, virtualization platforms, and so on) is implemented for the organization's sole use as part of your private cloud resources. These hardware/physical resources must be supported; failed hardware must be replaced. For public cloud resources, the hardware and physical resources are provided and supported by the service provider of the public cloud resources.

- You get the greatest flexibility of access to computing resources via the internet or private networks.

- Private clouds are not necessarily disconnected from public cloud resources. Access may be provided by a private managed network such as ExpressRoute to allow a hybrid cloud approach.

- You get the greatest flexibility in security, protection, and compliance control.

- Traditional **Windows Server Active Directory** can provide access to computing resources as the primary identity and authentication layer. **Microsoft Entra ID** (formerly named **Azure AD**) can also be utilized when connecting to public cloud computing resources through a hybrid model by using directory synchronization as the link between the two identity providers for a consistent, common, or single sign-on experience.

- Physical servers can be deployed within the private and public clouds, but you cannot own them in the public cloud; they can only be rented.

- You get the greatest flexibility of the expenditure model, that is, the ability to choose CapEx or OpEx, whichever is most appropriate for the computing resources.

**Azure Stack** connected to Azure is an example of a hybrid cloud platform. This scenario could have on-premises virtual machines being replicated and backed up to Azure or an on-premises instance of **Azure Virtual Desktop** or **Azure Kubernetes Service**, for example.

You learned about the different cloud computing delivery models, how they compare, and the characteristics of each. You will take the same approach to looking at the cloud computing service models in the next section.

## What Are Cloud Computing Service Models?

**Cloud computing** is generally considered to have four service models; these are also referred to as categories. These service models are as follows:

- IaaS

- PaaS

- **Function as a Service (FaaS)**/serverless

- SaaS

*Figure 1.9* shows the relationship between these service models. Every cloud computing resource will fit into one of these categories; a solution will comprise one or more resources from each of these categories, and you select the resources from each category based on each solution's needs, taking a mix-and-match approach to tailoring a set of technology resources to map to business needs.

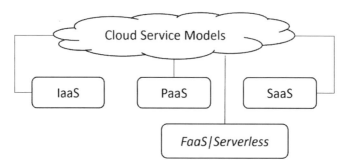

Figure 1.9 – Cloud computing service models

In this next section, you will cover quite a lot of ground as there are many concepts and aspects to present information on, not only for the exam but for knowledge beyond. You will look closely at each service model and compare and contrast the characteristics in more detail.

## A Closer Look at the Cloud Computing Service Models

**Cloud computing** is all about **abstraction**. This abstraction model approach removes layers that you no longer need to care about; the layer still exists, but it is being handled by somebody else and frees up resources to concentrate on other, more valuable layers.

The service models or categories of cloud computing define what layer of access and control the cloud service provider is responsible for and what the consumer of the cloud resources is responsible for (*Figure 1.10*).

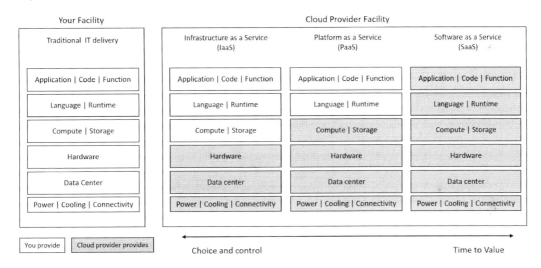

Figure 1.10 – Cloud computing service models—layer providers

You will see when looking at serverless in the next section, how you can change the unit of scale from hardware in the traditional computing model to applications or business logic (functions).

*Figure 1.10* is translated into the analogy of pizza processing (*Figure 1.11*):

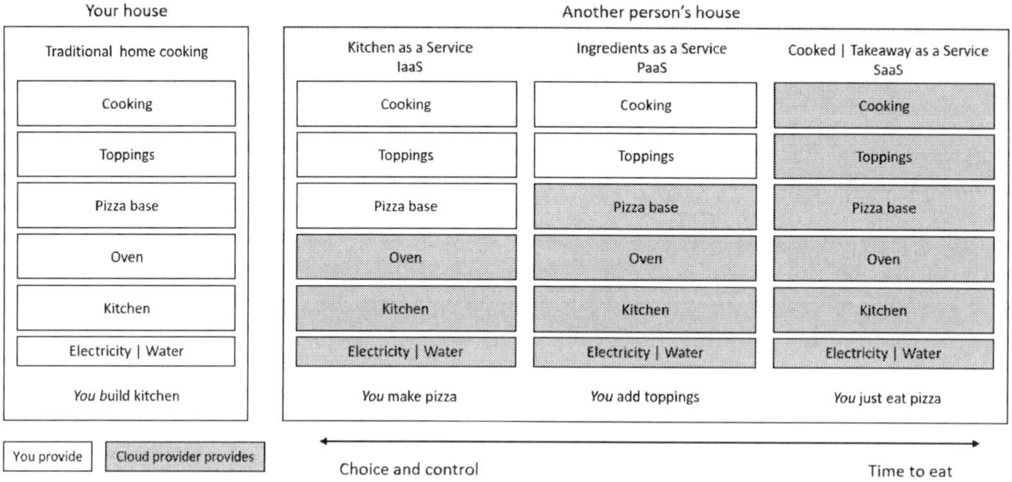

Figure 1.11 – Cloud computing service models—layer analogy of pizza processing

As you can see in *Figure 1.11*, the service model you go for is determined by the level of input and control you need.

Do you want to enjoy eating pizza as quickly as possible and you're fine to let somebody else make it, select the toppings, and cook it? The trade-off is that you do not get a say in what ingredients they use to make the pizza base, what size it is, what toppings, or how well it is cooked. But in this scenario, you accept that you do not need to know or care, so this may be the perfect scenario for you. This is an example of **SaaS**, a ready-cooked and prepared meal ready to consume, that is, "takeaway as a service."

However, to contrast that example, you may need to eat pizza but have some requirements you wish to specify. Maybe you want a particular ingredient to be used in the pizza base; maybe this is imperative as you have a specific intolerance or medical condition, so you must have control over the ingredients. You cannot guarantee this with the takeaway example as you only get that choice and control when you cook it yourself at home. So, the option with the most control is the "kitchen as a service," or **IaaS**, model.

But maybe the pizza base is not of concern; you do not want the trouble of making your pizza, as that requires time, effort, and skill even to know how to make a pizza base. So, you will let somebody else provide that for you, and it will probably be better, faster, and cheaper than you could make it. This leaves you to focus on choosing your toppings, as this is where the value and fun bit is. Pizza bases are boring, but selecting the toppings is where it gets exciting, and you want to focus on the topping ingredients. This is where the "ingredients as a service," or **PaaS** model now appeals the most.

In summary, each model has its place, depending on your needs.

In the following section, you will learn about the concept of serverless computing to know its positioning with the three service models of IaaS, PaaS, and SaaS, which you looked at in this section.

## What Is Serverless Computing?

The following is Microsoft's definition of serverless computing:

> **Serverless** *computing enables developers to build applications faster by eliminating the need to manage infrastructure. With serverless applications, the cloud service provider automatically provisions, scales, and manages the infrastructure required to run the code.*

The term **serverless** itself is a bit of a misnomer, as in reality, there are servers involved, much like how **wireless** does have wires involved at a certain point in the solution. The servers do exist, but you do not need to know that they exist for you to have your desired outcome met. This comes back to the topic of abstraction: the same layers still exist, and there are still servers that execute the code passed down from the runtime layer. It is just that the server layer is now further abstracted from you than it was in the IaaS and PaaS models.

The benefit of this further abstraction is that there are even fewer components to create and manage. This allows development teams to focus on writing their core code without considering what's running it; the provider automatically provides the resources needed to run the code. That means faster and more productive development teams, fewer operational overheads for DevOps teams, more significant innovation, and quicker time to value and return on investment for development resources.

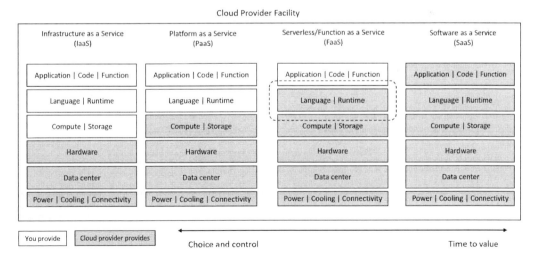

Figure 1.12 – Cloud computing service models—compare and contrast

Some of the caveats of serverless are as follows:

- Event-based workloads are the best use case

- Long-running tasks are not well suited to serverless

- The execution environment cannot be customized

- The cloud provider supports specific languages and runtimes

You learned, in this section, about the four **service models** of cloud computing: **IaaS**, **PaaS**, **FaaS/serverless**, and **SaaS**.

In the following section, these cloud computing **service models** will be compared.

# Comparing the Cloud Computing Service Models

Each service model has its characteristics. The most appropriate model is defined by how much you want or need to control, secure, and manage your resources, for example, your apps, code, data, networks, and security. In the last section, you learned about the service models. In this section, you will look at the characteristics of each model in more detail to know when you may choose one service model over the other.

## Characteristics of IaaS

In a nutshell, IaaS is a model where you can host your virtual machines and infrastructure services on hardware provided for you and shared with other tenants.

The cloud provider is responsible for providing all layers up to and including the hardware. You are responsible for providing all layers above the hardware layer (refer to *Figure 1.12*).

The following are the characteristics of IaaS:

- You create the **Virtual Machine** (**VM**) (installing the OS and software), storage, and computing resources as you would in a traditional on-premises computing model; this can be likened to a virtual data center. There is the ability to provide fault tolerance and redundancy through availability solutions in case of failure within an Azure data center, zone, or region.

- You can increase resources such as processors, memory, and virtual machine storage by using self-service without requiring redeploying or creating a new virtual machine of the required specifications.

- Based on the **OpEx** model, you only pay for resources you consume on a "pay-as-you-go basis." You only pay for a virtual machine while it's running; therefore, your month-to-month running charges may differ across virtual machines if you run them for different amounts of hours in the month. You will not be charged while a machine is in the stopped/deallocated state. Storage costs will still be charged if you persist data on disks.

- You get the greatest control and flexibility to deploy, configure, manage, and support resources as you require. IaaS requires the greatest management, administrative, and operations overhead.

- You have direct access and complete control over virtual machines, the OS, and any roles/ services, such as web servers, application servers, and SQL servers, that may be required to be installed/running on the virtual machines. You also have complete control over networking, security, and protection decisions.

The following are examples of Microsoft IaaS resources:

- Azure Virtual Machines

- Azure Storage

- Azure networking

## Characteristics of PaaS

In a nutshell, PaaS is a model where you host your application, code, data, and business logic on compute, and storage resources that are secured and isolated from other tenants.

The cloud provider is responsible for providing all layers up to and including the compute layer. You are responsible for providing all layers above the compute layer (refer to *Figure 1.12*).

The following are the characteristics of PaaS:

- PaaS provides a ready-to-use environment and platform for the fast deployment of hosting web applications, code, business logic, data, and so on. Using pre-deployed resources, development frameworks, languages, and runtimes provided as a service, there is a quicker time to value and consumption of the service.

- PaaS provides on-demand autoscaling.

- You have the ability to increase resources by changing the pricing tier of the service by using self-service. You must still select underlying compute resources sizing to host your app, code, and so on.

- You have no direct access to or control over the virtual machines or any applications, services, or roles that may be installed. Also, you do not get to specify or control which versions are available.

- PaaS gives you the least control and flexibility because the service provider is responsible for the compute and storage resources layer. Still, it requires the least management, administrative, and operations overhead.

The following are examples of Microsoft PaaS services:

- Azure App Service
- Azure SQL Database
- Cosmos DB
- Azure Files
- Azure Active Directory Domain Services

## Characteristics of FaaS (Serverless)

In a nutshell, **FaaS** is a model where you provide your code and business logic, and the cloud provider hosts it in their language, runtime, and compute environment, which is shared with other tenants.

The cloud provider is responsible for providing all layers up to and including the language, runtime, and compute. You are responsible for providing all layers above, that is, the business logic layer (refer to *Figure 1.12*).

The characteristics of FaaS are as follows:

- Azure Functions is a serverless code engine. It has the use case of events that trigger code; the Azure Functions code that is executed is a response or action based on an event trigger.
- Azure Logic Apps is a serverless workflow engine. It has the use case of events that trigger workflows. A Logic Apps workflow is a response or action based on an event trigger.
- You only have control over your application, code, and business logic layers. All other layers are provided as a service that you have no access to or control over. Essentially, you take the layers supplied to you and use them to execute (run/launch) your code/workflow. Using the pizza analogy covered earlier in this chapter, this is much like what could be described as a "take-and-bake" approach. Ultimately, you are still responsible for cooking. Still, the FaaS has provided all the layers below that, so the solution is ready to cook, as it were, much like a microwave meal.
- FaaS provides the least control and flexibility but abstracts all the layers below, providing the least amount of deployment, configuration, and maintenance, so you can focus on the application, code, and business logic layers, where the value is, without needing to be concerned about the lower layers.

The following are examples of Microsoft serverless resources:

- Azure Functions
- Azure Logic Apps

## Characteristics of SaaS

In a nutshell, SaaS is a model where you consume an application provided for you and share it with other tenants.

The cloud provider is responsible for providing all layers up to and including the applications. You are not responsible for any layers other than the configuration and consumption of the app (see *Figure 1.12*).

The following are the characteristics of SaaS:

- The cloud provider installs the application/solution and is responsible for its updates, scalability, availability, and security.

- SaaS provides the best time to value as there is no development time or resources required to create an application. It can be directly configured as needed and used instantly.

- In the pizza analogy, all the layers are taken care of, so all you need to do is just eat; this is the classic **takeaway** approach.

- SaaS provides the minimum amount of control and input on the lower layers.

The following are examples of a Microsoft SaaS solution:

- Microsoft Teams
- Microsoft Exchange Online
- Microsoft SharePoint Online
- Microsoft OneDrive
- Microsoft Dynamics 365

The following are examples of other vendors' SaaS solutions:

- Zoom
- Salesforce
- Dropbox
- Google Mail/Google Docs

This section covered the service models of IaaS, PaaS, and SaaS and introduced the concept of serverless computing as an extension of PaaS. You compared and contrasted each service model and outlined the characteristics unique to a particular model and those common across the models. This concludes the learning content for this chapter.

## Summary

This chapter included complete coverage of the AZ-900 Azure Fundamentals exam skills area: **Describe cloud concepts**.

In this chapter, you learned how to define cloud computing; describe the shared responsibility model; define cloud models, including public, private, and hybrid; identify appropriate use cases for each cloud model; describe the consumption-based model; describe IaaS; describe PaaS; describe SaaS; and identify appropriate use cases for each cloud service (IaaS, PaaS, and SaaS).

Further knowledge beyond the required exam content was provided to prepare you for a real-world, day-to-day, Azure-focused role. In the next chapter, you will look at the benefits of using cloud services.

## Exam Readiness Drill – Chapter Review Questions

Apart from a solid understanding of key concepts, being able to think quickly under time pressure is a skill that will help you ace your certification exam. That is why working on these skills early on in your learning journey is key.

Chapter review questions are designed to improve your test-taking skills progressively with each chapter you learn and review your understanding of key concepts in the chapter at the same time. You'll find these at the end of each chapter.

> **How To Access These Resources**
>
> To learn how to access these resources, head over to the chapter titled *Chapter 11, Accessing the Online Resources*.

To open the Chapter Review Questions for this chapter, perform the following steps:

1.  Click the link – `https://packt.link/AZ900E2_CH01`.

    Alternatively, you can scan the following **QR code** (*Figure 1.13*):

Figure 1.13 – QR code that opens Chapter Review Questions for logged-in users

2.   Once you log in, you'll see a page similar to the one shown in *Figure 1.14*:

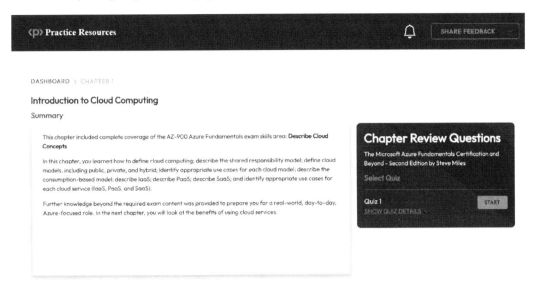

Figure 1.14 – Chapter Review Questions for Chapter 1

3.   Once ready, start the following practice drills, re-attempting the quiz multiple times.

## Exam Readiness Drill

For the first three attempts, don't worry about the time limit.

### ATTEMPT 1

The first time, aim for at least **40%**. Look at the answers you got wrong and read the relevant sections in the chapter again to fix your learning gaps.

### ATTEMPT 2

The second time, aim for at least **60%**. Look at the answers you got wrong and read the relevant sections in the chapter again to fix any remaining learning gaps.

## *ATTEMPT 3*

The third time, aim for at least **75%**. Once you score 75% or more, you start working on your timing.

> **Tip**
> You may take more than **three** attempts to reach 75%. That's okay. Just review the relevant sections in the chapter till you get there.

# Working On Timing

Target: Your aim is to keep the score the same while trying to answer these questions as quickly as possible. Here's an example of how your next attempts should look like:

| Attempt | Score | Time Taken |
| --- | --- | --- |
| Attempt 5 | 77% | 21 mins 30 seconds |
| Attempt 6 | 78% | 18 mins 34 seconds |
| Attempt 7 | 76% | 14 mins 44 seconds |

Table 1.1 – Sample timing practice drills on the online platform

> **Note**
> The time limits shown in the above table are just examples. Set your own time limits with each attempt based on the time limit of the quiz on the website.

With each new attempt, your score should stay above **75%** while your "time taken" to complete should "decrease". Repeat as many attempts as you want till you feel confident dealing with the time pressure.

# Additional Information and Study References

This section provides links to additional exam information and study references:

- **Microsoft Learn certification further information**:

  - AZ-900 - Microsoft Azure Fundamentals exam guide: `https://learn.microsoft.com/en-us/learn/certifications/exams/az-900/`

  - AZ-900 - Microsoft Azure Fundamentals study guide: `https://learn.microsoft.com/en-us/credentials/certifications/resources/study-guides/az-900`

- **Microsoft Learn training further information**:

  - AZ-900 - Microsoft Azure Fundamentals course: `https://learn.microsoft.com/en-gb/training/courses/az-900t00`

# 2

# Benefits of Using Cloud Services

In *Chapter 1, Introduction to Cloud Computing*, you learned to define cloud computing, describe the delivery and service models, and compare characteristics and use case scenarios.

This chapter will outline the benefits and value of cloud computing and its position as a digital transformation enabler; you'll get the cloud mindset that should be adopted compared to the traditional computing mindset.

This chapter will also cover cloud computing's operations model and close with the economics of cloud computing and the foundational change of the cost expenditure model.

This chapter primarily focuses on the **Describe cloud concepts** module from the *Skills Measured* section of the AZ-900 Azure Fundamentals exam.

> **Note**
>
> You can find a detailed AZ-900 Azure Fundamentals exam skills area in the *Appendix, Assessing AZ-900 Exam Skills* of this book.

By the end of this chapter, you will be able to answer questions on the following confidently:

- High availability and scalability in the cloud
- Reliability and predictability in the cloud
- Protection and recovery in the cloud
- The consumption-based model
- Cloud pricing models

In addition, this chapter's goal is to take your knowledge beyond the exam content so you are prepared for a real-world, day-to-day Azure-focused role.

# Cloud Computing as a Digital Transformation Enabler

**Digital transformation** is disruptive, a growth catalyst, and foundational in changing how an organization will deliver "time to value."

*Figure 2.1* outlines the value that cloud computing as a digital transformation enabler can realize for an organization:

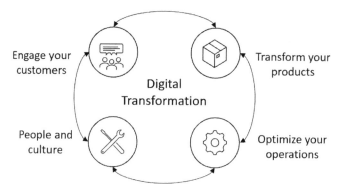

Figure 2.1 – Cloud computing as a digital transformation enabler

**Cloud computing** can be seen as a vital part of any digital transformation journey. However, the reality is that it is less about the "technology model" and more about the "business model," the "people," and the "process."

It is a fact that people do not like change and generally only change direction when they have to. However, there must be a "trigger" to induce the action.

Next, you will look at digital transformation triggers.

## Digital Transformation Triggers

The reason to adopt any disruptive technology, especially one that can have a business impact, must start with a "trigger" that's relevant to the stakeholder's pain points or objectives and any business operations or technical operations drivers.

This move often begins with a "business directive-led" discussion rather than a "technology-led" one. A business leader will always ask a technology leader what the benefits are, **not** the features.

The approach to digital transformation comprises steps to identify and resolve triggers. Once triggers have been identified, an approach can be planned. You can think of the triggers as the "why" and the approach as the "how."

*Figure 2.2* outlines some of the triggers for digital transformation initiatives:

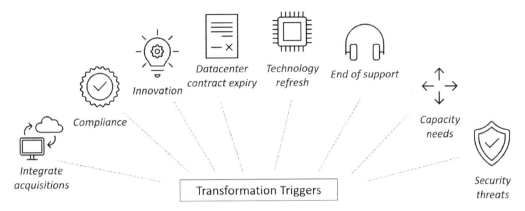

Figure 2.2 – Digital transformation triggers

These triggers are an important aspect of defining your cloud adoption strategy and driving your priorities. Knowing the rationale and motivation for adopting cloud resources and migrating your workloads is important. The following section looks at the migration approach.

## Migration Approach

The next step in the transformation journey is to grasp the processes, methods, and services that could be used to execute the transition to cloud services. This is outlined in the following list, along with the example services that can be applied:

1.  **Phase 1 | Assess**: This phase is an exercise in learning an organization's business operations and technical operations. It starts with discovery, which provides an inventory of people, processes, apps, data, infrastructure, and, critically, any dependencies. This will help you decide on the best strategy for each area of the captured inventory.

    Here are some example services for this phase:

    *   Azure Migrate Assessments: `https://packt.link/kco1y`

    *   Azure TCO calculator: `https://packt.link/Mvleh`

2.  **Phase 2 | Move**: This phase is the physical exercise of moving inventory items to their cloud services target, for instance, moving to **Software as a Service (SaaS)**, **Infrastructure as a Service (IaaS)**, **Platform as a Service (PaaS)**, or serverless cloud computing services.

    An example service for this phase is Azure Migrate migrations:
    `https://packt.link/Pqxsr`

3. **Phase 3 | Optimize**: This phase occurs after a period of bedding in – typically a period of months. This may include right-sizing activities better to suit the workload for cost and performance benefits.

   Here are some example services for this phase:

   - Azure Advisor: `https://packt.link/BMrtC`

   - Cost Management: `https://packt.link/pWPJc`

4. **Phase 4 | Secure and Manage**: This ongoing operations phase should include governance and control, security, and the protection of the network, app, data, and identities.

   Here are some example services:

   - Azure Monitor: `https://packt.link/qVNZd`

   - Azure Policy: `https://packt.link/CCvK6`

   - Microsoft Defender for Cloud: `https://packt.link/Nk8FJ`

   - Microsoft Sentinel: `https://packt.link/YdwLd`

   - Azure Backup: `https://packt.link/KfDYD`

   - Azure Site Recovery: `https://packt.link/JLP5V`

   - Azure Firewall: `https://packt.link/oZNM9`

   - Azure App Gateway/Web Application Firewall: `https://packt.link/sWRl1`

You have explored cloud computing as a digital transformation enabler, the triggers, and the migration approach in this section. The following section will look closely at the cloud computing mindset.

# Cloud Computing Mindset

The biggest challenge to cloud adoption is not technology but changing the "mindset" and "culture" within an organization.

The same thing has been happening with **DevOps** over the years. The realization over time has been that "DevOps" is not a technology or a job title but a "cultural shift" in a people and process model. To facilitate knowledge, this chapter will explain the terms, such as **Capital Expenditure (CapEx)** and **Operating Expenditure (OpEx)**, referenced in the following section.

The next section explores different mindsets that have been helpful in the adoption of cloud computing.

## What Is a Traditional Computing Model Mindset?

The following is an outline of the traditional computing model mindset:

- CapEx cost expenditure model

- Over-provision for peak demand and build in five-year growth from day one

- Fixed size and scaling approach

- Placing an order three months before you need it due to procurement lead times and project deployment times

- Monolithic, tightly coupled infrastructure stack approach

- Always-on 24/7 operation

The following section compares and contrasts the traditional computing model mindset with the cloud computing mindset.

## What Is a Cloud Computing Mindset?

The following outlines a cloud computing model mindset that you can compare with a traditional computing mindset:

- OpEx cost expenditure model

- Usage versus provisioning; just-in-time, demand-driven provisioning

- Cloud computing is designed to be elastic, scale in and out, and burst to meet demand

- Consume and pay for what you use for as long as you need it when you need it; shut down or pause when you do not

- Microservices, loosely coupled, business logic-centric approach

- Cloud-agnostic thought pattern

Now that you have learned about the cloud computing mindset and how it differs from the traditional cloud computing mindset, the following section looks at the computing operating model, one of the key differentiators between traditional and cloud computing.

# Cloud Computing Operations Model

Cloud computing is "elastic," "scalable," "agile," "fault-tolerant," highly "available," and helps with "disaster recovery." These operational model characteristics in cloud computing add value and benefit an organization's operational model.

These inherent and defining characteristics allow a workload deployed into a cloud computing environment to become highly available and scale in and out (both vertically and horizontally), which maps closely to demand. This ability to be elastic in nature allows the agility to provide a highly effective operations and economics model to flex with the changing demands of a business.

By optimizing running hours and right-sizing resources in line with demand and changing requirements, switching to a consumption-based system of paying as you use resources allows monitored spending without the over-commitment of a traditional computing cost model.

*Figure 2.3* outlines the computing resources demand model and shows the implications of actual demand against implemented resources based on predicted demand:

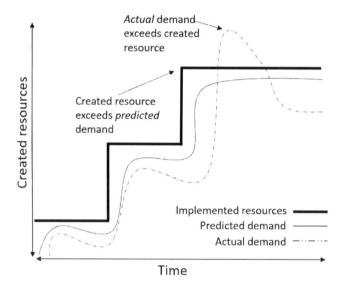

Figure 2.3 – Cloud computing resource demand model

You can also see the traditional computing mindset from the last section in *Figure 2.4*. This traditional computing mindset means over-provisioning resources to meet predicted demand, leaving many resources underutilized. When actual demand exceeds the predicted demand, no resources are available as there is no burst capacity or scale to meet the demand. To compound things, this demand has dropped off by the time these extra resources have been implemented and are no longer needed.

With the cloud computing mindset, resource utilization can be tracked and right-sized to demand. So, there is never a case of over-provisioning and paying for more resources than are needed.

With this knowledge of the cloud computing operations model, you will look more closely at the characteristics of cloud computing that deliver benefits and value over the traditional computing model.

## Operational Benefits of Cloud Computing

This section will look at the operational benefits cloud computing can add to an organization compared to those provided in a traditional computing model. Cloud computing platforms primarily provide the following operational benefits over traditional computing models:

- Scalability

- Elasticity

- Agility

- High availability (and geo-distribution)

- Disaster recovery

- Cost model

These operational benefits may be an inherent built-in platform function that provides features as part of the service, as is typically the case with **PaaS** or **Function as a Service** (**FaaS**) and SaaS. These operational benefits just need to be enabled in some cases, if not automatically included as part of the services.

These operational benefits could also be something that needs to be designed into part of the solution as an individual set of resources that need to be implemented to enable these characteristics.

For example, **IaaS** virtual machines will not provide scale, elasticity, high availability, and disaster recovery without these being designed into the solution and then implementing resources to provide the functionality to provide each of these characteristics.

The key takeaway is that cloud platform providers will generally provide these functions and characteristics. You may layer on additional functionality as your needs dictate.

Of course, not everything is perfect with the cloud computing model. Here are some challenges that can be overcome but must be considered and provided for:

- Network dependency—that is, reliability, stability, quality, and performance

- **Confidentiality, Integrity, Availability** (**CIA**) of users, apps, and data

- Access control and operational governance

- Cost control

With the operational benefits and challenges considered in this section, it is time to look at the benefits of cloud computing in more detail.

## What Is Scalability?

**Scalability** refers to how to react to and increase resources based on demand, usually in an automated way triggered upon a metric such as a time or resource threshold being reached. The following two concepts are related to the scalability of computing resources:

- **Scaling up** (vertical scaling): This means capacity is increased within the resource, such as increasing the processor or memory by resizing a virtual machine; the opposite is "scaling down," where resource capacity is decreased.

- **Scaling out** (horizontal scaling): This means additional resource instances, such as adding other virtual machines or compute node/scale units; the opposite is "scaling in," where resource instances are de-allocated.

Scalability should not be confused with **fault tolerance**, which moves a workload automatically to another resource or system when it detects a failure or unhealthy state.

## What Is Elasticity?

**Elasticity** refers to the ability to shape the resources needed automatically, to burst and scale to meet any peak in demand, and to return to a normal operating baseline.

## What Is Agility?

**Agility** means deploying and configuring resources effectively and efficiently in a short space of time to meet any change in requirements or operational needs.

## What Is High Availability?

**High availability** and **geo-distribution** mean deploying resources to operate within the required or mandated **Service-Level Agreement (SLA)** for those resources. An **SLA** sets out an expected level of service that a customer can expect from their service provider. This agreement will set out terms such as availability metrics, service availability, responsibilities, claims, and credit processes, as well as the vocabulary and terminology that will be used to express these aspects of the agreement.

The SLA is a guaranteed measure of uptime, which is the amount of time services are online, available, and operational. The following are the concept of availability in the context of computing and systems:

- **Availability** is the percentage of time a resource is available to service requests.

- **Service availability** is expressed as the uptime percentage over time, for example, 99.9%.

- Availability depends on **resilient systems**, meaning that a system can continue to function after recovering from failures.

- Increasing availability often results in an increase in costs due to the complexity of the solutions required to deliver the level of availability.

- **Failover** is another critical factor in availability. This means one system takes over from another when a resource fails and becomes unavailable and is part of an availability and disaster recovery strategy.

Microsoft defines an SLA as follows:

> *Microsoft's commitments to uptime and connectivity, meaning the amount of time the services are online, available, and operational.*

Microsoft provides each service with an individual SLA that will detail what is covered by the agreement and any exceptions. For any service that does not meet the guarantees, a percentage of the monthly fees are eligible to be credited; each service has its own defined SLA.

While you see lots of references to **availability** and **uptime** when looking at an SLA that will be provided for a service, the customer and consumer of the services will want to know what that means in the real world and what impact any breach may have on them. Therefore, it is often the case that the real metric that matters is **downtime**, which means for a given SLA, how long is that service permitted to be down (that is, the service is not available from the service provider)? You should scrutinize any SLA to determine whether that level of downtime is acceptable.

The service availability depends on the number of nines (as in the three nines is 99.9% and five nines is 99.999%) of the SLA. Microsoft SLAs are expressed on a monthly basis, so **99.9%** would have an allowed service downtime of **43.2 minutes** per month.

*Table 2.1* illustrates examples of SLA commitments and downtime permitted per month as part of an SLA:

| SLA of a Service | Permitted Downtime Per Month |
| --- | --- |
| 99.9% | 43m 28s |
| 99.95% | 21m 44s |
| 99.99% | 4m 21s |
| 99.999% | 26s |

Table 2.1 – The SLA for a service indicating the acceptable level of downtime per month

Observe that 99.9% is the minimum SLA that Microsoft provides; 99.999 % is the maximum. It should be noted that 100% cannot be provided by Microsoft.

You should also be aware of the concept of a **composite** SLA; this means that when you combine services (such as virtual machines and the underlying services such as storage, networking components, and so on), the overall SLA is lower than the individual highest SLA on one of the services. This is because each service that you add increases the probability of failure and increases complexity.

The following actions will "positively" impact and "increase" your SLA:

- Using services that provide an SLA (or improve the service SLA), such as **Entra ID Premium editions** and **Premium SSD managed disks**

- Adding redundant resources, such as resources to additional/multiple regions

- Adding availability solutions, such as using availability sets and availability zones

The following actions will "negatively" impact and "decrease" your SLA:

- Adding multiple services due to the nature of **composite SLAs**

- Choosing **non-SLA-backed** services or free services

The following actions will have **no** impact on your SLA:

- Adding multiple tenancies

- Adding multiple subscriptions

- Adding multiple admin accounts

The Azure status page (`https://packt.link/DdVgV`) provides a global overview of the service health across all regions; this should be the first place you visit, should you suspect there is a wider issue affecting the availability of services globally. From the status page, you can click through to Azure Service Health in the Azure portal, which provides a personalized view of the availability of the services that are being used within your Azure subscriptions.

**Service credits** are paid through a claims process by a service provider when they do meet the guarantees of the agreed service level; each service has its own defined SLA. You should evaluate all your services to ensure that, where required, you always have an SLA-backed service; as they say, there is often an operational impact that's felt from "free services".

If you suspect that your services have been affected and that Microsoft has not been able to meet its SLA, then it is your responsibility to take action and pursue credit; you must submit a claim to receive service credit. For most services, you must submit the claim the month after the month the service was impacted. If your services are provided through the Microsoft **Cloud Solution Provider** (**CSP**) channel, they will pursue this claim on your behalf and provide the service refunds accordingly.

> **Note**
> You can find more details about Microsoft SLAs for Azure services and the composite SLA at `https://packt.link/X5G0B` and `https://packt.link/qzOnf`.

### What Is Disaster Recovery?

**Disaster recovery** is based upon a set of practices or measures to ensure that, when a system fails, it can be restored to operation by failing over to a replicated instance in another region.

A "disaster recovery strategy" will be determined by the required **Recovery Time Objective (RTO)** and **Recovery Point Objective (RPO)**. Replication technologies allow for much shorter RTOs and RPOs that can be achieved with backups. The following are the crucial elements in creating comprehensive disaster recovery plans:

- **RTO**: This refers to the maximum duration of acceptable **downtime** for the system.
- **RPO**: This refers to how much **data loss** is acceptable to a system.

This is represented in *Figure 2.4*:

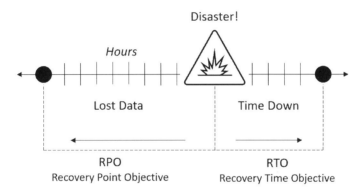

Figure 2.4 – RTO and RPO

Having grasped the operational benefits, read on to compare disaster recovery to high availability and backup concepts.

## Comparing Disaster Recovery, High Availability, and Backup

High availability and disaster recovery can be classified as **system protection**, whereas backup can be classified as **data protection**. The following concepts help in building robust and resilient systems in cloud computing environments like Microsoft Azure:

- **High availability**: When systems fail and are not available, you can run a second instance in the same Azure region.
- **Disaster recovery**: When systems fail and are not available, you can run a second instance in another Azure region.
- **Backup**: When data is corrupted, deleted, lost, or irretrievable (perhaps due to ransomware), you can restore the instance from another copy of the system.

*Figure 2.5* outlines the three preceding points of high availability, disaster recovery, and backup:

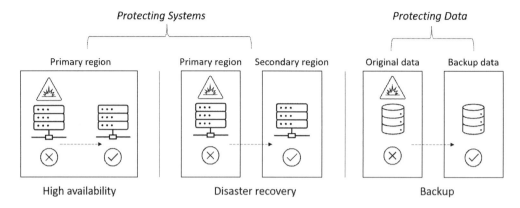

Figure 2.5 – Comparing backup, high availability, and disaster recovery

High availability, disaster recovery, and backup should not be an "either-or" decision in a strategy for business continuity; any strategy should include "all three" as they serve different purposes.

**Fault tolerance** is a means of providing high availability in systems. It is similar to Auto Scale, in which workloads can be moved from one system to another. The trigger for fault tolerance is a health check on a failed system, as opposed to a system under load from demand.

## Challenges of Implementing Business Continuity

**Cost**, **complexity**, and **compliance** are the biggest challenges for business continuity. These challenges result in systems that are often not covered by disaster recovery or protected by backups, which challenges your ability to comply with any regulatory or internal mandatory policy.

While you may be familiar with the traditional causes of a disaster or business disruption, a threat to business operations can also come from a "global pandemic." Mitigation and planning for a pandemic have not often been included in a disaster recovery or business continuity strategy.

While not a disaster or outage, a "pandemic" certainly causes a significant business disruption that almost nobody can foresee. It is reasonable to say that those who had already adopted some form of cloud services and a remote working strategy before the COVID-19 pandemic were probably better prepared than others.

*Figure 2.6* shows that when you adopt a cloud computing model, your cost model changes; you may have reduced complexity, and your compliance levels may increase:

Figure 2.6 – Challenges to implementing business continuity

Adopting a cloud strategy utilizing Microsoft Azure can address many of these challenges. The challenges are often centered around costs, and the benefit and driver can be the changing cost model that can be provided by the cloud.

An additional benefit is that there is no need to maintain and purchase the resources required for a secondary site. With Microsoft Azure as the secondary site, only what is used is paid for in a consumption-based model.

From the content in this section, you have now learned about the cloud computing operations model, including aspects of the demand model, and operational benefits, as well as comparing disaster recovery, high availability, and backup. The following section will cover the economics of cloud computing, the consumption model, and the cost-expenditure model.

# Economics of Cloud Computing

This section will look at the **consumption-based model**, one of the two economic characteristics of cloud computing. The second economic characteristic that cloud computing is based on is the **cost-expenditure model** of **operational expenditure**.

## Consumption Model

In a nutshell, a consumption model means paying only for the time you use the resource. This can be likened to leasing/renting something instead of purchasing and owning the asset outright.

Some resources, such as virtual machines, can be stopped and started to reduce costs, so you only pay while running them. This is one of the key business benefits of the cloud computing cost model over a traditional computing cost model.

Now take a closer look at the cost-expenditure models.

## Defining the Expenditure Models

It is essential to know the finance terms CapEx and OpEx. The details are as follows:

- **CapEx**: This is the "upfront commitment" of a large amount of money to purchase assets, such as investment in data center facilities, network circuit implementation, physical hardware, or software, as a "one-off payment" that you then own for the lifespan of those assets. You can liken this to the model of purchasing a vehicle or a mobile phone handset outright with a sum of money. You own it until it needs replacing, so you have to find another lump sum of money to reinvest to purchase another one in a few years.

- **OpEx**: Essentially, a **pay-as-you-go** model for consuming assets and resources is the ongoing running costs, which require a recurring payment when the asset or resource is required and in use to deliver services or functionality to a business. This could include staffing costs, data center facility management costs, power, and software that is not purchased outright but leased on a subscription basis.

    There is no upfront commitment of money to buy assets. Every month, you pay only for the amount you use during a certain period. You can liken this to the model of renting a vehicle or mobile phone handset and paying every month. You never own the asset but use it for as long as you need. You may swap it, upgrade it, and downgrade it as you wish within the terms.

*Figure 2.7* aims to represent this:

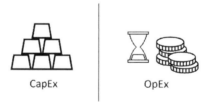

CapEx                OpEx

Figure 2.7 – Cost expenditure models

The value of cloud computing to a business is not so much the **technology** but the **economic model** it provides. The utilization of the cost model is often the value driver, with the technology being secondary.

You have learned about the cost expenditure models for a business that apply to cloud computing and traditional computing models. It is time to look at how those expenditure models are used and the benefits and value of cloud computing's cost model.

## Applying Cost Expenditure Models to Cloud Computing

In the traditional computing model (pre-cloud platforms), hardware resources and software were purchased upfront with a one-off lump sum. These business assets would be seen as depreciating assets; this is the CapEx model.

In contrast to the public cloud computing model, resources provided by the cloud platform are shared with others. This means there has been "no CapEx" to provision hardware, so you can start using these resources on demand. These resources are treated as day-to-day "OpEx."

The exception is **reserved instance resources**, where you can commit to a usage term of one to three years, paying upfront (or monthly) on a CapEx basis to reserve predicted resource usage. This is more cost-effective over a one- to three-year period than paying on the pay-as-you-go consumption model.

In the case of the private cloud computing model, cloud computing technologies are hosted on dedicated, single-tenant hardware resources. Typically, these technologies are self-hosted on hardware in a facility (colocation) but may also be hosted with a third-party hosting provider. In this model, there is an element of CapEx and OpEx. The most significant portion is CapEx for purchasing hardware and assets, with usage (and often licensing and software) as OpEx.

The **hybrid cloud** approach will give the greatest flexibility in the expenditure model. This approach will allow you to decide the resources and respective expenditure models that they utilize to fit the business's needs best (*Figure 2.8*):

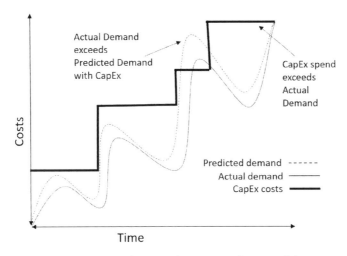

Figure 2.8 – Application of cost expenditure models

The consumption cost model of cloud computing ensures not committing large amounts of capital expenditure on depreciating assets. Instead, by keeping that money within the business to use for day-to-day expenses, paying for what you need when you need it, and only for as long as you need it, you can keep your costs much closer to actual demand rather than over-committing to costs for a predicted demand. When resource demand exceeds predicted demand, the nature of the cloud computing model will ensure you have resources that can be scaled in and out to meet that demand.

The economics of cloud computing were covered in this section. You looked at the consumption model and how the cost expenditure models are applied, in addition to the benefits and value of the OpEx model of cloud computing. This concludes this chapter.

# Summary

This chapter included complete coverage of the **Describe the benefits of using cloud services** skills area of the AZ-900 Azure Fundamentals exam.

In this chapter, you learned about the benefits of using cloud services. You looked at cloud computing as a digital transformation enabler, the triggers, the cloud migration approach, and adopting a cloud mindset. In addition, you learned about various aspects of a cloud operations model and the economics of cloud computing.

Further knowledge beyond the required exam content was provided to prepare you for a real-world, day-to-day Azure-focused role.

The next chapter will look at **Azure's Core Architectural Components**.

# Exam Readiness Drill – Chapter Review Questions

Apart from a solid understanding of key concepts, being able to think quickly under time pressure is a skill that will help you ace your certification exam. That is why working on these skills early on in your learning journey is key.

Chapter review questions are designed to improve your test-taking skills progressively with each chapter you learn and review your understanding of key concepts in the chapter at the same time. You'll find these at the end of each chapter.

> **How To Access These Resources**
>
> To learn how to access these resources, head over to the chapter titled *Chapter 11, Accessing the Online Practice Resources*.

To open the Chapter Review Questions for this chapter, perform the following steps:

1.  Click the link – `https://packt.link/AZ900E2_CH02`.

    Alternatively, you can scan the following **QR code** (*Figure 2.9*):

Figure 2.9 – QR code that opens Chapter Review Questions for logged-in users

2. Once you log in, you'll see a page similar to the one shown in *Figure 2.10*:

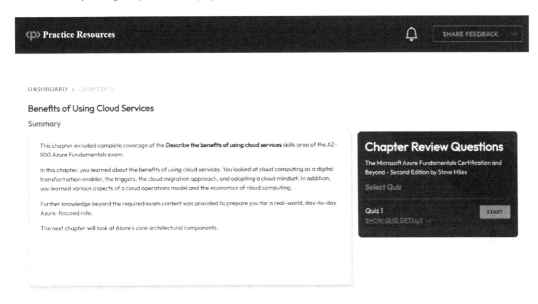

Figure 2.10 – Chapter Review Questions for Chapter 2

3. Once ready, start the following practice drills, re-attempting the quiz multiple times.

## Exam Readiness Drill

For the first three attempts, don't worry about the time limit.

### ATTEMPT 1

The first time, aim for at least **40%**. Look at the answers you got wrong and read the relevant sections in the chapter again to fix your learning gaps.

### ATTEMPT 2

The second time, aim for at least **60%**. Look at the answers you got wrong and read the relevant sections in the chapter again to fix any remaining learning gaps.

## *ATTEMPT 3*

The third time, aim for at least **75%**. Once you score 75% or more, you start working on your timing.

> **Tip**
>
> You may take more than **three** attempts to reach 75%. That's okay. Just review the relevant sections in the chapter till you get there.

# Working On Timing

Target: Your aim is to keep the score the same while trying to answer these questions as quickly as possible. Here's an example of how your next attempts should look like:

| Attempt | Score | Time Taken |
|---------|-------|------------|
| Attempt 5 | 77% | 21 mins 30 seconds |
| Attempt 6 | 78% | 18 mins 34 seconds |
| Attempt 7 | 76% | 14 mins 44 seconds |

Table 2.2 – Sample timing practice drills on the online platform

> **Note**
>
> The time limits shown in the above table are just examples. Set your own time limits with each attempt based on the time limit of the quiz on the website.

With each new attempt, your score should stay above **75%** while your "time taken" to complete should "decrease". Repeat as many attempts as you want till you feel confident dealing with the time pressure.

# Additional Information and Study References

This section provides links to additional exam information and study references:

- **Microsoft Learn certification further information**:

    - AZ-900 - Microsoft Azure Fundamentals exam guide: `https://packt.link/dfOv9`

    - AZ-900 - Microsoft Azure Fundamentals study guide: `https://packt.link/musyY`

- **Microsoft Learn training further information**:

    - AZ-900 - Microsoft Azure Fundamentals course: `https://packt.link/YNKhL`

# 3

# Azure Core Architectural Components

In *Chapter 2, Benefits of Using Cloud Services,* you gained the skills to outline the benefits and value of cloud computing and its positioning as a digital transformation enabler, the audience of cloud platforms, and the cloud mindset that should be adopted compared to the traditional computing mindset.

This chapter will outline the core architectural components from a physical and logical perspective. From the "physical component" perspective, you will look at the data centers that host the cloud computing resources, the global networks connecting them and connecting users to their resources, the global regions that provide the cloud platform resources, and the availability of these resources.

From the "logical component" perspective, you will look at all aspects of resource management. You will also cover management groups that act as a mechanism for managing governance. You will learn about Azure subscriptions, which act as a mechanism and boundary for billing and access management. Next, you will cover **Azure Resource Manager** (**ARM**) and resource groups, which form the basis for access management and governance.

This chapter primarily focuses on the **Describe Azure architecture and services** module from the *Skills Measured* section of the AZ-900 Azure Fundamentals exam.

---

> **Note**
> You can find a detailed AZ-900 Azure Fundamentals exam skills area in the *Appendix, Assessing AZ-900 Exam Skills* of this book.

---

By the end of this chapter, you will be able to answer questions on the following confidently:

- Azure regions, region pairs, and sovereign regions

- Availability zones

- Azure data centers

- Management groups

- Azure resources and resource groups

- Subscriptions

- The hierarchy of resource groups, subscriptions, and management groups

- Azure Resource Manager

In addition, this chapter's goal is to extend your knowledge beyond the exam content so you are prepared for a real-world, day-to-day Azure-focused role.

# Azure Global Infrastructure

The key components of the Azure global infrastructure are the "physical data centers," the "edge infrastructure," and the "global network," sometimes called **premises** and **pipes**.

An **Azure physical data center** is a secure facility that hosts the "physical" computing, storage, and networking facilities that provide the Azure cloud computing platform resources. Each data center has independent, isolated, redundant power supplies and cooling systems for resilience against outages.

**Edge locations** are secure facilities where traffic enters and leaves the Microsoft global network. These locations can provide computing resources to be closer to users for improved network latency, allowing fewer network hops through fewer providers. If required, the traffic can stay longer on the Microsoft backbone network without transiting the internet.

The **Microsoft global network** is one of the largest private networks in the world, with global/cross-ocean fiber that is leased or owned by Microsoft. This global network connects data centers to regional gateways and edge locations where traffic can enter and leave the Microsoft **Wide Area Network (WAN)**.

Microsoft also provides **ExpressRoute**, a service that allows customers to create private network connections to Azure regions from specific peering locations. This allows traffic from a customer's **Multiprotocol Label Switching (MPLS)** WAN to enter the Microsoft network, bypassing the internet entirely and offering a "low-latency" private connection. *Figure 3.1* outlines the topology of the Azure global infrastructure components:

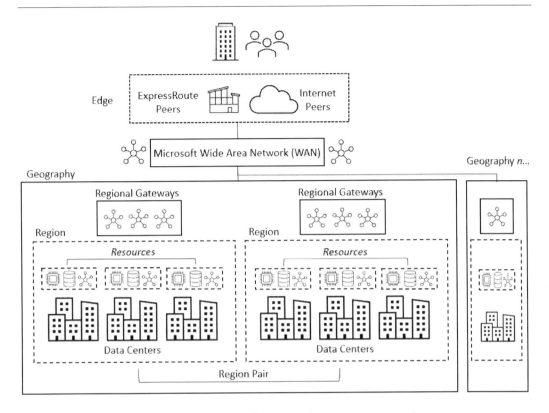

Figure 3.1 – Azure global infrastructure key component topology

The location for a **resource** will be the one that best meets the organization's needs. It may be a **technical driver**, such as service capability and availability or latency in that region, or a **business driver**, such as compliance, data residency, or even cost.

You will now learn about Azure regions and geographies to provide redundancy and high availability for resources.

## Azure Regions and Geographies

Microsoft data centers are grouped into collections across different sites to provide redundancy and high availability for the resources, such as computing and storage hosted within the data centers.

These sets of grouped data centers are known as **regions** and are exposed as the deployment location when creating resources. There are multiple geographies, such as Europe, the UK, the US, and Asia, which contain **multiple regions** with **multiple data centers** in each region.

The following are some example regions within different geographies:

- The **Europe** geography:

  - North Europe region, located in Ireland

  - West Europe region, located in the Netherlands

- The **UK** geography:

  - UK South region, located in London

  - UK West region, located in Cardiff

- The **US** geography:

  - Central US region, located in Iowa

  - East US region, located in Virginia

  - East US 2 region, located in Virginia

  - East US 3 region, located in Georgia

  - North Central US region, located in Illinois

  - South Central US region, located in Texas

  - West Central US region, located in Wyoming

  - West US region, located in California

  - West US 2 region, located in Washington

  - West US 3 region, located in Arizona

- The **Asia Pacific** geography:

  - East Asia region, located in Hong Kong

  - Southeast Asia region, located in Singapore

> **Note**
>
> The complete list of geographies and regions can be found here:
> `https://packt.link/0KdxT`.

The data centers in a region are connected by a "low-latency network" for availability, which provides the basis for **availability zones**, which you will cover in the next section.

**Regions** belong to a particular **geography** and are deployed in "pairs" for disaster recovery. These regions are located 300 miles or more apart where possible. This is to ensure that they are far enough from each other to be protected from local disasters that would impact service availability. It is possible that when a region has an outage, services will automatically failover to the other region in the pair.

A **geography** can have multiple regions and defines a "data residency" and "compliance" boundary. *Figure 3.2* shows the relationship between Azure **regions** and **geographies**:

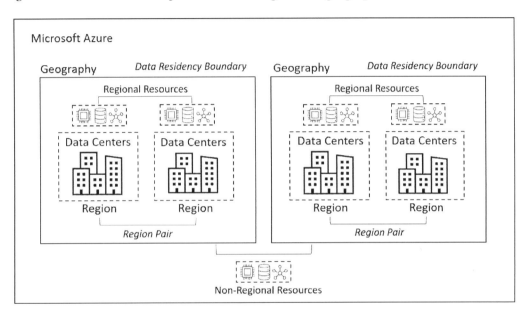

Figure 3.2 – Azure regions and geographies relationship

Although Azure resources are physically located in data center facilities, these data centers are not considered individual facilities in which you can create resources. When creating an Azure resource, such as a virtual machine, it is not possible to directly select a particular data center; **only a region** can be selected.

*Figure 3.3* shows `Region` selection in the Azure portal when creating resources:

Figure 3.3 – Azure region selection for creating resources

When creating Azure resources, regions are categorized under the `Recommended` or `Other` headings. The appropriate option should be selected for the scenario.

A **Recommended** region is designed to support "availability zones," now or planned for the future. Regions categorized as **Other** (not shown in *Figure 3.3*) refer to the data pairing of regions to provide the data residency boundaries and low latency for disaster recovery purposes. These are the regions that do not support **availability zones**.

Once the appropriate option is selected, a resource, such as a virtual machine, is created in any of the data centers in that region. These resources, such as virtual machines, are called **regional services** as they are dependent on being co-located in that specific region's data centers.

However, not all resources and services are available in all regions. New resources and services are often initially available in the US or a specific region and then rolled out to the rest of the world. Some resources are **non-regional**, meaning they are not dependent on or bound to a particular region's data center and are a global service. However, that service's metadata can have a location that can be specified for compliance. Some examples of non-regional services are **Traffic Manager** and **Front Door**. In contrast, **DNS** and **Microsoft Entra Domain Services** (Formerly **Azure Active Directory Domain Services**) are "geo-based" to ensure data is kept within that geography.

When planning to create resources between regions, it should be considered that any data transfer leaving a region or **egress** is billed; however, traffic "within" a region or **ingress** is free.

It is now time to learn about Azure Edge Zones.

### *Azure Edge Zones*

Microsoft is extending the Azure platform to incorporate edge computing. **Edge computing** allows data processing and code to be executed closer to the end user when sensitivity to network latency is critical.

**Edge Zones** can provide the application with consistent Azure computing resources. The workload processing is completed outside the Microsoft data center regions but within Microsoft **Point-of-Presence (POP)** locations (locations outside of Microsoft data regions that have Azure-hosted services for processing workloads) or third-party data center locations, or processed at the customer's data center locations. An organization can choose to run some resources in Azure regions and some in Azure Edge Zones based on its requirements. *Figure 3.4* shows the positioning of Azure data center regions and the Azure Edge Zones:

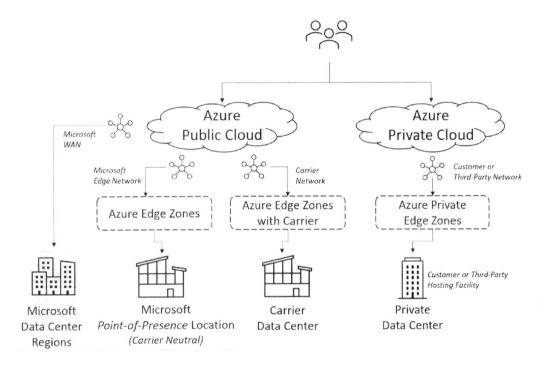

Figure 3.4 – Azure Edge Zone relationships

The following describes the three Edge Zone scenarios:

- **Azure Edge Zones**: These are still Azure public cloud (shared) platform resources (Microsoft hardware) within Microsoft's POP edge locations. These edge locations provide services such as ExpressRoute, CDN, and the Azure Front Door service. These zones are connected to Microsoft's global network.

- **Azure Edge Zones with the carrier**: These are still Azure public cloud (shared) platform resources (Microsoft hardware) but are now shipped to exist within the carrier's data center locations. These zones are part of the carrier's global network.

- **Azure private Edge Zones**: These are a part of the Azure Stack (private) cloud platform (customer or third-party hardware) within the customer's location or a third-party hosting provider. These zones are part of the customer or hosting provider's private network and not of a carrier or Microsoft network. These zones can be connected to Microsoft data center regions using a VPN or ExpressRoute to establish hybrid connectivity if required.

With your knowledge of the concepts of Azure Edge Zones, you can now explore Azure sovereign regions.

### Azure Sovereign Regions

Azure provides what is referred to as **sovereign regions**, which support greater compliance for specific markets. These are isolated cloud-platform regions that run dedicated hardware and isolated networks in the regions where these sovereign regions are located, as shown in *Figure 3.5*:

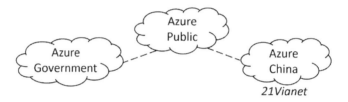

Figure 3.5 – Provided Azure sovereign regions

The sovereign region platforms also have their own portals with different URLs and different service endpoints in the DNS. Here are some examples of the URLs and endpoints to connect to in the DNS:

- **Azure Government**: This is a separate instance of the Azure platform operated by Microsoft. It is solely used by US government bodies (and partners):

  - The Azure portal can be accessed via a dedicated URL at `https://packt.link/jp8gg`.

  - The service endpoints to connect to in DNS are in the form of `*.azurewebsites.us`.

  - You can find more information on Azure Government at `https://packt.link/Dwohy`.

- **Azure China (21 Vianet)**: This is a separate instance of the Azure platform operated by 21 Vianet. It is for compliance with Chinese government regulations:

  - The Azure portal can be accessed via a dedicated URL at `https://packt.link/rsMLZ`.

  - The service endpoints to connect to in DNS are in the form of `*.chinacloudsites.cn`.

  - You can find more information on Azure China (21 Vianet) at `https://packt.link/6KMo0`.

You have now grasped the concept of Azure regions and geographies along with edge computing, Edge Zones, and Azure sovereign regions. The next section will focus on the availability components and the risk model.

## Availability Components

When creating resources in Azure, you should think back to the cloud computing services models of **Infrastructure as a Service (IaaS)**, **Platform as a Service (PaaS)**, **Serverless/Functions as a Service (FaaS)**, and **Software as a Service (SaaS)** with the same principles and approach being applied to responsibility as for the "availability" of resources.

This means you should consider how you will make data, app, compute, and other services available in the case of a failure at the app or virtual machine, hardware, data center, or region level.

Depending on the service, Microsoft is responsible for providing a range of availability options. Still, you are responsible for implementing them to ensure you have designed an availability strategy that meets your **Service-Level Agreement (SLA)** requirements. Microsoft's SLAs for its services are based on financial compensation when the defined SLA is not met; although this is not paid automatically and must be claimed by the customer.

> **Note**
> Microsoft SLAs for all services can be found at `https://packt.link/GMblA`.

*Figure 3.6* summarizes these components by looking at virtual machines and storage resources. You will see how you can increase the SLA and durability by using the following components:

| Single Virtual Machine | Availability Sets | Availability Zones | Region Pairs |
|---|---|---|---|
| SLA 99.9% | SLA 99.95% | SLA 99.99% | Protection across a region |
| For premium or ultra ssd disks *(99.5% when using standard SSD disks)* *(95% when using standard HDD disks)* | Protection within a data center | Protection within a region | |

Figure 3.6 – Azure availability components relationship

An availability solution is based on the resources to be protected, the nature of the failure to protect the resources, and the SLA requirements.

Here are the "availability" components that Azure can provide to build a solution. The following components can be considered as building blocks to use as required:

- Within a data center component:

  - **Example failures that could occur**: Hardware rack failure, power, or network.

  - **Availability component**: "availability set" in the case of a virtual machine or locally redundant storage in the case of storage.

- Within a region component:

  - **Example failures that could occur**: Data center failure, power, network, or cooling.

  - **Availability component**: The "availability zone" in the case of a virtual machine or zone-redundant storage in the case of storage; synchronous replication is used.

- Across a region component:

  - **Example failures that could occur**: Entire region failure—multiple data centers in a region suffer failures such as power, network, or cooling.

  - **Availability component**: "Azure Site Recovery" in the case of a virtual machine, or in the case of storage, "geo-redundancy" with "asynchronous replication."

The next section looks at adopting a risk model.

### Adopting an Availability Model

Much like in the security area, where you looked at a **Risk Model**, and you took a **defense-in-depth** approach, you should consider taking a similar approach to implementing **availability** in a solution.

You should know the possible failures at the level you are concerned with, determine the **impact** and **probability**, and then implement the most appropriate solution. This availability model should be driven by determining your required SLA, that is, the uptime required for a resource. The SLA of a resource can be increased by combining different availability components.

Now let's look at availability sets.

### Availability Sets

In a nutshell, **availability sets** are logical groupings of virtual machines that provide the availability of the virtual machines within a data center and provide the virtual machines with a 99.95% SLA.

Availability sets deploy virtual machines across different hardware instances through what is known as a **fault domain**, meaning the virtual machines are placed on hardware that is in "physically separated racks" when they are created. If there is a "within-rack failure," then all virtual machines are not impacted; only a subset will be impacted as you have "spread your eggs between several baskets." However, without availability sets, you have kept all your eggs in the same basket.

Without virtual machines being part of an availability set, the best SLA for a single virtual machine will be 99.9% when ultra or premium SSD disks are used. This drops to 99% when standard SSD disks are used and 95% when a standard HDD is used.

These SLAs equate to the following figures:

- 99.5% availability results in a period of allowed downtime/unavailability of 3h 37m 21s.

- 99.9% availability results in a period of allowed downtime/unavailability of 43m 28s.

- 99.99% availability results in a period of allowed downtime/unavailability of 4m 21s.

*Figure 3.7* helps to visualize resource placement in an availability set:

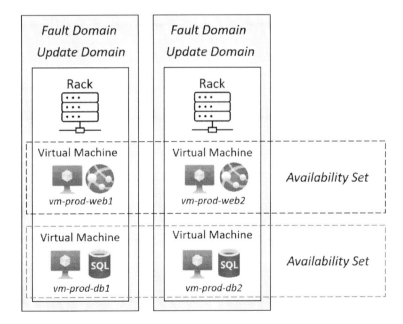

Figure 3.7 – Providing Azure availability set functionality in a solution

Availability sets also act as an update "patching" boundary. An update domain is automatically assigned to all virtual machines that are part of an availability set. Updates to one set of virtual machines are isolated from other virtual machines to ensure that only one update domain gets updated at a time. If an update impacted the service of virtual machines in one update domain, that update would not be applied to other update domains.

Some points to consider regarding availability sets are as follows:

- Availability sets are not billable items.

- A virtual machine is part of a single availability set.

- Virtual machines can only be added to an availability set when created. It is not possible to add to an availability set or change the availability set after the virtual machines have been created. In such cases, you would need to delete the virtual machine and redeploy it, but this time as part of an availability set. Therefore, planning is critical for this purpose.

- You might consider deploying a single virtual machine from the start as part of an availability set. While it will not help meet the availability set SLA, as that requires at least two instances or more, it would prepare your workload for the future without needing to redeploy.

- You will need to create the virtual machine in the same resource group as the availability set to be able to add the virtual machine to the availability set.

- Three fault domains and five update domains (a maximum of 20 can be configured) are part of an availability set.

- The assignment is carried out automatically and horizontally in sequence—that is, vm1 in fault domain #1, vm2 in fault domain #2, and vm3 in fault domain #3—as you have only three fault domains in this example. This means that vm4 will be assigned to fault domain #1.

The next section looks at how fault and update domains are indispensable.

### Fault Domains

A **fault domain** is a group of resources in a data center rack that share the same power and network. When a failure occurs in a fault domain, all resources in that fault domain become unavailable.

*Figure 3.8* shows each web server and database server in a separate fault domain:

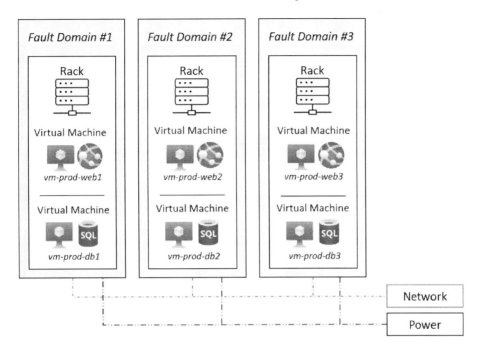

Figure 3.8 – Providing availability set fault domain functionality in a solution

A failure can occur in one of the fault domains, but only one web server and one database server will be offline. As discussed earlier, this is the approach of "spreading your eggs across different baskets." If the servers shared the same fault domain, the failure would affect all of them.

You can now read on to learn about update domains.

## Update Domains

**Update domains** are similar to fault domains but relate to "patching schedules."

You should put each web server in its own update domain so they are rebooted independently and there is always a web server available to handle requests. The same approach should be taken for the database servers so that a database server is always available to handle requests from the web servers. This precludes both database servers from being rebooted simultaneously and potentially both being unavailable.

*Figure 3.9* helps to visualize the assignment of virtual machines across update domains:

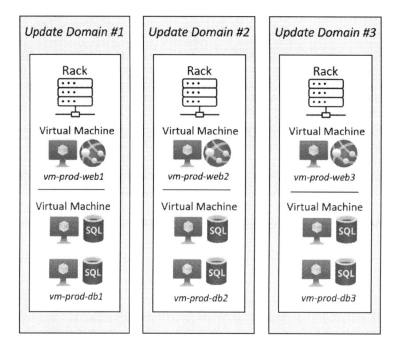

Figure 3.9 – Providing availability set update domain functionality in a solution

In a nutshell, all virtual machines in the same update domain will receive updates and be rebooted simultaneously.

> **Further knowledge**
>
> The key takeaway from this section is not to put two web servers, for example, in the same update domain, as both will be rebooted simultaneously.

This next section looks at availability zones.

### Availability Zones

Some regions are further divided into availability zones, although they are not available in all regions, and not all resources support availability zones.

The purpose of an **availability zone** is to provide redundancy within a region, that is, to protect against a "data center failure" so that a failure related to something such as power, cooling, or connectivity does not impact the operations of any resources running in a single data center.

> **Note**
> Availability zones protect resources from a **data center** failure and not from a **region** failure. The scope of availability sets is to protect a virtual machine from an **in-rack** failure, for example, within a data center.

*Figure 3.10* outlines the Azure availability zone topology:

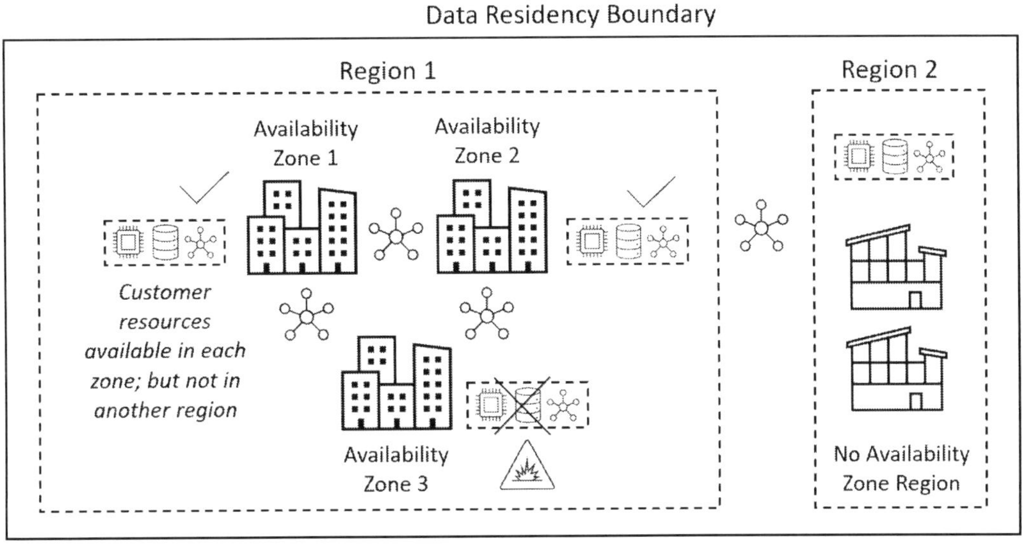

Figure 3.10 – Azure availability zones providing redundancy within a region

The availability of resources running in a zone is provided by each zone being protected using independent power, cooling, and networking from other zones. A service outage in one zone will not affect resource availability in other zones.

Microsoft can provide a higher-level SLA when you choose to use availability zones for your deployed resources for those that support this functionality and in those regions where this is available.

In the example of providing availability for virtual machines, a 99.99% uptime is guaranteed by Microsoft if a minimum of two virtual machines are deployed into two or more zones. There is synchronous replication of virtual machines, which is automatically taken care of by Microsoft.

Without an availability zone, if the data center where your resource is running has a failure, your resource will be offline until that data center is back online and services are restored.

Availability zones allow resources, connectivity, and traffic to remain within the primary region but are hosted within a different physically isolated and distanced set of data center buildings.

To protect against an entire region becoming unavailable, resources can be replicated in a secondary region to protect against a service failure within the primary region where the resources are running. The issue may be that you do not want or cannot have your services failing over or running from another region for reasons such as compliance, latency, or connectivity. You may rely on ExpressRoute or VPNs that are not configured to be available in the secondary region. There may also be many other dependencies; for example, having another region as a redundancy option is not viable.

Azure resources are placed into one of three categories as outlined here:

- **Zonal services**: These provide the ability to select an availability zone for the resources. For instance, resources can be pinned to a specific zone based on your needs, performance, or latency.

- **Zone-redundant services**: The replication of resources across zones is automatic, and you cannot define the replication settings governing how the resources are distributed across the zones.

- **Non-regional services**: Services are available in all geographies and are not affected by zone-wide or region-wide outages.

### Proximity Placement Groups

**Proximity placement groups** are a logical entity and an architectural component that should be considered in any solution design where low latency between Azure infrastructure and compute resources is required. Proximity placement groups ensure the compute resources are physically adjacent and collocated within the same physical data center and not across data centers.

Proximity placement groups are important where **latency** is considered. Placing the resources closer within a single availability zone is possible, but the challenge is that an availability zone can expand to span multiple physical data centers. The virtual machines that are part of the web frontend tier for the solution may be in one data center, but the database tier is in a different data center's racks; the latency impact here should be readily apparent. Virtual machine-accelerated networking was one solution to latency; however, proximity placement groups alleviate this.

*Figure 3.11* outlines the placement of virtual machines without a proximity placement group:

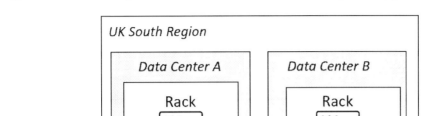

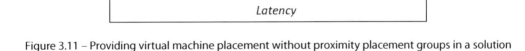

Figure 3.11 – Providing virtual machine placement without proximity placement groups in a solution

In *Figure 3.11*, two virtual machines that need to communicate with each other could be placed by Microsoft in different data centers several kilometers apart. This may cause issues due to latency.

*Figure 3.12* outlines the Azure proximity placement groups topology and how this can reduce latency. Observe that the virtual machines are now located within the same data center, and the latency is now reduced to within the same rack:

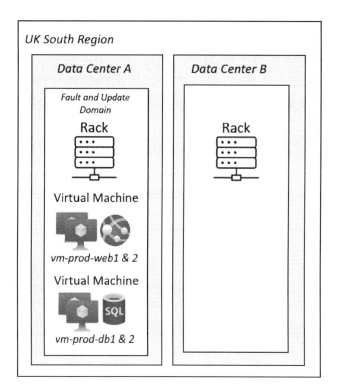

Figure 3.12 – Providing virtual machine placement with proximity placement groups in a solution

*Figure 3.12*, while solving a latency problem, introduces an availability issue. Now, as both virtual machines are located in the same rack, they also share the same **fault** and **update** domains. This issue can be resolved using an "availability set" to place each virtual machine in a **different** rack with its own fault and update domains. *Figure 3.13* outlines this concept:

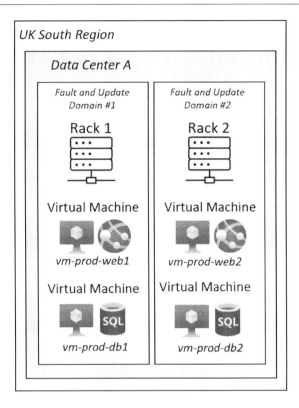

Figure 3.13 – Providing proximity placement groups and availability sets in a solution

Here are a few things to note concerning proximity placement groups:

- They are Azure resources and need to be created before they can be used.

- They can be used with virtual machines, Virtual Machine Scale Sets, and availability sets.

- When creating the compute resource, specify the proximity placement group previously created.

- To move existing compute resources into a proximity placement group, the resource will need to be stopped (deallocated).

- They are set at the resource level, not the individual virtual machine level, for availability and Virtual Machine Scale Sets.

- A workload such as SAP HANA with SAP NetWeaver is a good example of the importance of having the machines separated for high availability/SLA but close enough to not face latency issues in communication.

In this section, you learned about the Azure global infrastructure and how to reduce latency with proximity placement groups. The following section explores the concept of resource management. You start this section by looking at Azure management scopes.

# Azure Resource Management

It is important to ensure that any data or workloads running in a cloud computing environment are managed in a **governed**, **controlled**, **secured**, and **protected** manner as they would be for a traditional computing model. *Figure 3.14* illustrates these aspects:

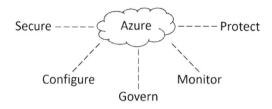

Figure 3.14 – Azure resource management

Azure resource management solutions should include the following:

- **Availability**: This is managed through redundancy, replication, and traffic management.
- **Protection**: This is managed through backup and disaster recovery.
- **Security**: This is managed through threat protection and security posture management.
- **Configuration**: This is managed through automation, scripting, and update management.
- **Governance**: This is managed through access control, compliance, and cost management.
- **Monitoring**: This is managed through the collection of security incidents, events, resource health, performance metrics, logs, and diagnostics.

The foundation for all management within Azure is ARM, which is an **Application Programming Interface** (**API**) and the **management** and **deployment** service for Azure.

All user and resource interactions pass through the **ARM API**. You can think of the ARM API as the "brain" or "engine" of Azure. It provides a single consistent management layer and orchestration engine that processes all requests for every interaction with the Azure platform. Be it the portal, command-line interfaces, templates, Microsoft utilities, or third-party software, they all call the ARM API.

This section introduced the concepts of Azure resource management.

> **Further knowledge**
>
> The key takeaways from this section are that **governance** and **planning** are essential stages when creating resources in Azure. Doing this correctly can prevent re-work and potentially tearing down aspects that may have been implemented without fully appreciating what should be considered and grasping all options and their benefits and limitations on the desired outcome. The following section looks at Azure management scopes.

## Azure Management Scopes

Azure provides the following four management scopes so that **Role-Based Access Control** (**RBAC**) and Azure Policy can be targeted at the following levels:

- Management group level
- Subscription level
- Resource group level
- Resource level

*Figure 3.15* outlines these four management scopes and their hierarchy:

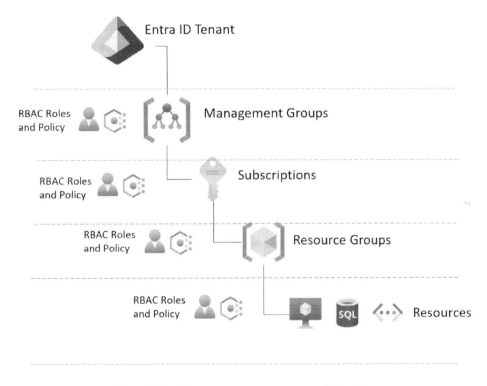

Figure 3.15 – Azure management scopes relationship

This section detailed the concepts of Azure management scopes—the levels at which access control and policies can be applied. The following section looks at Azure management groups and how they relate to the management scopes for access control and policies.

## Azure Management Groups

**Azure management groups** are **logical containers** that group together Azure subscriptions; they can be considered a governance and management layer to implement access control and policies. Management groups are the most effective governance scope when multiple Azure subscriptions exist in a tenant.

However, there are some limitations of management groups to be aware of:

- Management groups can only contain other management groups and subscriptions. They cannot include resource groups or resources.

- The scope is per tenant and not across tenants.

- The parent management group cannot be deleted or moved. However, it can be renamed.

- Only one parent management group is supported, and only one parent hierarchy is a single tenant.

- They can support many child management groups (up to 1,000).

- A hierarchy of up to six levels is supported.

This hierarchy may be applied across business units, regions, or environments, wherever you may need to define billing or access control boundaries. In this scenario, planning is everything.

*Figure 3.16* shows just one example of the hierarchy and the relationships between the different subscription types within a business:

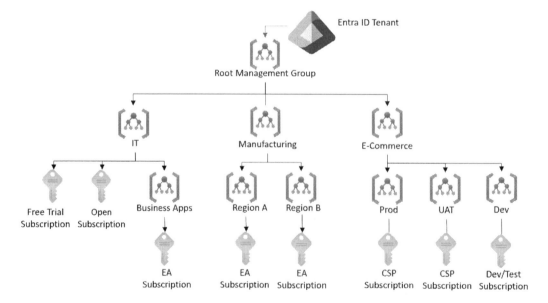

Figure 3.16 – Azure management group and subscription relationships

Now that you have learned about Azure management groups and their relationship to Azure subscriptions, let's move on to explore Azure subscriptions.

## Azure Subscriptions

**Azure subscriptions** can be considered the "logical containers" of Azure resources that share the same "billing" and "access control" boundaries.

An Azure subscription is a billing mechanism for the Azure resources you consume within a tenancy. It can be likened to a **bar tab**—a method of paying for everything you have consumed, all together and itemized at the end of the night, instead of paying individually each time you order a drink.

To continue the analogy, when a bar tab is opened, a payment method (such as a credit card) must be provided so that there is one bill to settle for everything put on the tab at the end of the night.

Every time a resource is created within Azure, an Azure subscription must be selected for the allocation of the consumption of resources (or "tab" in the previous example). This means the Azure subscription(s) are created first before creating any resources. At the end of the month, all the Azure resources created in that subscription will be billed in a single itemized invoice.

*Figure 3.17* outlines Azure subscriptions:

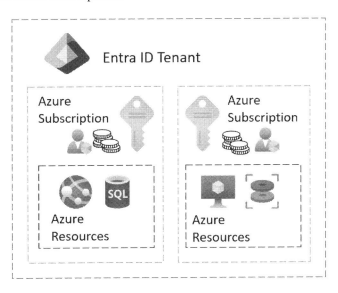

Figure 3.17 – Relationship between Azure subscriptions and resources within a tenant

The Azure subscription should first be created in a **new** or **existing** Entra ID tenancy, as this is the foundation and starting point. **Management groups** and **resource groups** are then planned as needed.

Subscriptions cannot be merged; however, resources can be moved into another subscription. The subscription that no longer holds any resources after the move can be deleted or allowed to expire. When a subscription is deleted, all resources within the subscription are deleted. However, when a subscription expires, the resources remain. In either case, the tenancy remains in place and is not removed.

The billing owner of the subscription can also be changed, much like a bar tab could be run up and transferred to somebody else to take it over and settle the tab.

When planning to start creating resources in Azure, you must first define access and billing control. Defining these will shape the subscription and resource group strategy. You should create the tenancy, subscription, and resource groups in that order.

Planning is necessary for your subscriptions, and you need to determine whether multiple subscriptions will exist within a tenancy. You may wish to have one for production resources and another for development and testing purposes to isolate access to the resources through the subscription or to control who will receive the invoice for any resources created within each subscription. This will depend on your needs, and you will look at creating additional subscriptions later in the *Additional Subscriptions* section in this chapter.

Now it is time to look at the relationships between subscriptions and tenants.

### Relationship between Tenants and Subscriptions

As you saw in the last section, there are certain relationships between Azure subscriptions and Entra ID tenants. The relationships also extend to other entities, such as resource groups and Azure resources. There are existing relationships between users, groups, and apps, such as a Microsoft 365 subscription. **Resource groups** are logical containers for resources, and you will explore this later in this chapter.

*Figure 3.18* outlines the relationship between these entities:

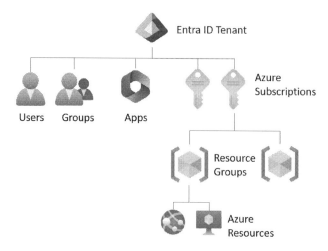

Figure 3.18 – Azure subscription and tenant relationship

In a nutshell, the following relationships exist:

- **Entra ID tenant**: This contains users, groups, and Microsoft 365 subscriptions.
- **Azure subscription**: This contains resource groups, which includes resources.

Here are a few things that should be observed in these relationships:

- Each subscription in Azure can be associated with **only one** Entra ID tenant in a parent-and-child relationship, with the Entra ID tenant being the parent.
- A subscription can be moved to a different Entra ID tenant.
- The subscription billing owner can be changed, such as moving from being invoiced by Microsoft to being invoiced by a Channel Cloud Solution Provider.
- Each subscription can have multiple resource groups. Each resource group can be part of **only one** subscription.
- Each resource can be associated with **only one** resource group. In a parent-and-child relationship, the resource group is the parent.
- Each user can be associated with **only one** Entra ID tenant, with the Entra ID tenant being the parent.
- Each user can access **more than one** Entra ID tenant.
- Each group can be associated with **only one** Entra ID tenant, with the Entra ID tenant being the parent.
- Each **Microsoft 365 subscription** can be associated with **only one** Entra ID tenant (a domain), with the Entra ID tenant being the parent.

It is now time to explore more on Azure subscription management.

## Multiple Subscriptions

An organization is not limited to a single subscription. Resources can be consumed from multiple subscriptions within the same tenant or another tenant the organization owns. Any additional subscriptions can be created for access control management or billing management purposes, as a subscription acts as a billing and resource management boundary.

There are subscription soft quota limits, which means you need to contact Microsoft support to increase resource quota limits through a service request. Typically, this request would be for a virtual machine core count that has exceeded the value set for the number of cores in the subscription quota. The subscription quota would need to be increased to set the number of virtual machine cores needed.

A subscription can be a boundary of **access control**. A subscription could be created for each environment, such as creating a subscription for user acceptance testing, production, or staging. Alternatively, a subscription could be created per team or project, as shown in *Figure 3.19* in this section.

This approach to access control ensures control of access to resources, with individuals or groups having the least amount of access they need to the minimum amount of resources. This is one of the core principles of governance and compliance, and through RBAC, the approach and principle of "least privilege" can be adopted. The subscription can also be used as a layer to enforce **Azure Policy**.

In addition to being used as a boundary of access control, a subscription can also be used as a boundary of "billing control." This means costs incurred from Azure resources created can be allocated with a "charge-back" or "show-back" approach. The relevant entity can see precisely what environment, team, or project incurred the costs without all resource costs being aggregated into one subscription.

> **Note**
>
> Tags can be used to break down resources within a subscription. Since they are out of the scope of this section, they will be covered in *Chapter 8, Azure Governance and Compliance*.

*Figure 3.19* outlines the relationships between multiple subscriptions, tenants, and resources.

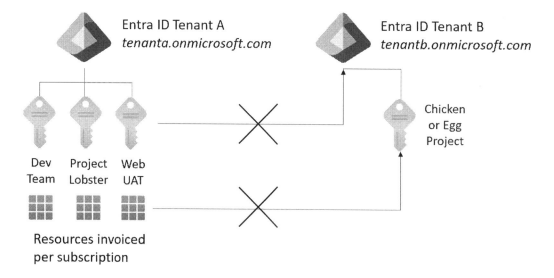

Figure 3.19 – Multiple Azure subscriptions

Looking back to the "bar tab" analogy from the previous section, each resource can only be billed to one bar tab. However, resources can be moved between subscriptions so that another subscription can be used to pick up the bill (their own bar tab) for those resources consumed.

For instance, some resources that you no longer wish to be billed for under the existing resources' subscription can be moved to another subscription that may be more appropriate to pay the bill for those consumed resources. The resource move is a simple operation that can be done within the Azure portal.

You can see from the example shown in *Figure 3.19* that the three subscriptions associated with `Tenant A` cannot be associated with `Tenant B` simultaneously. These subscriptions can only have their own parent owner.

Likewise, resources can only exist within one subscription that acts as the billing mechanism for the consumption of those resources. The resources cannot be associated with another subscription within another tenancy simultaneously. They can move owners from subscription to subscription within the same tenancy and from the parent subscription to a "different" subscription in a "different" tenancy.

You learned about Azure subscription management in this section, including the reasons for and benefits of creating multiple Azure subscriptions in a tenancy. Now, in this next section, you will explore more about **Azure Resource Manager** and the functionality it provides.

## Azure Resource Manager (ARM)

In a nutshell, **ARM** is the **deployment** and **management** service for Azure. It provides a consistent management and control layer for the creation, update, and deletion, of resources as well as control access, application of policy, governance, and compliance. *Figure 3.20* outlines the ARM architecture:

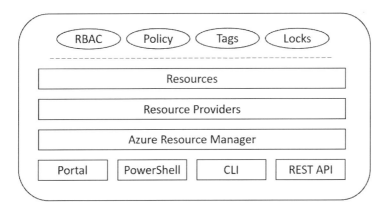

Figure 3.20 – ARM architecture showing the relationship between its components

ARM provides the following functionality:

- Deployment, management, and monitoring as it pertains to resource grouping rather than individual resources
- Application of access control and policies at the resource group level, inherited by all resources in that group
- Application of tags to resources for billing logical grouping and management
- Repeatable life cycle deployments that result in a consistent state
- Use of deployment template files through **JavaScript Object Notation (JSON)** or **Bicep** to define the deployment of resources
- Creation of resource dependencies

As the name implies, ARM takes a resource-centric approach to every Azure object or entity classed as a resource.

The main component of the ARM logical architecture is the resource group. The resource group can then be a target for applying access control and policies instead of individual resources.

Here are some terms to know about when working with ARM:

- **Resource**: In a nutshell, this is a billable item that is consumed, the lowest-level element that can be broken down in Azure. These can be thought of as the cells, molecules, or building blocks of all services and solutions for the Azure platform. Billing takes place on the resource level, and each resource will have an ID with a billing meter that calculates the amount consumed and the rate at which the customer should be billed. Billing meters are not used for Entra tenants, subscriptions, management groups, resource groups, and so on. These are logical entities and have no billing meters.
- **Resource group**: A logical container for resources. Resources that are to be managed together as a life cycle are grouped to target access control and compliance through policies. Resources are grouped into resource groups in the most appropriate way for management purposes.
- **Resource provider**: These are not logical, but rather the actual service that contains and provides Azure resources. You could consider a book as a reading resource and the library as the provider.
- **Resource Manager templates**: These are **JSON** or **Bicep** files that provide a repeatable and automated deployment methodology. These form the foundation of the **Infrastructure as Code (IaC)** methodology and use a **declarative** syntax instead of an **imperative** syntax, which is the approach with PowerShell.

You have now grasped the concept of ARM. The next section looks at resource groups.

## Resource Groups

Resource groups are one of the core foundational elements of the Azure platform and ARM. The Azure platform is built around resource-centric principles. Resource groups are **logical containers** for Azure resources and are used as a "management scope" for access management and policy.

The relationship between a resource group, subscription, and the resource itself is outlined in *Figure 3.21*:

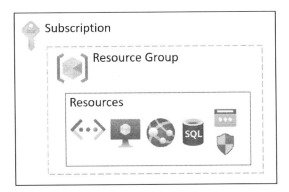

Figure 3.21 – Azure resource group relationships

This section introduced the concept of resource groups. The key takeaway from this section is the flexibility that using resource groups provides, and how you can use resource groups to logically group resources in a way that means something to a given organization. For instance, it may be grouped by resource type, environment, business unit, project, or location.

The following section looks at some of the characteristics of resource groups.

## Resource Group Characteristics

The following are the characteristics of resource groups:

- Resources must belong to a resource group and can only exist in one resource group. However, they can be moved between resource groups.

- Resources can interact with other resources in the same resource group, other resource groups, and subscriptions.

- Resources work at the data plane level, while resource groups and subscriptions work at the management plane level.

- Resource groups do not have to use the same region. They can include resources from other regions.

- Resource groups do not contain subscriptions, but subscriptions contain resource groups.

- Resource groups are not physical. They are logical entities and not billable items.

- Resource groups contain metadata about the resources they include.

- Resources inherit all permissions set at the resource group level they belong to by default.

- When adding new resources to a resource group, they inherit those permissions and any access assignments.

- When moving resources, the resources lose the permissions of the resource group they belonged to and inherit those of the new resource group they are moved to.

- If access and permissions are assigned at the resource group level, all resources in that resource group can be managed.

- Deleting a resource group will remove all resources within that resource group. However, it would not delete the subscription or tenant.

- Since all resources are contained in the same resource group, it is easy to act on all resources with a single activity. All resources within the resource group inherit the access assignments and policies set at the resource group.

- When assigning tags to a resource group, the resources in that resource group do not inherit those tags. You would have to individually apply the tags to each resource in that group.

Now that you have explored the characteristics of resource groups, it is time to learn more about resource group logical organization.

## Azure Resource Group Organization

You must first define access and billing control when planning to create Azure resources. This will shape the **subscription** and **resource group** strategy. Here is the order in which these elements should be created:

- Tenancy

- Subscription

- Management groups

- Resource groups

The resource group is typically used to group all resources that share the same **life cycle** or have some form of "dependency" or the same "access control" or "management" requirements. The resources could be grouped by **environment**, **business unit**, **region**, or another combination as appropriate.

Creating the appropriate resource group requires planning to find the optimal way to organize all the Azure resources logically. This will become increasingly important as the environment grows to hundreds or thousands of resources. It is best to plan a strategy for both the logical grouping of resources and a naming convention to make identifying resources easier for management purposes.

This resource group organization is entirely subjective as it all depends on the organization's decision on how resource groups will be used. Some may like to see **location** grouping, and some **resource type** groupings, such as networks or virtual machines. *Figure 3.22* outlines the different methods that could be taken:

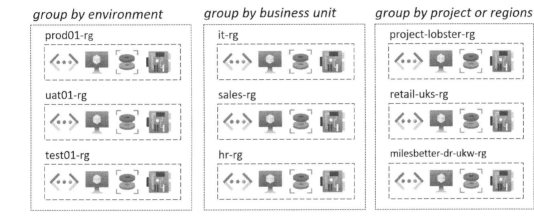

Figure 3.22 – Azure resource group organization showing grouping methodologies

When managing resource groups as part of day-to-day operations, you can delete individual resources as well as the resource group and all the resources associated with it. Deleting at the resource group level is useful in cases when several resources in the resource group are no longer needed, and allows a bulk delete, rather than deleting each resource. This can also be risky, as there may be resources in a resource group that have dependencies and are required not to be deleted.

To avoid this, governance controls can be put in place—that is, removing the ability to delete resource groups through RBAC. In addition, **locks** can also be used to prevent deletion, which will be covered in *Chapter 8, Azure Governance and Compliance*.

You learned in this section all about the components of ARM, which concludes this chapter on *Azure Core Architectural Components*.

## Summary

This chapter included complete coverage of the AZ-900 Azure Fundamentals exam skills area: **Describe Azure architecture and services**.

In this chapter, you learned both the physical and logical aspects of the core Azure architectural components: the data centers that host the Azure platform resources, the regions they exist in, the networks connecting them, and the related aspects of availability. You now also know about Azure subscriptions and all aspects of Azure resource management, including management groups and management scopes, ARM, and resource groups.

The next chapter will deal with **Azure Core Resources** to follow Microsoft's intended guided learning path for the AZ-900 exam.

## Exam Readiness Drill – Chapter Review Questions

Apart from a solid understanding of key concepts, being able to think quickly under time pressure is a skill that will help you ace your certification exam. That is why working on these skills early on in your learning journey is key.

Chapter review questions are designed to improve your test-taking skills progressively with each chapter you learn and review your understanding of key concepts in the chapter at the same time. You'll find these at the end of each chapter.

> **How To Access These Resources**
>
> To learn how to access these resources, head over to the chapter titled *Chapter 11, Accessing the Online Practice Resources*.

To open the Chapter Review Questions for this chapter, perform the following steps:

1.  Click the link – `https://packt.link/AZ900E2_CH03`.

    Alternatively, you can scan the following **QR code** (*Figure 3.23*):

Figure 3.23 – QR code that opens Chapter Review Questions for logged-in users

2.  Once you log in, you'll see a page similar to the one shown in *Figure 3.24*:

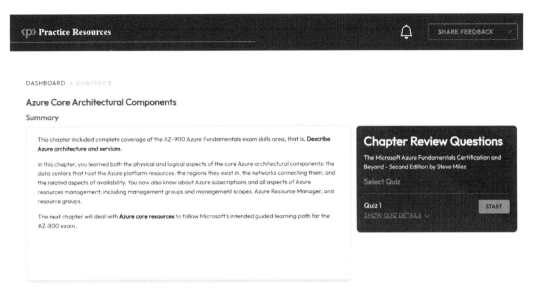

Figure 3.24 – Chapter Review Questions for Chapter 3

3.  Once ready, start the following practice drills, re-attempting the quiz multiple times.

## Exam Readiness Drill

For the first three attempts, don't worry about the time limit.

### ATTEMPT 1

The first time, aim for at least **40%**. Look at the answers you got wrong and read the relevant sections in the chapter again to fix your learning gaps.

### ATTEMPT 2

The second time, aim for at least **60%**. Look at the answers you got wrong and read the relevant sections in the chapter again to fix any remaining learning gaps.

## *ATTEMPT 3*

The third time, aim for at least **75%**. Once you score 75% or more, you start working on your timing.

> **Tip**
> You may take more than **three** attempts to reach 75%. That's okay. Just review the relevant sections in the chapter till you get there.

# Working On Timing

Target: Your aim is to keep the score the same while trying to answer these questions as quickly as possible. Here's an example of how your next attempts should look like:

| Attempt | Score | Time Taken |
|---|---|---|
| Attempt 5 | 77% | 21 mins 30 seconds |
| Attempt 6 | 78% | 18 mins 34 seconds |
| Attempt 7 | 76% | 14 mins 44 seconds |

Table 3.1 – Sample timing practice drills on the online platform

> **Note**
> The time limits shown in the above table are just examples. Set your own time limits with each attempt based on the time limit of the quiz on the website.

With each new attempt, your score should stay above **75%** while your "time taken" to complete should "decrease". Repeat as many attempts as you want till you feel confident dealing with the time pressure.

# Online Hands-On Activities

Once you complete this book, complete the hands-on activities that align with this chapter. These are available on the accompanying online platform. Perform the following steps to open hands-on activities:

1. Navigate to the `Dashboard`.
2. Click the `Hands-On Activities` menu.
3. Select the activity you want to attempt.

4.  The following activities align with this chapter:

    I.  Set 1 – Azure Subscriptions (Accessible at `https://packt.link/activity4`)

    II. Set 2 – Management Groups (Accessible at `https://packt.link/activity5`)

    III. Set 2 – Resource Groups (Accessible at `https://packt.link/activity6`)

Each activity will have a set of tasks. Complete all the tasks to shore up your practical knowledge. For example, *Figure 3.25* shows the tasks aligned with the activity *Azure Subscriptions*:

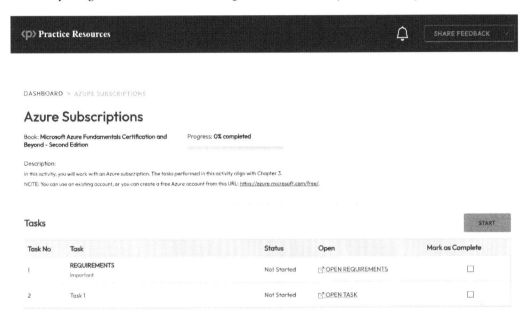

Figure 3.25 – Tasks in Azure Subscriptions activity

# Additional Information and Study References

This section provides links to additional exam information and study references.

- **Microsoft Learn certification further information**:

  - AZ-900 - Microsoft Azure Fundamentals exam guide: `https://packt.link/2i3TL`

  - AZ-900 - Microsoft Azure Fundamentals study guide: `https://packt.link/aURjD`

- **Microsoft Learn training further information**:

  - AZ-900 - Microsoft Azure Fundamentals course: `https://packt.link/PboSF`

# 4

# Azure Core Resources

In *Chapter 3, Azure Core Architectural Components*, you gained knowledge of the Azure platform's core components, from both the physical and logical perspectives.

This chapter will outline the core building block resources available in Azure; you will look at the components of **compute**, **networking**, and **storage**.

This chapter primarily focuses on the **Describe Azure architecture and services** module from the *Skills Measured* section of the AZ-900 Azure Fundamentals exam.

> **Note**
> You can find a detailed AZ-900 Azure Fundamentals exam skills area in the *Appendix, Assessing AZ-900 Exam Skills* of this book.

By the end of this chapter, you will be able to answer questions on the following confidently:

- Azure compute resources
- Azure network services
- Azure storage services

In addition, this chapter's goal is to take your knowledge beyond the exam content, so you are prepared for a real-world, day-to-day, Azure-focused role.

# Azure Resources

In *Chapter 3, Azure Core Architectural Components*, you covered resource groups and learned that they are a **logical grouping** of Azure resources; but what is a "resource" in Azure?

An **Azure resource** is an **Azure entity** that can be "managed." These resources are the building block components combined to create services, and you use these services to provide solutions. These services and resources can be broken down into more manageable identities and categories, forming a service catalog of Azure services that you can browse through and select to build your solution. You can build a solution using any of the services within the Azure service catalog, which comprises several thousand individual resources.

To build a solution, you need compute, storage, and network resources, as well as identity, security, and management services, among others. The following sections will explore the compute, storage, and networking resources.

# Azure Compute Resources

Compute resources are one of the core resources you will look at in this chapter. The term **compute** can be described simply as a "platform to execute code on"; it runs your **software** and processes your **data**.

The next sections will review the following compute resources outlined in the AZ-900 exam's **Skills Measured** section:

- Virtual Machines (VMs) and Scale Sets
- Containers
- App Service
- Functions
- Azure Virtual Desktop

## Virtual Machines

This section will introduce **Virtual Machines (VMs)**, as outlined in the AZ-900 exam's **Skills Measured** section: **Describe Azure compute and networking services**.

> **Note**
>
> You can find a detailed *Certification Skills Measured* section in the *Appendix, Assessing AZ-900 Exam Skills* of this book.

**VMs** are **Infrastructure-as-a-Service (IaaS)** "compute service resources," the common "building blocks" of any Azure solution. VMs are the **virtualization** of the physical computer resources of CPU and memory. They are a software emulation of physical hardware computers.

VMs are the most appropriate compute service in the following scenarios:

- When there is a need to provide complete control of the **Operating System (OS)** and any software installed.

- When there are customization requirements, such as customizing the OS, the software/applications, and their runtimes. Custom and Azure Marketplace images can also be used. The OS can be Windows or Linux distributions.

- When the workload cannot be containerized.

- When there is a need to extend on-premises computing capacity, perhaps for development and testing, disaster recovery, and business continuity scenarios. VMs can be connected to an organization's network using a VPN and the internet to route the traffic or the **Microsoft ExpressRoute** service, a private network connection that bypasses the internet for better performance and low-latency requirements. Alternatively, Azure VMs can be isolated and not connected to on-premises environments.

Creating VMs in your solution as an IaaS resource component means that there are tasks you are still responsible for under the shared responsibility model. These are tasks you need to carry out as you would for on-premises compute resources, such as configuring and patching the OS, installing, and configuring any software, creating backups, securing the VM with network security controls, and managing/securing user account access.

The next section will look at the differences between physical machines and virtual machines and the benefits of virtual machines over physical machines.

### *Physical Machines versus Virtual Machines*

To grasp the benefits of virtual machines over physical machines, you will first explore the physical hardware operating model.

Historically, for each application that an organization wishes to operate, there is typically a one-to-one mapping between the application and a dedicated instance of an OS and physical machine, meaning that each app requires its own physical machine. In this scenario, many physical machines would be required: an organization would have to have individual dedicated physical machines to run Exchange, SharePoint, Active Directory, files, print, the web, databases, line-of-business applications, and so on.

*Figure 4.1* outlines this typical traditional physical hardware operating model, which has a common shared infrastructure connecting and supporting multiple physical machines:

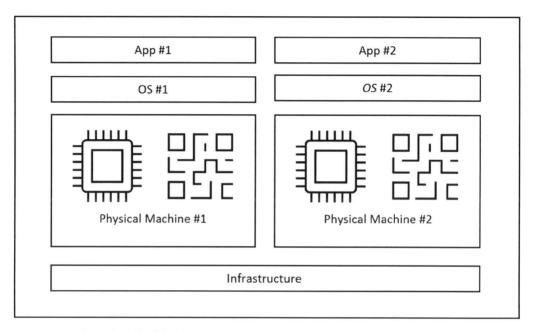

Figure 4.1 – Traditional approach supporting a single app per physical machine

*Figure 4.1* illustrates the traditional approach to deploying one physical machine per app. It was (and still is) a costly and operationally inefficient model. However, **virtualization** is an alternative to this and has many benefits to an organization when running on-premises.

When running virtual machines on a cloud platform, there can be even greater operational and financial benefits and value, as you learned in *Chapter 1, Introduction to Cloud Computing*. Adopting public cloud virtualization involves no longer having to purchase and maintain hardware in an on-premises facility and finance it all with a CapEx cost model (although on-premises hardware may also be leased as OpEx).

Before you switch to the virtualization model, you need to know what virtualization is as a technology concept, its benefits, and what value it provides to an organization's technology and business personas.

**Virtualization**, as a technology concept, is based on **abstraction** and, specifically, "hardware abstraction." The technology layer that is used to achieve hardware abstraction is known as a **hypervisor**.

**Abstraction** means "removing a dependency" and filtering out the facts of some characteristics no longer relevant, which allows you to focus on what is important. So, for example, in the case of virtualization, the VM is "no longer dependent on the hardware." If you have abstracted or removed the hardware from the equation, you no longer need that layer or its detail. The hardware is somebody else's issue to handle; you just take what you need from it.

Likening this to the analogy of pizza processing and the Pizza-as-a-Service example from *Chapter 1, Introduction to Cloud Computing*, you could say that your favorite franchised pizza outlet has abstracted the cooking process in that they have abstracted the ingredients, the recipe, the oven, as well as the whole kitchen; for example:

> *You request from a pizza outlet a specific pizza size that meets your requirements and all you have to do is consume it; you have removed/filtered out (no longer your concern or care) the details of stocking the ingredients and knowing recipes, the ability to cook, having a special pizza oven, the actual cooking process, and so on.*

In the *Virtualization versus Containerization* section, you will see that **containerization** is all about abstraction at the **OS level**, while **virtualization** means abstraction at the **hardware level**.

*Figure 4.2* visualizes the approach of virtualization:

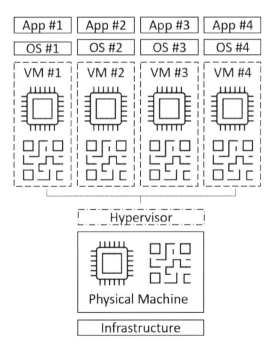

Figure 4.2 – Virtualization approach supporting multiple apps per physical machine

This model allows fewer physical machines to run more applications. In *Figure 4.1*, you had two physical machines to run two apps. With virtualization, you can now run four applications from just one physical machine.

Each VM shares the underlying hardware resources on which the VM is located, referred to as the "host resources." You can create many virtual CPU and memory resources from one physical CPU resource. How many VMs you can create on from a physical host machine will vary depending on the underlying host's resources… your mileage may vary.

Now that you know about the differences and benefits of the virtualization approach, it is time to look at the different types of VMs available to run your workloads.

### VM Types

Different workloads have different requirements and therefore need different solutions. To address this, Azure has different VM types, and each VM type is tailored to a specific use case and workload type.

VM types are broken down into categories and family series. The family series identifier is a leading "alphabetic character." In addition, a naming convention is used to break down the VM types based on their intended use case. Some examples of this include the following:

- Subfamilies

- The number of virtual CPUs (this can be expressed as the number of vCPUs)

- Additive features

- Versions

You will take a closer look at VM naming conventions later in this section.

---

**Further knowledge**

VMs also support nested virtualization, which allows you to run Hyper-V inside a VM. It is mainly used for testing, training, development, and non-production workloads. Not all VM sizes support nested virtualization; however, this is liable to change. You can find the latest information at `https://packt.link/w0XYb`.

---

As mentioned earlier, the family series identifier is a leading alphabetic character. Now, take a look at the following categories, family series, and intended purpose of various VMs:

- **General purpose** (A, B, and D family series): These VMs have a balanced CPU-to-memory ratio. They are best suited for testing and development (A series only), burstable workloads (B series only), and general-purpose workloads (D series only).

- **Compute optimized** (F family series): These VMs have a high CPU-to-memory ratio. They are best suited for web servers, application servers, network appliances, batch processes, and any workload where bottlenecks and a lack of resources will typically originate in the CPU over memory.

- **Memory optimized** (E and M family series): These VMs have a high memory-to-CPU ratio. They are best suited for relational databases, in-memory analytics, and any workload where bottlenecks and a lack of resources will typically originate in the memory over the CPU.

- **Storage optimized** (L family series): These VMs have high disk throughput and I/O. They are best suited for data analytics, data warehousing, and any workload where bottlenecks and a lack of resources will typically relate to the disk over the memory and CPU.

- **GPU optimized** (N family series): These VMs have graphics processing units (GPUs). They are best suited for compute-intensive, graphics-/gaming-intensive, visualization, and video conferencing/streaming workloads.

- **High performance** (H family series): These are the most powerful CPU VMs that Azure provides, offering high-speed throughput network interfaces. They are best suited for compute and network workloads such as SAP HANA.

Knowledge of these family series is all you need for the exam objectives. However, as the book aims to take your skills beyond the exam objectives to prepare you for an Azure role, this section will take a closer look at the Azure naming conventions involved. These naming conventions can help you identify the many VMs you can choose from when you create a VM.

For simplicity and readability, the core aspects can be presented as follows:

```
[Family] + [Sub-Family] + [# of vCPUs] + [Additive Features] +
[Version]
```

Here is some information on the core aspects represented in the VM series naming:

- **Family**: This represents the VM family series.

- **Sub-Family**: This represents the specialized VM differentiations.

- **# of vCPUs**: This represents the number of vCPUs of the VM.

- **Additive Features examples**:

  - a: This indicates an AMD-based processor.

  - d: This indicates a VM with a local temp disk.

  - i: This indicates an Isolated size.

  - l: This indicates a low memory size.

  - m: This indicates memory-intensive size.

- s: This indicates the presence of Premium Storage capabilities. However, some newer VM options without this attribute can still support Premium Storage.

- t: This indicates a tiny memory size.

- **Version**: This represents the version of the VM family series.

Some example breakdowns are as follows:

- **B2ms**: B series family, two vCPUs, memory-intensive, Premium Storage-capable

- **D4ds v5**: D series family, four vCPUs, local temp disk, Premium Storage-capable, version 5

- **D4as v5**: D series family, four vCPUs, AMD, Premium Storage-capable, version 5

- **E8s v3**: E series family, eight vCPUs, Premium Storage-capable, version 3

- **NV16as v4**: N series family, NVIDIA GRID, 16 vCPUs, AMD, Premium Storage-capable, version 4

You now know the different VM types you can use to run your workloads. Next, you will look at what else to consider when choosing VMs for the compute service to host your workloads.

### VM Deployment Considerations

When it comes to deploying VMs on an Azure subscription, you should think of your solution more broadly, not just focusing on deploying resources in isolation without further consideration of other elements such as the operational aspects. Some additional elements to consider when creating VMs for a solution are outlined in this section and visualized in *Figure 4.3*:

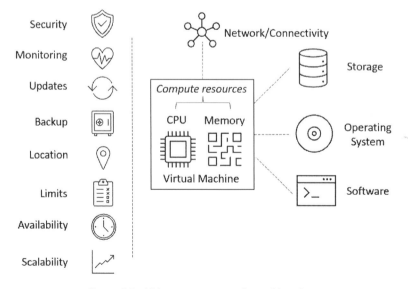

Figure 4.3 – VM components and considerations

Now, explore the following additional elements in more detail:

- **Additional VM resources**: A VM includes a virtual CPU and memory as its core components. However, you will need to provide an OS, software, storage, networking, connectivity, and security for the VM at a minimum, the same as you would for a physical computer.

- **Location and data residency**: Not all VM types and sizes are available in all regions. Check whether the VM types and sizes required for your solution are available in the region where you will be creating resources. Data residency may also be an important point to ensure you meet any compliance needs mandated for your organization. Different regions will also have different costs for VM creation.

- **VM quota limits**: Each Azure subscription has default quota limits that could impact the creation of VMs. In addition, there are limits on the number of VMs, the VM's total cores, and the VMs per series. The specific default limits depend on the Azure subscription billing type. Quota limits for SQL VMs and virtual desktop VMs that require the NV series type, for example, can commonly be exceeded, but this can be resolved by requesting a quota limit increase from Microsoft Support.

> **Note**
> You can find further information on these limits at `https://packt.link/1HREg`.

- **Monitoring**: It is vital to have visibility into the performance metrics and operational and security event logs to gain insights; you cannot respond to what you do not know about. Unfortunately, Microsoft does not automatically monitor VMs or their resources. There are automatically captured activity logs, but this is more of an audit and governance control than performance metrics or operational and security event logs; to have more visibility, you must enable monitoring.

  You can use both **Azure Monitor** and **Azure Advisor** to gain insights into your VM's performance and operational health. In addition, a cloud-native **Security Incident and Event Management** (**SIEM**) solution such as **Microsoft Sentinel** can be used as a single pane of glass and provides a bird's-eye view across all Azure, other clouds, and on-premises resources.

- **Backup**: Microsoft does not automatically back up the OS or software running on your VMs. Under the shared responsibility model, you have complete control of that aspect, and it is your responsibility to protect it. However, Microsoft's responsibility is to protect the underlying host's hardware and software.

- **Update management**: Microsoft does not automatically update the OS or software running on your VMs. As with backups, you have complete control over this aspect, and it is your responsibility under the shared responsibility model. However, **updating** the underlying host's hardware and software is Microsoft's responsibility. This leads to the next important aspect, the question of availability.

- **Availability**: This is the percentage of time a service is available for use. The two core components for addressing SLA requirements for VMs are **availability sets** and **availability zones**, each providing an SLA. This is important to consider because, as your VM is provided by Microsoft's hardware and infrastructure, it can and will fail in unavoidable ways. It is more a case of how you handle the failure when it happens than preventing it.

  It may be a planned or unplanned update/maintenance event that Microsoft carries out. So, it may not be an outright failure; it may mean that your VM gets rebooted or moved to another host. This could result in a short service interruption.

  These interruptions do not impact how your service operates when you implement measures provided by Microsoft, such as availability sets and availability zones. It is important to note that these measures need to be actioned by you, as they are not configured by default.

- **Scalability**: This is the ability of a system to handle increased loads while still meeting availability goals. VMs do not typically support scaling or auto-scaling; however, an IaaS resource solution such as **Scale Sets** can provide this functionality for VMs.

  A **Scale Set** is an IaaS resource service with built-in "auto-scale" features for VM-based workloads such as web and application services and batch processing. You specify the number of VMs and OS type to be deployed in the Scale Set, and a number of identical VMs will then be created. You benefit from "multiple fault domains" and "update domains" with Scale Sets as they are automatically deployed in availability sets and compatible with availability zones to protect against data center failures. This provides the automatic scaling, load balancing, availability, and fault tolerance functionality expected from a cloud model.

This section explored the factors that you need to consider when choosing VMs as the compute service to host your workloads. You learned the differences between physical machines and virtual machines, as well as VM types and deployment considerations. In the next section, you will look at containerization and compare and contrast it to VMs as a compute service, as well as Azure Container Instances and the Azure Kubernetes platform.

## Container Services

**Container services** are a form of compute service outlined in the exam's **Skills Measured** section: **Describe Azure compute and networking services**.

The Azure container services are described as follows:

- **ACI**: This is a **Platform-as-a-Service (PaaS)** service for containers running in Azure.

- **Azure Container Apps**: These have additional benefits over ACI for running your containers by providing scaling and load balancing and permitting greater flexibility in your design. They remove the need for container management and also run as a PaaS service.

- **AKS**: This is a container-hosting platform and orchestration service for managing containers at scale.

Before looking at container services, it is a sound idea to first explore the differences between virtualization and containerization.

### Virtualization versus Containerization

These compute service approaches can be defined as follows:

- **Virtualization**: This is an approach where the "hardware is abstracted." This allows many compute instances (VMs) to share a single host's hardware resources. Each compute instance runs with its own isolated OS.

- **Containerization**: This is an approach where the "OS is abstracted." Here, abstract means to remove—that is, remove the requirement to provide that layer. You make the abstracted (removed from thought and consideration) layer the cloud provider's responsibility to keep available, maintain, and so on; you still consume resources from it, but it is a layer that you no longer need to know or care about.

**Containers**, as a concept, are built around encapsulation and creating standardized software units, packaging an application's code and its dependencies such that they can be deployed equally seamlessly into a development or production environment with expected, repeatable, and consistent results. They are advantageous as they are intended to be portable, self-contained computing environments.

A **container** is a compute unit similar to a VM. Containers and VMs have the same goals—that is, to "host" and "execute" code. However, VMs have a lot of overhead, are big, utilize a lot of resources, and have slow boot times. You can consider a container an anti-VM as their characteristics are the complete opposite. They are lightweight, smaller in size, utilize fewer resources, and have quicker boot times. So, they are more agile, have more efficient compute units than a VM, and are therefore a perfect fit for your digital transformation journey and modernizing your data center and workloads. You may even be brave enough to say that containerization, at some point, will do to virtualization what virtualization did to the process of installing an OS in the physical server bare-metal approach.

This containerization approach allows many compute instances (containers) to share the host software resources of one OS of a single host. Thus, it can be thought of as more of an application delivery model than a virtualization model.

*Figure 4.4* visualizes the concepts of virtualization and containerization against the traditional physical approach:

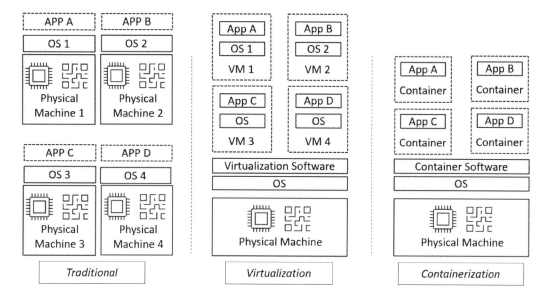

Figure 4.4 – Concept differences in traditional versus virtualization versus containerization

Looking closely, you will observe that *Figure 4.4* visualizes the different approaches that can be used to host your application. These are explained in detail as follows:

- **Traditional approach**: Before virtualization and containerization technologies, applications were installed on an OS that was installed directly on the hardware. This process is usually referred to as being installed on **bare metal**. This means there is no software (such as a hypervisor) between the OS and the hardware.

  The early physical approaches installed many apps on one OS and one physical server (often referred to as a "piece of tin"), but this often resulted in resource starvation, where the resource-hungry app would consume all the resources or raise software conflicts with processes and libraries (referred to as **Dynamic Link Libraries** (DLL) hell).

  This was solved by running each application on its own physical server. However, this brought other problems as you had over-resourced and under-utilized servers, costing a lot of money with little output. In addition, it brought physical tin sprawl across the data center, which meant that you needed more physical rack space. Expanding physical rack space required more floor space, cabling, power, cooling, and so on. Finally, this meant that the IT focus was on data center capacity management, and this distracted engineers from their core task—the job of deploying and operating apps for the business.

The bottom line is that the ability of one physical server to deliver one app introduced an inefficiency-of-scale problem that was seen as a cost to the business. Hence, IT was seen as a cost center, not an innovation or value-creation center.

- **Virtualization approach**: Virtualization was an opportunity to change the previous scenario of one app per physical server. This ability allowed abstracting (removing dependency on) the hardware.

  The benefits that virtualization provides include tackling the two key challenges of the traditional physical approach i.e., **scale** and **utilization**. Virtualization meant that you could run multiple VMs and, therefore, multiple applications on one physical server, meaning greater resource utilization and less floor space, power, and cooling are required.

  In conclusion, fewer physical servers are required to deliver more apps, translating to fewer costs to deliver the same applications to the business. Due to this, you have a leaner, more agile, tangible, and value-delivering IT team.

- **Containerization approach**: Containerization is another evolution in delivering applications to a business. This approach changed from abstracting the hardware to abstracting (removing dependency on) the software bringing about the benefits of containerization.

  The key benefits and metrics are greater resource utilization, efficiency, and isolation, smaller sizes, faster boot-up, agile app deployment, and no requirement to provide a guest OS for each app, as they all share the underlying host OS kernel.

  The bottom line is that fewer physical servers and OS instances are required to deliver more apps, which, again, means fewer costs to deliver more applications to the business in a more demand-driven, agile, and standardized manner.

Now you have grasped the concepts of virtualization versus containerization, you will look at ACI.

## Azure Container Instances (ACI)

What is **Azure Container Instances (ACI)**? In a nutshell, it is a multitenant, serverless **Containers-as-a-Service (CaaS)** platform intended to run single-instance containers in isolation.

What does this mean? Simply put, this means it is a PaaS service for containers running in Azure. You just create a single instance of a container and start using it as you would a VM. There is no need to manage the VMs to host the containers and no additional services are required to create or manage them.

Containers share the kernel of the host OS they are running on. This means containers are very lightweight and have faster boot times. ACI containers can be available in seconds, compared to VMs, which have to host their own guest OSs and have much slower start times. The important fact is that there is no overhead when creating container platforms, no need to manage VMs, and no orchestration components. Both Windows and Linux containers are supported on the ACI container platform.

It should be noted that there "are" VMs underneath; it is that misnomer of **serverless** again. This term just means that you do not need to concern yourself with the details. Microsoft provides and manages the underlying hosts, the VMs, the container engine, the orchestration components, and so on, leaving you with a compute unit to host and execute your code.

The primary benefit is that it allows for the most straightforward and quickest entry point to start running your apps in Azure containers without the need to manage servers or orchestration components.

ACI is best suited to running jobs that are rarely used or scheduled (quarterly, yearly, ad hoc), including batch processing, and those that are temporary or demand-driven/event-driven. This also includes jobs that do not interact with other container instances/services or require advanced orchestration, load balancing, or autoscaling, given that these are single-instance containers and are best for single-use and isolated jobs. Now that you know about ACI, it's time to take a look at Azure Container Apps.

### Azure Container Apps (ACA)

What is **Azure Container Apps**? In a nutshell, it's a fully managed serverless container service platform that is powered by the **Kubernetes**, **DAPR**, **Kubernetes Event-Driven Autoscaling** (**KEDA**), and **envoy** open-source technologies.

It allows Kubernetes-style applications and microservices to be built without having to manage the complexities of container orchestration. No direct access is given to the underlying APIs, control plane, and cluster management of Kubernetes.

You can learn more about DAPR and KEDA at the following URLs:

- `https://packt.link/xfBsd`
- `https://packt.link/PEP7a`

Now that you have looked at Azure Container Apps, it's time to learn about the AKS compute service.

### Azure Kubernetes Service (AKS)

What is the **Azure Kubernetes Service** (**AKS**)? In a nutshell, it is a container "hosting platform" and "orchestration service" for "managing containers at scale."

This approach brings the power of the open-source Kubernetes platform but is delivered as a PaaS-managed platform by Microsoft; think of this as CaaS. The service is designed for highly customizable, scalable, and portable workload scenarios.

When comparing ACI with AKS, it is important to know the non-functional aspects of cost, complexity, and operations. In other words, you can think of each of these solutions at opposing ends of the scale. ACI is the simplest in terms of how it operates and also has the lowest cost, while AKS has the greatest functionality, features, and scale. However, this means AKS comes with complexity in terms of how it operates and it is also expensive.

*Figure 4.5* visualizes the difference between the ACI and AKS container services:

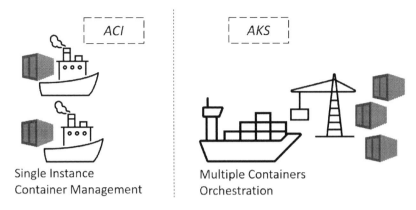

Figure 4.5 – ACI versus AKS for containerization compute services

The AKS service architecture has two essential elements—the master node and the worker node. The master node is the control plane managed by Microsoft, while the worker nodes contain Pods that the customer manages.

*Figure 4.6* shows the high-level AKS service architecture:

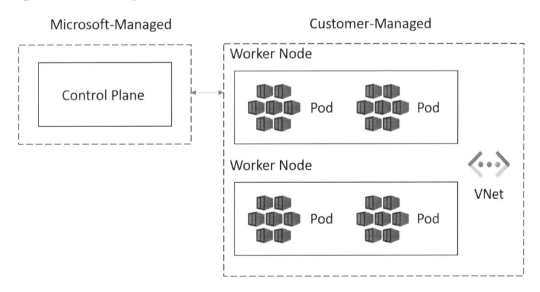

Figure 4.6 – AKS high-level service architecture showing Microsoft's
responsibilities versus the customer-managed components

While the **master node** is responsible for scheduling the underlying **worker nodes**, **Pods,** and the **worker nodes** are the VMs that run the node's components and the container runtime. *Figure 4.7* shows the high-level worker node service architecture:

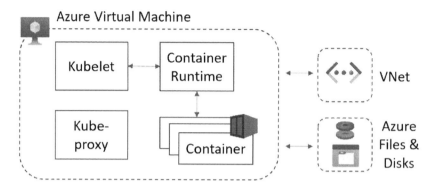

Figure 4.7 – Worker node high-level service architecture

You should size and scale out the VMs in your nodes to support the performance and capacity demands you need to meet. The Azure VM for cluster nodes is based on Windows Server 2019 or Ubuntu Linux. Microsoft manages the process of creating and scaling these VMs. These nodes are billed as regular VMs so discounts such as reservations can be applied.

This section introduced the AKS compute service. You learned the differences between the ACI and AKS container services, as well as the AKS service architecture components of the master node and worker node. In the next section, you will look at Azure App Service as an Azure compute service for hosting code, websites, and applications.

## Azure App Service

Azure App Service is a compute service outlined in the exam's **Skills Measured** section: **Describe Azure compute and networking services**.

**Azure App Service** is a PaaS resource and provides a website and code-hosting platform fully managed by Microsoft. The platform supports Windows and Linux workloads, multiple frameworks, and programming languages such as .NET, .NET Core, Node.js, Python, PHP, and more.

*Figure 4.8* visualizes how you can host a website or code in the IaaS model versus the PaaS model:

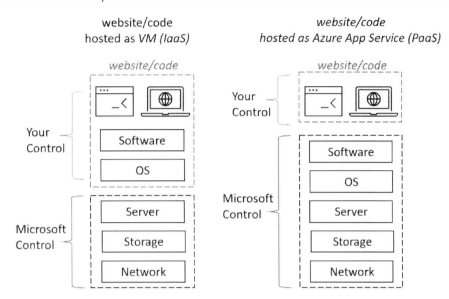

Figure 4.8 – IaaS hosting with Azure VM versus PaaS hosting with Azure App Service

Being a **PaaS** service means that this is a hosting platform managed by Microsoft; Azure App Service is responsible for the underlying compute service that will host your website or code. Therefore, you do not need to manage VMs or containers as you are only responsible for providing the website or code to be hosted.

Each app service runs inside an "App Service plan." You can think of the App Service plans as a TV subscription service plan or a mobile/broadband service provider plan. Each has a tariff with a set of features and functionalities you have enabled and can access as a subscriber. The more fully-featured the plan is, the more choices and options you will have. You just need to choose a plan with the most appropriate features that meet your needs.

*Figure 4.9* outlines the relationship between all the components of Azure App Service:

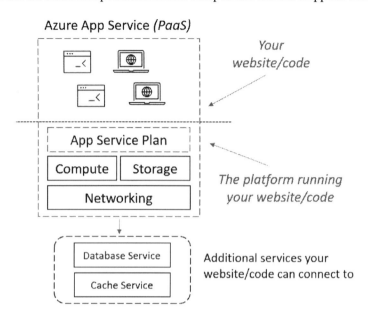

Figure 4.9 – Azure App Service plan components relationship

In reality, the App Service plan is closer to that of a server farm; it defines the number of VMs your App Service instance will use, the type and size of VM and its properties, and the region the VMs will be created. One App Service plan (server farm) can be used to host multiple web apps if enough resources are available from the underlying VM resources.

A web app can only be hosted on a single App Service plan (one set of compute instances, one server farm), but an App Service plan may host many web apps. A web app, when being created, can be added to an existing App Service plan. Alternatively, you can create a new App Service plan to host your web app/code.

You can select an OS to host your app/code, as well as a runtime stack such as .NET, PHP, or Java and its version. You can also select the region where your website/code will be hosted. This could have cost or data compliance implications if you must use certain regions based on compliance rules.

App Service has pricing tiers that define the features and functionality available in each tier. The following are the price tiers available:

- **Free and shared**: This is intended for development and testing purposes. No SLA is provided, and your app will run on the same compute service resources as other customers. There is no support for autoscaling, hybrid, or VNet connectivity. Also, custom domains are only available in the shared tier.

- **Basic service plan**: This is intended for low-traffic usage that does not require advanced autoscaling and traffic management features. It has built-in basic load balancing across instances. Custom domains and hybrid connectivity are supported, but not VNet connectivity.

- **Standard service plan**: This is intended for running production workloads. It supports custom domains, autoscaling, hybrid, and VNet connectivity.

- **Premium V2/V3**: This is intended for larger-scale and performance production workloads. It provides all the features of Standard, plus private endpoints.

- **Isolated/Isolated V2**: This is intended for mission-critical workloads required to run on a virtual network in a private, dedicated environment.

An App Service plan is billed even when no web apps are running. This is because the VM is created as part of the plan and will remain running until it is deleted, even with no web apps running on the VMs. The only way to stop billing is to delete the App Service plan.

An App Service plan has **scale-up** and **scale-out** properties in the portal when configuring an App Service plan. The scale-up property adds functionality and features. These are part of a pricing tier, and you are, in effect, selecting a VM with a pre-configured runtime stack such as .NET, PHP, and Java. You can select any of the different versions available.

The amount of compute instances that can be scaled is determined by the pricing tier. This compute instance scaling is only available for the Basic, Standard, and Premium pricing tiers. An App Service pricing tier can be changed after creation. Changing this will modify the functions, features, and the number of compute instances available to run your web app.

The scale-out property adds additional compute instance resources to support running these apps. You can scale manually or set up custom autoscaling on a schedule based on any metric available. Your pricing tier will determine your scale-out limit, which could be either Basic, Standard, or Premium.

This section looked at Azure App Service. You learned how you can use a PaaS approach to host a website or code versus the IaaS approach, as well as getting to know the components' relationship embodied in the Azure App Service plan. Next, you will take a brief look at another Azure compute function, Azure Functions.

## Azure Functions

**Azure Functions** is a "serverless code engine." It is a **Function-as-a-Service (FaaS)** or serverless model where you provide your code and business logic, and the cloud provider hosts it in their language, runtime, and compute environment shared with other tenants.

Azure Functions is used for events that trigger code. The **Functions** code being executed is a response or action based on an event trigger.

Microsoft is responsible for providing all layers up to and including the language, runtime, and compute. You are responsible for providing the business logic layer.

Equipped with this knowledge of Azure Functions, you will now learn about the Azure Virtual Desktop service.

## Azure Virtual Desktop Service

The Virtual Desktop service is a compute service that you must learn about, as outlined in the exam's *Skills Measured* section: **Describe Azure compute and networking services**.

Microsoft's Azure **Virtual Desktop service** is a desktop and application virtualization service that provides access to your desktop and applications from virtually anywhere and on any device.

It is provided as a **PaaS service** that allows remote users to connect from their devices to their hosted desktops and remote applications in Azure. This access is provided securely and reliably from any location with an internet connection or over a private managed network such as Microsoft's ExpressRoute service. Many device types and virtual desktop clients are available to provide the broadest range of connectivity and access methods. The following are some of the benefits of virtual desktops:

- It provides a full Windows client and Office 365 experience.

- It delivers the only multi-session Windows 10/11 experience.

- It paves a migration path for **Remote Desktop Services (RDSs)**.

- It deploys and scales in minutes.

- It allows access to the cloud service from anywhere, from a web client to a desktop client such as Windows or macOS, and iOS, Android, and Linux devices.

- It provides centralized identity management and security using Entra ID for role-based access control with Conditional Access, Microsoft Intune, and Microsoft Defender support.

- It provides improved remote access security using reverse connect technology, meaning no inbound ports to the session host's VMs, thus reducing the attack surface area.

- It provides the most cost-effective service using pooled desktops through the traditional RDS session host model approach, where many users share one session host VM. Alternatively, virtual desktops can provide the most performant and secure solution through the traditional VDI approach, where power users or security requirements mandate a level of isolation between user sessions, with one user per VM (where a desktop cannot be shared between users). This is the personal desktop approach.

- If you do not wish to provide users with access to a full desktop, you can publish the applications that have been installed on the VMs.

*Figure 4.10* visualizes the Azure Virtual Desktop approach and its components:

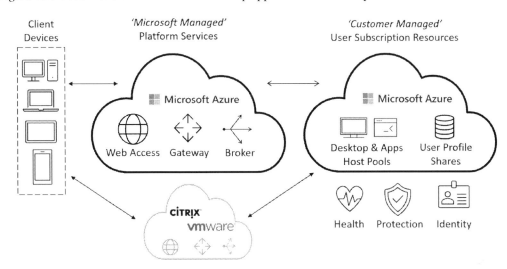

Figure 4.10 – Azure Virtual Desktop service providing access from virtually anywhere

As shown in *Figure 4.10*, the Azure Virtual Desktop service has the following elements:

- **Microsoft-provided and -managed platform services**: These are PaaS functions where Microsoft provides the managed services of the web access, gateway, and broker roles. These provide the secure connectivity service layer that connects users with their desktops and published apps.

- **Host pools**: These are collections of VMs. They are the user-assignable entities that will run your users' desktops and publish the remote applications. For example, you may have multiple host pools to meet your needs, and each pool is a collection of VMs that share the same image and configuration that may be assigned to a different set of users. Different images and configurations could be available to different users and teams based on Azure AD group assignments to different pools.

  In addition, there are two load-balancing methods—that is, depth mode and breadth mode. **Depth mode** saves costs by fully utilizing a single VM to host users' sessions before placing a session on the next VM. This is known as **vertical load balancing**. On the other hand, **breadth mode** is the best load-balancing method for performance since each user session is created on the next available VM and never on the same VM as the last session it was connected to (where two or more VMs are available in the host pool). This is known as **horizontal load balancing**.

- **Customer-created desktops**: These are the infrastructure resources that will provide the user's desktops and apps. Host pools contain the session host VMs that provide the user's desktop, published apps, and file shares; file shares will be required to host the user's profile containers.

- **Customer-created remote applications**: Applications no longer need to be installed on the VM OS itself or included as part of the image. Through the MSIX app attach functionality, the apps are decoupled from the OS and are then dynamically attached to the VM that a user is connected to for their remote session.

- **User profiles**: Here, the **FSLogix** profile container technology is used, which allows a user profile to be stored on a **Virtual Hard Disk (VHD)** in the file share location. This is then dynamically attached to the VM that a user is connected to for their remote session, whether it be the full desktop or just the application that has been published.

- **Third-party provided and managed virtual desktop platform services**: Vendors such as Citrix and VMware are part of the ecosystem that provides additional functionalities. You can utilize their presentation and management layers to connect to your virtual desktops and apps.

- **Cost savings**: Cost savings can be made by using autoscaling and running the VMs only when users connect to them. You can also consider using ephemeral disks to negate the need to persist disks in storage. In contrast to shutting VMs down to save costs, if the VMs must be running 24/7, then you can save on pay-as-you-go metered pricing by committing to a one- or three-year commitment to reserve the compute capacity, which is called **Reserved Instances (RI)** or **VM reservations**. Note that this only discounts the compute costs of the VM. You will still have to pay the OS costs for storage, networking, and so on.

  Finally, through the **Azure Hybrid Use Benefit (AHUB)**, you can also negate the OS costs for the VMs if you have eligible software licensing. You should contact Microsoft Support or a licensing specialist partner for guidance in this area.

This concludes the Azure compute services content for this chapter. You learned about the Azure Virtual Desktop service, looking at its components and benefits. In the next section, you will look at the network services available in Azure; you will cover virtual networks, peering, connectivity services, and name resolution.

## Azure Network Services

Azure provides a range of network services you can use to communicate with Azure resources. You must know about the following Azure network services since they are outlined in the exam:

- **Virtual Network (VNet)**
- VNet peering
- Virtual Private Network (VPN) gateway
- ExpressRoute
- Azure DNS

Azure networking provides the following capabilities:

- **Communication between Azure resources**: Communication paths between Azure resources, such as VMs, are provided through VNets. Communication between VNets is enabled using VNet peering (within the same region and across regions). Additionally, service endpoints are used to connect PaaS resources such as storage services and database services.

- **Communication with on-premises resources**: You can extend your local on-premises networks into Azure through VPNs, which provide encrypted connections over the internet, or ExpressRoute, which allows private, low-latency connections that bypass the internet.

- **Communication with third-party services**: You can communicate with other cloud providers, carriers, hosting and data center service providers, and software vendors, for example, to access the APIs or services offered by these third parties.

- **Communication with the internet**: Azure can be used as an internet breakout point for Azure resources or for on-premises purposes to access Azure resources. Azure resources such as VMs can accept incoming internet traffic through a public IP address. However, all VMs will typically have private IP addresses for security purposes, and the public IP address should be assigned via a load balancer, NAT Gateway, or other internet-facing gateway resource.

- **Isolation and segmentation of network traffic**: VNets are communication boundaries that provide isolation of the address space(s) (also referred to as **prefixes**) used within that VNet. To allow VNets to communicate, a VPN gateway, **Network Virtual Appliance** (**NVA**), or VNet peering must be used. In addition, a VNet's address space can be segmented with subnets to allow traffic filtering and routing to be defined at the subnet level. Typically, a VNet will contain one or more private address spaces, although public prefixes are supported.

- **Routing of network traffic**: Azure uses a set of default system routes or traffic direction/destination paths. You can think of this as a set of defined **Satellite-Navigation** (**Sat-Nav**) traffic routes that define how to get to a destination when coming from a given location. These routes will direct traffic between the subnets of all interconnected VNets to on-premises networks and the internet; no traffic inspection or filtering is applied by default. You can also apply **User-Defined Routes** (**UDRs**), which you will read about in the *Internal Virtual Network (VNet) Routing* section.

- **Filtering of network traffic**: By default, no traffic filtering occurs within a VNet. However, a **Network Security Group** (**NSG**) can be used, which is a resource that allows you to define inbound and outbound allow and deny rules. You can filter this traffic based on factors such as source IP, destination IP, port, protocol, and more. Alternatively, you can use an NVA—a VM that runs network routing and traffic control/filtering software provided by a third party (Barracuda, Fortinet, and WatchGuard, to name a few). This acts as a firewall/packet filter in this scenario.

- **Encryption of network traffic**: Through a VPN gateway, traffic that has been sent and received from on-premises or another VNet can be encrypted.

- **Name resolution services through DNS services**: Azure has an integrated name resolution service for all resources in a VNet. You can configure the VNet with a custom DNS entry for any internal or external DNS server you have. For example, you can set the custom entry to the IP addresses of domain controllers if these handle the DNS for your VMs.

- **Cost implications**: No traffic entering (**ingress**) a VNet within a region is billed, but all traffic leaving (**egress**) a VNet and region is. This also applies to VNet peering; traffic between VNets will be billed for egress, not ingress.

Next, take a closer look at Azure VNets.

## Azure Virtual Networks

**Azure VNet** is an IaaS resource that enables communication with Azure resources. A VNet represents a software-defined, single-tenant, private network in a single Azure region that your resources communicate on. A VNet is dedicated to you and is not shared with other tenants in Azure.

Resources in the Azure VNet can access the internet and on-premises resources via public and private networks. Users and on-premises resources can also access and communicate with resources in the Azure VNet via these public and private networks. You may have one or more VNets; each can be connected or isolated to meet your goals. In addition, several connectivity options support inter-VNet and cross-premises connectivity scenarios.

*Figure 4.11* visualizes the VNet and connectivity approach:

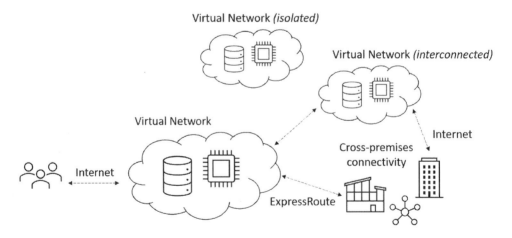

Figure 4.11 – Azure virtual networks schema showing communication between resources

The following are some characteristics of VNets:

- VNets act as "communication boundaries"; by default, Microsoft routes traffic to all the resources in a VNet to allow them to communicate with each other. However, if you wish to ensure that, by default, the VMs don't communicate (such as for compliance reasons), place each VM in a separate VNet.

- If you want the VMs in different VNets to communicate with each other, you must ensure that VNet peering or a VPN is used to connect them.

- You can control traffic into a VNet using a VPN gateway (one per VNet), an NSG, or a firewall. A VPN or NSG is a per-VNet control. If you have multiple VNets to control traffic, then an Azure firewall or third-party NVA is the most efficient option. This has a one-to-many ratio in that one firewall or NVA can control access to multiple VNets across multiple subscriptions. An NSG cannot be applied at the VNet level, but only at the subnet or network interface level.

- A VNet belongs to a resource group that belongs to a subscription and can only be part of one region. VNets can span across data center zones but are not available across regions.

- VMs in different subscriptions can communicate with each other so long as they are part of the same VNet or VNet peering, or if a VPN gateway connects the VNets and they don't have conflicting IP ranges.

- All traffic entering (ingress) a VNet and region is "not billed," but all traffic leaving (egress) a VNet and region is "billed." This also applies to VNet peering, since the traffic between these VNets will be billed for egress, not ingress.

- VNets contain one or more IP address spaces. Private IP prefixes are typically used, but public address spaces can also be used.

- VNet address spaces can be segmented into smaller subnets, the same as on-premises networks. However, note that Azure networking does not allow control at **Layer 2** (Data Layer | MAC address) of the **Open Systems Interconnect** (**OSI**) model; only **Layer 3** (Network Layer | IP address) can be controlled. The OSI model of network functions is beyond the scope of this book and exam objectives, but it has been mentioned here to give a fuller picture.

- If you are connecting Azure VNets to on-premises networks, you should ensure that these addresses do not overlap and are not duplicated. For example, you must ensure the same matching address space(s) does not exist on-premises. In this scenario, you should create Azure VNets with unique address spaces that differ from those used on-premises.

Now you will learn about VNet segmentation—a set of communication paths.

## VNet Segmentation

VNets, in their simplest form, are a set of communication paths that interconnect systems and other resources and services. You can think of them as corridors or elevators in a building. There are always entry and exit points in buildings. These are known as doors, but in VNets they can be considered gateways; there are external doors on the buildings and internal doors that separate rooms from corridors. You also have different floors, and you may even have buildings connected by interconnecting walkways or skyways in a campus environment.

In VNets, you can create similar constructs to segment a network into smaller sections called **subnets**. In the building example, a VNet is a building, an address space (also referred to as an address prefix) is a floor (VNets can have multiple address spaces, similar to how a building can have multiple floors), and the subnets are rooms. These subnets are then all connected by corridors, stairs, and elevators, which act as the (human) traffic paths. When you create a VNet, you define an address space; this can be broken down into subnets. Each resource within the VNet will be assigned an IP address.

*Figure 4.12* visualizes this concept of VNets and segmentation:

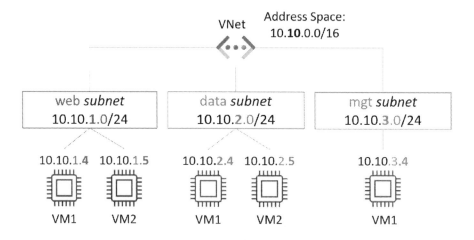

Figure 4.12 – The concept of segmenting a VNet into subnets

*Figure 4.12* shows an address space created using the **Classless Inter-Domain Routing** (**CIDR**) format of 10.10.0.0/16. This has been further segmented into smaller subnets (/24), with each resource assigned an IP address from this range. By default, all traffic can be routed between all the resources in all subnets, routed to other VNets, and routed externally to the internet and on-premises. You can define your routes based on how traffic travels to its destination through UDRs.

It is recommended that you use the following private non-routable (RFC1918) address ranges with Azure VNets:

- 10.0.0.0 to 10.255.255.255 (10/8 prefix)

- 172.16.0.0 to 172.31.255.255  (172.16/12 prefix)

- 192.168.0.0 to 192.168.255.255 (192.168/16 prefix)

Azure reserves five IP addresses in any subnet. When creating a VM, you will notice that the first IP assigned in any given subnet will be a .4 address because Azure reserves the first four IP addresses (ranges start at 0, not 1) and the last IP address. They are detailed as follows:

- The **first IP address** is reserved for the VNet's network address—that is, x.x.x.0.

- The **second IP address** is reserved for the VNet's default gateway—that is, x.x.x.1.

- The **third** and **fourth IP addresses** are reserved for the VNet's Azure DNS—that is, x.x.x.2 and x.x.x.3, respectively.

- The **fifth IP address** is reserved for the VNet broadcast address—that is, x.x.x.255.

The following section looks at internal routing.

### Internal Virtual Network (VNet) Routing

As you learned earlier in this chapter, VNets have a set of communication paths that interconnect systems. Azure uses a set of default "system routes" or traffic direction/ destination paths that allow resources to communicate with each other.

You cannot edit or remove these routes, but you can create custom route tables to control (redirect) the direction of traffic (packets). This is called **UDR** and allows you to override the default Azure system routes. Again, similar to the Sat-Nav analogy, this allows you to load in your custom traffic directions to override the manufacturer's predefined ones.

You can apply UDR through a "route table" resource within a VNet, combined with an NVA. This approach allows network segmentation and traffic control to occur much as it would in a traditional network.

*Figure 4.13* outlines this approach:

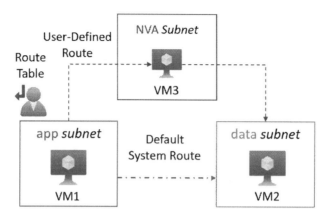

Figure 4.13 – VNet showing internal routing and segmentation through the use of an NVA

*Figure 4.13* shows that, in the default system routing, there is a communication path between VM1 and VM2. This could mean that if VM1 were to be compromised, it could contact VM2. However, if you apply a route table to the subnet where VM1 is, then any traffic leaving VM1 will be overridden by the UDR route table and directed to VM3. VM3 will then inspect the traffic and either block or allow the traffic based on the security rules set on the appliance (firewall). In this scenario, if VM1 is compromised, it will no longer communicate directly with VM2 and must be passed to VM3 first.

Next, you will look at external VNet routing.

### External Virtual Network (VNet) Routing

**External routing** is where traffic leaving (egressing) Azure has its path to its destination determined by cold-potato routing. The alternative to this is hot-potato routing. These terms are defined as follows:

- **Cold-potato routing**: This ensures that traffic remains on the Microsoft global network for as long as possible before it is handed off to a downstream "ISP edge" **Point of Presence (PoP)** to be delivered to its final destination. This is the most expensive form of egress data from Microsoft regions but has the lowest latency, the best quality, and the fastest performance. This can be likened to a plane courier versus a boat postal service.

- **Hot-potato routing**: This means that traffic leaves (egresses) the Microsoft global network at the earliest opportunity and travels to its destination via the internet, which means passing the packet between points (hops) on the internet multiple times. When the packet arrives at a point, it is passed on as soon as possible, if not immediately. This is where the analogy of passing a hot potato comes from. This is the cheapest option for data egress as it does not stay on the Microsoft network for any length of time. It exits onto the public network as quickly as possible and is the closest point to the data center. It is delivered by a cheaper, slower, less reliable boat postal service.

*Figure 4.14* outlines the hot- versus cold-potato routing approach. In the diagram, the cold-potato-routed traffic gets delivered to its final destination quicker with lower latency and more reliability as it stays on the Microsoft global backbone network for longer:

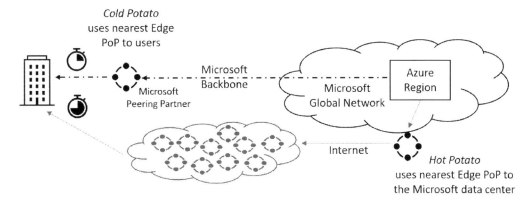

Figure 4.14 – Hot- versus cold-potato routing to carry traffic to its destination

*Figure 4.15* likens this to delivering a packet to its final destination by using the perspective of air travel versus shipping:

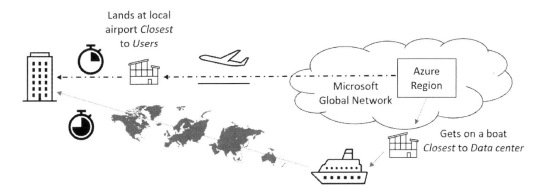

Figure 4.15 – Air travel versus shipping routes—similar to hot- versus cold-potato routing

The next section will look at VNet peering.

### Virtual Network Peering

**VNet peering** allows two or more VNets to be connected seamlessly so that, from a communication point of view, the traffic flow appears as though it is on the same network.

Unlike a VPN gateway whose traffic must be routed over the internet, traffic between the VNets, when using VNet peering, is routed over the Microsoft backbone, meaning fast, reliable, low-latency, and secure connectivity between your resources in different VNets. This is the same as traffic being routed between resources within the same VNet. *Figure 4.16* visualizes this inter-VNet connectivity:

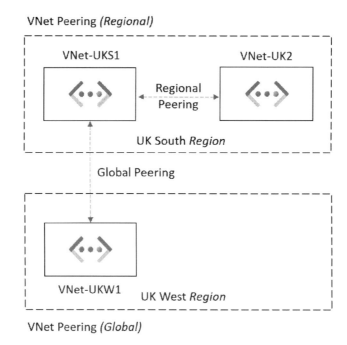

Figure 4.16 – Inter-VNet connectivity shown using peering

VNet peering also supports **regional** and **global** VNet peering, as shown in *Figure 4.16*. They are detailed as follows:

- **Regional VNet peering**: This is used to connect VNets from the same region
- **Global VNet peering**: This is used to connect VNets from different regions

As seen in *Figure 4.16*, a hub-and-spoke design is the most common deployment topology.

Now you will explore the VPN gateway service.

## Virtual Private Network (VPN) Gateways

A **VPN gateway** is a service that allows encrypted traffic to be sent through private and secure connections between resources in an on-premises location and an Azure VNet by using the internet. This allows users and resources to seamlessly connect as though they were part of the same local network. A VPN gateway requires several resources to be deployed. They are detailed as follows:

- **VNet**: A VNet can only have one VPN gateway, which is a resource that can be associated with only one VNet. When connecting Azure VNets to on-premises networks, you should ensure that these addresses do not overlap, are not duplicated, and that the same matching address space does not exist on-premises. In this scenario, you should create Azure VNets with a unique address space that differs from those used on-premises.

- **Gateway subnet**: A dedicated subnet named **GatewaySubnet** is created within the VNet. The VNet address space must have enough space available to allocate this. A /27 (/26 ...) address or larger is recommended since this ensures enough IP addresses are available.

- **Public IP address**: This resource is the public IP address used to connect to the on-premises VPN device (or another VNet's gateway).

- **Local network gateway**: This resource is used to represent your on-premises network location. It defines the VPN appliance that connections will be made through, as well as the network address spaces (also referred to as address prefixes) that you will be connecting from to establish a connection to the Azure resources. A local network gateway can specify a single on-premises network address space or multiple network address spaces.

  The local network gateway is configured with an IP address or the **Fully Qualified Domain Name (FQDN)** of the on-premises VPN appliance you will make a connection to. You also specify the IP ranges from the local on-premises network location that you will connect from.

  You can modify your local network gateway to reflect any changes in your on-premises network. For example, you can add or remove address spaces (prefixes) if you added a new on-premises network and now need to connect to Azure resources over the VPN associated with this local gateway, and then add these new IP spaces to allow this communication.

  Suppose you needed to prevent a network from communicating, you could remove these on-premises network spaces from the local gateway. By doing this, they will no longer be able to access resources in Azure over the VPN.

- **Connection**: This resource creates a logical connection between the local network gateway and the VPN gateway.

*Figure 4.17* shows these resources and their relationships:

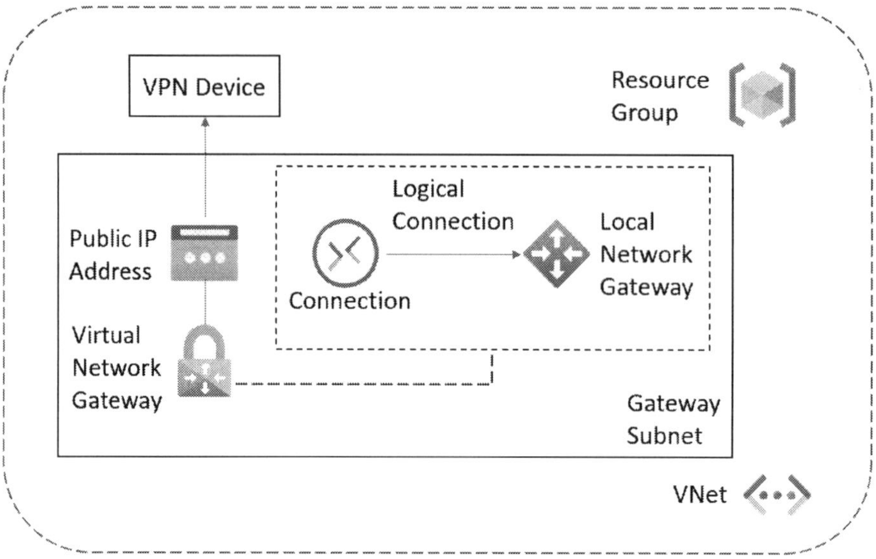

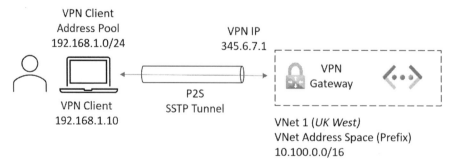

Figure 4.17 – VPN gateway resources allowing encrypted traffic to be sent through secure connections

A VPN gateway supports both the **Point-to-Site** VPN and **Site-to-Site** VPN connectivity methods. In the next few sections, you will look at these two connectivity methods in more detail.

The next section will look at the Point-to-Site VPN connectivity method.

### Point-to-Site VPN

This allows you to make a "secure encrypted connection" to Azure resources using a single user from a client device. This is intended for remote users who are not connected to the corporate network (and cannot use a Site-to-Site VPN), such as home workers or those traveling; the **OpenVPN**, **SSTP**, and **IKEv2** protocols are used. *Figure 4.18* shows a Point-to-Site VPN:

Figure 4.18 – Point-to-Site VPN

In *Figure 4.18*, a user initiates a VPN session through a VPN client to connect them to the Azure VNet. The user's device is allocated an IP address from the VPN client address pool, which is used for communication with Azure VNet resources.

Next, you will look at the Site-to-Site VPN connectivity method.

### Site-to-Site VPN

This allows you to make a secure encrypted connection to Azure resources in a cross-premises scenario to support a hybrid connectivity solution. The Azure VPN gateway service provides both "policy-based" VPNs (also referred to as static routing) and "route-based" VPNs (also referred to as dynamic routing).

**Policy-based VPNs** may be considered for more legacy scenarios since this is the older approach and is generally used to connect on-premises devices that only support policy-based (static) connections. This is typical since firewalls provide more VPN functionality than a fully-fledged and dedicated VPN device. Due to this, **route-based VPNs (dynamic)** are the recommended approach.

Both support the **Internet Protocol Security (IPSec)** protocol known as **Internet Key Exchange (IKE)**—both versions 1 and 2. The only authentication method that is supported is "pre-shared keys."

*Figure 4.19* shows how to connect an on-premises network to Azure using a Site-to-Site VPN. This topology requires a VPN device to be located at the on-premises site, and it must have a public IP address:

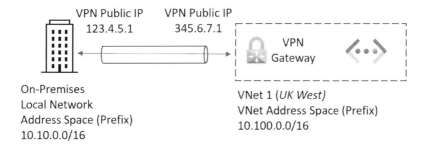

Figure 4.19 – Site-to-Site VPN

*Figure 4.20* illustrates how to connect two Azure VNets using a Site-to-Site VPN:

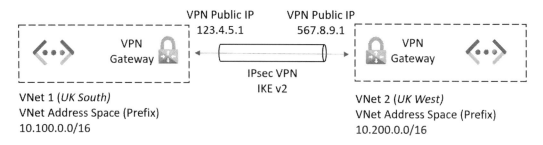

Figure 4.20 – VNet-to-VNet VPN

The alternative to using a Site-to-Site VPN to connect two Azure VNets is to use VNet peering. However, this uses private addresses and does not encrypt the traffic between the two VNets. This is a private connection that stays on the Microsoft backbone network, so it may not be a suitable alternative requirement.

Now, let's examine the ExpressRoute service.

### ExpressRoute

**ExpressRoute** (using an **ExpressRoute circuit**) is a true extension of your on-premises networks into Microsoft's data centers. It provides a fast, low-latency, enterprise-quality (reliable, stable) connection to your Azure resources for cross-premises scenarios.

Unlike a VPN network, traffic does not route (traverse) the internet. Traffic is carried over a privately managed network between your resources and Microsoft's data centers. This network is facilitated by a global telecom carrier, which acts as the connectivity provider.

As expected, this enterprise-grade connectivity has built-in redundancy that uses dynamic routing and the **Border Gateway Protocol** (**BGP**). *Figure 4.21* outlines the topology of an ExpressRoute circuit connection using a connectivity provider alongside a Site-to-Site VPN connection:

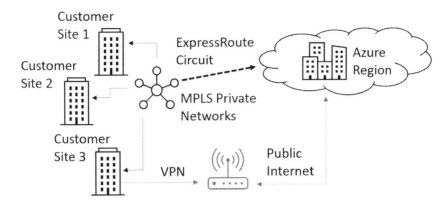

Figure 4.21 – ExpressRoute showing the connection for cross-premises to Azure resources

As you can see, by working with a connectivity provider, ExpressRoute circuits can make Azure data centers appear just like any other site on an MPLS circuit by extending the on-premises network's reach globally and the data center's capacity.

You learned about Azure virtual networks in this section, covering network segmentation, routing, and connectivity. You will now look at Azure DNS in the following section.

## Azure DNS

**Name resolution** in Azure can be provided by a traditional **Windows Server DNS** running on a VM or provided by **Azure DNS**, which is a managed service that is fully VNet-integrated to provide both "public" and "private" zones.

**Azure DNS** is a Microsoft-managed **DNS-as-a-Service** solution for the name resolution of Azure resources. You do not need to provide your own DNS servers for name resolution.

The Azure DNS service provides hosting for both your **public DNS zones** and **private DNS zones**, for which Azure can be authoritative. The following are the DNS services available:

- **Public DNS**: This hosts your DNS domains and provides name resolution for internet-facing domains.

- **Private DNS**: This allows for hostname resolution within a VNet and between VNets.

Once your DNS zones are "migrated" to Azure DNS, Microsoft's DNS Name Servers will respond to queries for resources in these zones. **Anycast DNS** is used by the DNS service, which means that the query will be responded to by the DNS server that is closest geographically to the query. The **Azure portal**, **Azure PowerShell**, or **Azure CLI** can create and manage the Azure public and private zones.

The following outlines the high-level steps to implement a public zone:

1.   Create a public zone.

2.   Add records to the zone.

3.   Validate name resolution for the zone.

The following outlines the high-level steps to implement a private zone:

1.   Create a private zone.

2.   Link (publish) the zone to the VNets for name resolution using the Azure DNS service.

3.   Add records to the zone if required and enable "auto-registration."

4.   Validate name resolution for the zone.

### Azure DNS Private Zones

For Azure DNS private zones, the following capabilities are provided:

- Automatic registration from a private zone linked to the VNet of VMs

- DNS resolution forwarding across private zone-linked VNets

- Reverse DNS lookup within the scope of the VNet

### Azure DNS Drawbacks

The following are some limitations of Azure DNS:

- There is no support for **conditional forwarding**. You should use your own DNS server in place of this if this capability is required.

- There is no support for **Domain Name System Security Extensions** (**DNSSEC**). You should use your own DNS servers in place of this if this capability is required.

- There is no support for **zone transfers**. You should use your own DNS servers in place of this if this capability is required.

- Reverse DNS is only possible with private address spaces linked to the VNet.

- You can only link one VNet to a private zone.

- There is a limit to the number of zones and records per subscription.

Next, you will look at Windows Server DNS hosted on Azure VMs.

# Windows Server DNS on Azure VMs

The **DNS server role** can be installed on Azure VMs running the Windows Server OS using Server Manager in the same way as an on-premises installation.

You can specify that a VNet uses your own Windows DNS servers instead of Azure DNS; these DNS servers could be Azure VM DNS servers or on-premises DNS servers connected to the Azure VNet.

You may decide to implement Windows Server DNS on Azure VMs to replace (or in addition to) Azure DNS in the following scenarios:

- When you have a need for name resolution between VNets

- When you have a need for name resolution of Azure resources from on-premises

- When you have a need for conditional forwarders

- When you have a need for zone transfers

Your own Windows DNS servers can be set in the Azure VNet **DNS Servers Custom** setting, as shown in *Figure 4.22*:

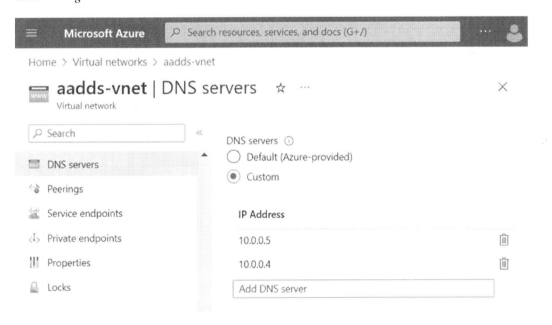

Figure 4.22 – Custom DNS server setting

In this section, you learned about hosting Windows Server DNS on an Azure VM. Next, you will get familiar with hybrid name resolution.

## Hybrid Name Resolution

**Hybrid name resolution** refers to an approach where names can be resolved for Azure-hosted and on-premises resources using both the Windows Server DNS and Azure DNS.

*Figure 4.23* illustrates hybrid name resolution:

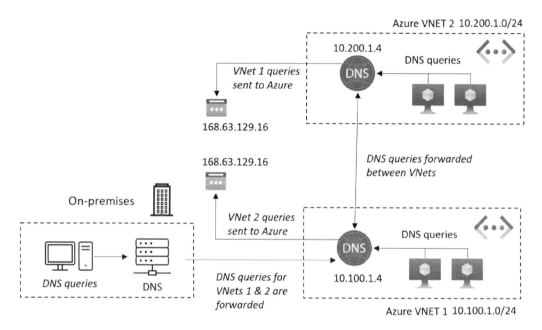

Figure 4.23 – An example solution demonstrating the hybrid name resolution approach

In *Figure 4.23*, Windows Server DNS servers attached to a VNet can respond to queries for its on-premises domain, such as its own authoritative zones, and use the recursive resolvers in Azure for forwarded queries that need to resolve Azure hostnames that it will not have a record of. The address to use for the Azure DNS recursive DNS resolvers is 168.63.129.16.

This section looked at Azure DNS and covered both public and private Azure DNS services, Windows Server DNS on Azure VMs, and hybrid name resolution. This concludes this chapter's content on Azure networking services. In the next section, you will look at the storage services available on Azure.

# Azure Storage Services

Azure provides various "storage services" to cater to various storage solution needs, each providing different capabilities and features to best match their intended purposes and usage patterns.

But first, you must know about the following Azure storage services since they are outlined in the exam:

- Azure Files, containers (Blob Storage), Queue Storage, and disk storage
- Storage accounts, tiers, replication, storage copying
- Data stores

The content in this section will take your knowledge beyond the exam's objectives to prepare you for a real-world, day-to-day, Azure-focused role.

The next section will look at the different Azure storage types.

## Storage Types

The following storage types are available in Azure:

- **Files**: This service provides fully managed, highly available serverless network file shares using the **Server Message Block** (**SMB**) protocol. These traditional mapped drives use port 445 and the SMB 3.x protocol for communication.

- **Binary Large Object** (**Blob**): This provides cost-effective, massive scale-out unstructured data storage. The following are the three types of Blobs available:

  - **Page Blob**: This is used to store random-access data objects, such as VM disks.

  - **Block Blob**: This is used to store ordered data objects, such as backups.

  - **Append Blob**: This is used to store data objects, such as log files, consecutively as they are added.

- **Table Storage**: This provides a data store for "non-relational" (NoSQL) "structured" and "semi-structured" data.

- **Queue Storage**: This provides a data store for large amounts of asynchronous messages.

Selecting the right data storage solution to match your workload type is a key design decision to provide an operational solution at optimal cost and performance. You may need to implement different storage types in a single solution as no Azure Storage service will meet all needs.

## File Storage

**File storage** provides serverless **SMB file shares**. Serverless PaaS deployments mean there are no file servers to manage. The file-server layer has been abstracted so you can focus on creating shares and managing their access.

These shares are highly available, fully managed network file shares that can be accessed using the traditional SMB protocol and from anywhere over port 445. You should ensure that this port and protocol are not blocked.

**Azure Files** supports a maximum file size of 4 TB and a maximum file share size of 100 TB (at the time of writing). It provides a traditional "mapped drives" storage solution to servers or Windows 10 in a lift-and-shift format.

Azure Files can also be used for backup and disaster recovery scenarios for file servers located on-premises. Azure File Sync can replicate file shares from on-premises file servers, providing a cloud tiering capability.

**Azure File Sync** uses Azure Files to keep file shares centralized in Azure but retains on-premises file servers to maintain existing operations, compatibility, and performance. Azure file shares can also be "cached locally" to on-prem file servers, so they are closest to the location where they are required. The file share data is still accessible locally via **SMB**, **Network File System (NFS)**, and **File Transfer Protocol (FTP)**.

The next section will look at container (**Blob**) storage.

## Container (Blob) Storage

**Container storage** provides massive-scale, cost-effective storage for unstructured data such as text, video, photos, files, and more. Containers are used to store Blob data objects. Here are the three forms of Blob data that can be stored in a container:

- **Page Blob**: This is used to hold random-access files, such as objects that have been randomly written and read, in no particular order. An example would be VM disks (managed disks are stored in Microsoft storage accounts).

- **Block Blob**: This is used to hold text or binary files, such as objects that have been ordered, are consecutive, and are not random. An example would be backups.

- **Append Blob**: This is used for objects that have been consecutively added after the last piece of information stored in the Blob. An example of its use is for storing log files.

With this knowledge of container storage, you will now learn about Queue Storage.

## Queue Storage

Asynchronous messages can be stored in **Azure Queues**. The message queues are managed within an application programmatically. The programmatic management of message queues is done when a URL is used to access messages in **Azure Queues**, and all requests are authenticated. A single message can have a maximum size of **64 KB**, and a message queue can have a maximum size of approximately **550 TB**. A message is given a "time-to-live," which is, by default, set to "seven days" (this can be changed for messages added to a queue). A message is "deleted" from the queue when the time-to-live value expires.

The next section will look at disk storage.

## Disk Storage

**Disk storage** provides disks that can be attached to VMs. These provide the OS disk and temp disk used in VMs. Data disks may also be attached to VMs to provide additional storage capacity and additional volumes to meet disk layout needs, such as a VM that will run SQL Server. In addition, these data disks may be used as an install path for applications or to store data that you cannot store on the system volume.

**Azure Managed Disks** are the recommended disk storage for Azure VMs for persistent data storage; Microsoft manages these disks.

The following are the types of managed disks that can be attached to a VM:

- **Standard HDD**: Low-cost storage

- **Standard SSD**: Consistent performance and low latency

- **Premium SSD**: High performance and low latency

- **Ultra disk**: Sub-millisecond latency

Now you will look at storage accounts.

## Storage Accounts

Storage accounts are Azure resources that act as repositories and boundaries to store all your data objects. In addition to working as data planes, they can also be considered management plane consoles. Storage accounts are used to define the settings and configurations that can be applied to the data held in the storage account, such as tiering, redundancy, security, access control, protection, monitoring, and so on.

Storage accounts are automatically encrypted for each storage service. They can be monitored using Azure Storage Analytics and Azure Monitor.

You can create your first storage account using the Azure portal, as illustrated in *Figure 4.24*:

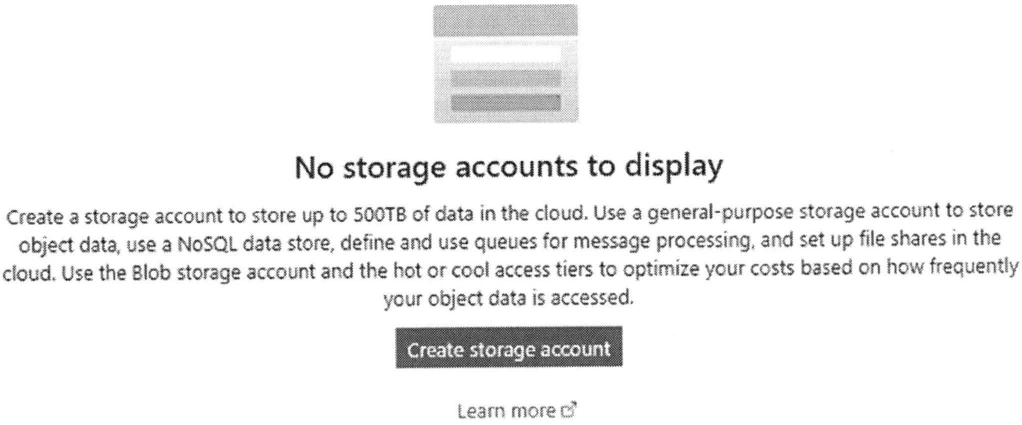

## No storage accounts to display

Create a storage account to store up to 500TB of data in the cloud. Use a general-purpose storage account to store object data, use a NoSQL data store, define and use queues for message processing, and set up file shares in the cloud. Use the Blob storage account and the hot or cool access tiers to optimize your costs based on how frequently your object data is accessed.

Create storage account

Learn more ⬀

Figure 4.24 – Creating a storage account in Azure

You can also use **PowerShell**, the **Azure CLI**, or an **IaC** deployment language such as **Terraform**, or **Bicep** with **ARM** templates.

Once created, the storage account can be accessed via **HTTP/HTTPS** through a globally unique namespace. These are known as endpoints and can be "public" or "private."

A "public endpoint" is assigned a **public IP** and can be accessed over the internet. A "private endpoint" is assigned a **private IP** address from a virtual network and is only accessible from the virtual network.

The following types of storage accounts can be created:

- **Standard general purpose v2**: This is a standard storage account that supports blobs, file shares, tables, and queues.

- **Premium block blobs**: This is a Premium Storage account that supports block blob and append blob types.

- **Premium page blobs**: This is a Premium Storage account that supports page blobs only.

- **Premium File shares**: This is a Premium Storage account type that supports file shares only.

*Figure 4.25* illustrates these storage account types:

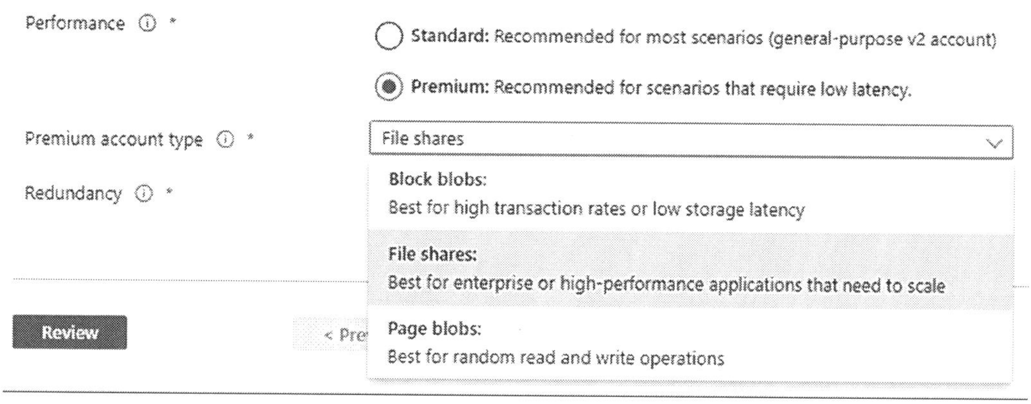

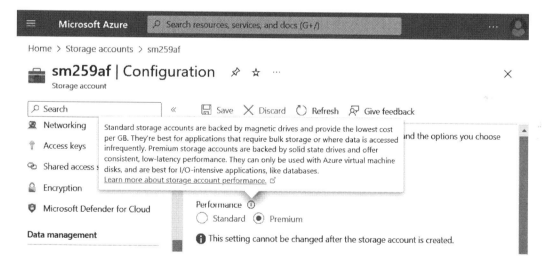

Figure 4.25 – Storage account types

You cannot change the performance type setting after creating a storage account. This is clearly stated, as shown in *Figure 4.26*:

Figure 4.26 – Storage account performance type setting

You must create a new storage account of the performance type you need and then move the data to the created storage account. The storage account also provides a unique namespace (and endpoint) for each data object to address each storage account uniquely. The unique identifier for a storage object is constructed in the following format:

```
https://<storage account name>.<service name>.core.windows.net
```

The following are the endpoints of each of the Azure storage services:

- **Blob storage**: `https://<storage-account>.blob.core.windows.net`
- **Data Lake Storage Gen2**: `https://<storage-account>.dfs.core.windows.net`
- **Azure Files**: `https://<storage-account>.file.core.windows.net`
- **Queue storage**: `https://<storage-account>.queue.core.windows.net`
- **Table storage**: `https://<storage-account>.table.core.windows.net`

The next section will look at storage tiers.

## Storage Tiers

**Azure storage services** provide different storage tiers to store your data objects in the most cost-effective and performant way that meets your needs. The tier you choose should be based on how frequently data is accessed and whether data can be moved between tiers at any time; you should also consider the data access/retrieval (rehydration) costs.

The three available storage tiers are as follows:

- **Hot tier**: This is optimized for frequently accessed data that are as follows:
  - The highest storage costs
  - The lowest access costs
- **Cool tier**: This is optimized for infrequently accessed data (stored for at least 30 days) that are as follows:
  - Lower storage costs
  - Higher access costs

- **Archive tier**: This is optimized for rarely accessed data (stored for at least 180 days) that are as follows:

  - The lowest storage costs

  - The highest access costs and data retrieval (rehydration) costs

  - Data is offline and will take several hours for the first byte to be accessible

Next, let's move on to storage replication.

## Storage Replication

Microsoft provides **redundancy** of your data in Azure through several **replication** options. You will look at all of that in this section.

However, note that under the **shared responsibility model**, you are "responsible" for ensuring your data is available and protected by selecting the most appropriate replication and protection model to meet your needs.

The following are the redundancy options that are available within a **primary region**, though some regions offer more replication types:

- **Locally Redundant Storage (LRS)**: This provides three copies of your data, replicated synchronously within a single physical location in the primary region. This is the lowest cost option but has the lowest availability and durability.

- **Zone-Redundant Storage (ZRS)**: This provides synchronously replicated copies of your data across three availability zones in the primary region. This is a higher-cost option but has the highest availability and durability within a region.

The following are the redundancy options that are available within a **secondary region**:

- **Geo-Redundant Storage (GRS)**: This provides three copies of your data, replicated synchronously within a single physical location in the primary region. Your data is also asynchronously replicated to a single physical location in the secondary region. This secondary region provides three copies of your data, replicated synchronously as LRS.

- **Geo-zone-redundant storage (GZRS)**: It provides synchronously replicated copies of your data across three availability zones in the primary region. Your data is also asynchronously replicated to a single physical location in the secondary region. This secondary region provides three copies of your data, replicated synchronously as LRS.

Let's move on to look at storage copying options.

## Storage Copying

Several native Azure platform capabilities can copy (move) data into and out of Azure and between Azure resources. The various Azure platform capabilities are as follows:

- **AzCopy**: This command-line utility helps you transfer data to or from a storage account.

- **Storage Explorer**: This GUI tool allows you to interact with your Azure storage resources. You can upload data and manage storage resources using Storage Explorer.

- **Azure Migrate**: This Azure discovery, assessment, and migration service can move your on-premises VM-based disk storage to Azure.

- **Databox**: This is an Azure service for transferring large amounts of data into Azure that may not be possible with other methods.

- **Azure File Sync**: This Azure service enables hybrid file shares. Windows Server can be utilized as a local cache for Azure file shares and provide centralized file storage in Azure while retaining on-premises local file servers.

> **Note**
> You can read more about the Azure platform's capabilities in the *Additional Information and Study References* section.

Next, you will look at data stores.

## Data Stores

Choosing the right **data store** to match your data type is a key design decision. No single storage solution fits all data types, and several stores might be needed to provide a complete and optimal solution. Your solution will largely be determined by the data type(s) you wish to store.

Here are the key factors in deciding on an optimal storage solution:

- How will you classify your data: structured, semi-structured, unstructured, streaming, relational, or non-relational data?

  - An example of structured data (also referred to as relational data) would be data stored in databases, such as a CRM system. This includes anything with a strict schema, such as most operational data stored in a SQL database or business data stored in a data warehouse for analysis and decision-making.

- Examples of semi-structured data are key/value pairs, JSON files, and XML files.

- Some examples of unstructured data include media files such as photos, videos, and audio; Office documents such as Word, PDF, and text; and log files.

- How will the primary operations use your data—analytical, transactional, read/write, search/lookup, upload, change, and so on—carried out on each data type?

- How can you get the best performance out of your application?

- How can you get the best durability, availability, recovery, and security?

- How can you be the most cost-effective?

*Figure 4.27* provides a simple data store selection guide (for clarity, not all the decision points have been shown):

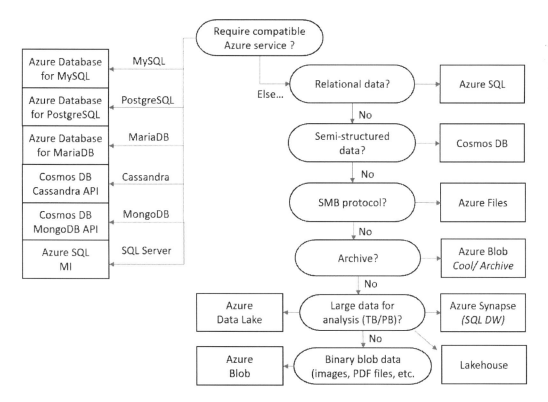

Figure 4.27 – The flow for choosing a data store

In this section, you learned about the Azure storage services and grasped the concepts behind storage types, account types, tiers, replication, copying, and data stores. This concludes this chapter's Azure storage services content.

# Summary

This chapter provided complete coverage of the AZ-900 Azure Fundamentals exam's following *Skills Measured* section: **Describe Azure compute and networking services** and **Describe Azure storage services**.

In this chapter, for the **compute** skills area, you learned how to compare compute types (including container instances, **virtual machines**, and functions), describe VM options (including Azure Virtual Machines, Azure Virtual Machine Scale Sets, availability sets, and Azure Virtual Desktop), describe resources required for virtual machines, and describe application hosting options, including the Web Apps feature of Azure App Service, containers, and virtual machines.

For the **network** skills area, you learned how to describe virtual networking, including the purpose of Azure VNet, routing, segmentation, peering, connectivity, and Azure DNS.

For the **storage** skills area, you learned how to compare Azure storage services and describe storage types, account types, tiers, replication, copying, and data stores.

In the next chapter, you will look at **Azure Identity and Access**.

# Exam Readiness Drill – Chapter Review Questions

Apart from a solid understanding of key concepts, being able to think quickly under time pressure is a skill that will help you ace your certification exam. That is why working on these skills early on in your learning journey is key.

Chapter review questions are designed to improve your test-taking skills progressively with each chapter you learn and review your understanding of key concepts in the chapter at the same time. You'll find these at the end of each chapter.

> **How To Access These Resources**
> To learn how to access these resources, head over to the chapter titled *Chapter 11, Accessing the Online Practice Resources*.

To open the Chapter Review Questions for this chapter, perform the following steps:

1.  Click the link – `https://packt.link/AZ900E2_CH04`.

    Alternatively, you can scan the following **QR code** (*Figure 4.28*):

Figure 4.28 – QR code that opens Chapter Review Questions for logged-in users

2.  Once you log in, you'll see a page similar to the one shown in *Figure 4.29*:

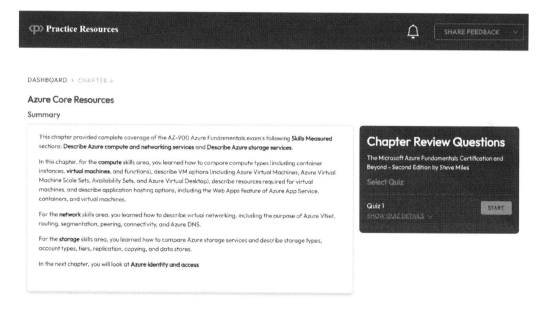

Figure 4.29 – Chapter Review Questions for Chapter 4

3.  Once ready, start the following practice drills, re-attempting the quiz multiple times.

## Exam Readiness Drill

For the first three attempts, don't worry about the time limit.

### ATTEMPT 1

The first time, aim for at least **40%**. Look at the answers you got wrong and read the relevant sections in the chapter again to fix your learning gaps.

### ATTEMPT 2

The second time, aim for at least **60%**. Look at the answers you got wrong and read the relevant sections in the chapter again to fix any remaining learning gaps.

### ATTEMPT 3

The third time, aim for at least **75%**. Once you score 75% or more, you start working on your timing.

> **Tip**
> You may take more than **three** attempts to reach 75%. That's okay. Just review the relevant sections in the chapter till you get there.

# Working On Timing

**Target**: Your aim is to keep the score the same while trying to answer these questions as quickly as possible. Here's an example of how your next attempts should look like:

| Attempt | Score | Time Taken |
|---|---|---|
| Attempt 5 | 77% | 21 mins 30 seconds |
| Attempt 6 | 78% | 18 mins 34 seconds |
| Attempt 7 | 76% | 14 mins 44 seconds |

Table 4.1 – Sample timing practice drills on the online platform

> **Note**
> The time limits shown in the above table are just examples. Set your own time limits with each attempt based on the time limit of the quiz on the website.

With each new attempt, your score should stay above **75%** while your "time taken" to complete should "decrease". Repeat as many attempts as you want till you feel confident dealing with the time pressure.

## Online Hands-On Activities

Once you complete this book, complete the hands-on activities that align with this chapter. These are available on the accompanying online platform. Perform the following steps to open hands-on activities:

1. Navigate to the `Dashboard`.

2. Click the `Hands-On Activities` menu.

3. Select the activity you want to attempt.

4. The following activities align with this chapter:

    I.  Set 2 – Virtual Networks (VNets) (Accessible at `https://packt.link/activity7`)

    II. Set 2 – Virtual Machines (VMs) (Accessible at `https://packt.link/activity8`)

    III. Set 3 – App Service Web Apps (Accessible at `https://packt.link/activity9`)

    IV. Set 3 – Storage Accounts (Accessible at `https://packt.link/activity10`)

Each activity will have a set of tasks. Complete all the tasks to shore up your practical knowledge. For example, *Figure 4.30* shows the tasks aligned with the activity *Virtual Networks (VNets)*:

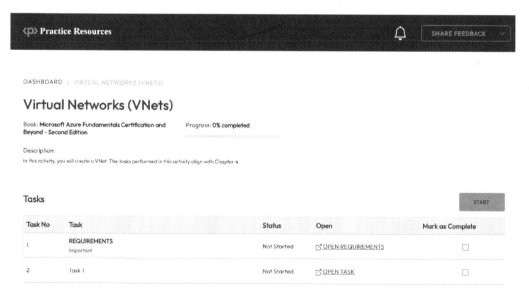

Figure 4.30 – Tasks in Virtual Networks (VNets) activity

## Additional Information and Study References

This section provides links to additional exam information and study references:

- **Microsoft Learn certification further information**:

  - AZ-900 - Microsoft Azure Fundamentals exam guide: `https://packt.link/m9ZM0`

  - AZ-900 - Microsoft Azure Fundamentals study guide: `https://packt.link/31W6E`

- **Microsoft Learn training further information**:

  - AZ-900 - Microsoft Azure Fundamentals course: `https://packt.link/QsTj3`

# 5

# Azure Identity and Access

In *Chapter 4, Azure Core Resources*, you looked at the core building block resources available in Azure of "compute", "storage", and "networking."

This chapter will outline the core building block service of "Identity and Access" available in Azure; you will look at directory services in Azure, authentication methods, external identities, conditional access, and role-based access control.

This chapter primarily focuses on the **Describe Azure identity and access** module from the *Skills Measured* section of the AZ-900 Azure Fundamentals exam.

> **Note**
>
> You can find a detailed AZ-900 Azure Fundamentals exam skills area in the *Appendix, Assessing AZ-900 Exam Skills* of this book.

By the end of this chapter, you will be able to answer questions on the following confidently:

- Authentication and authorization
- Microsoft Entra ID
- Identity and access management

In addition, this chapter's goal is to take your knowledge beyond the exam content so that you are prepared for a real-world, day-to-day Azure-focused role.

## Authentication and Authorization

Accessing resources is based on a two-stage concept of first **authenticating** and then **authorizing**; identifying "who you are" and determining "what you can do."

**Authentication**, also referred to as **AuthN**, is the process of establishing and proving the identity of a person (or service). This can be done by validating provided access credentials information against stored or known identifying information.

**Authorization**, also referred to as **AuthZ**, is the process of establishing what level of access the authenticated person (or service) has to the resources, that is, what they can access and what actions they may perform.

*Figure 5.1* visualizes the concepts of authentication and authorization.

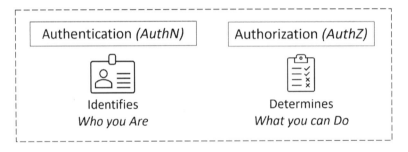

Figure 5.1 – The concepts of authentication and authorization

In this section, you looked at the concepts of authentication and authorization. The following section looks at Microsoft Entra ID.

## Microsoft Entra ID

**Microsoft Entra ID**, previously named (Azure Active Directory), is a multi-tenant cloud-based identity and access management solution that is part of Microsoft's Microsoft Entra "identity platform" product family.

Microsoft Entra ID is primarily a "cloud-based" centralized **Identity Provider** (**IDP**) and "directory service" for objects, which are stored in Microsoft Entra ID with attributes.

For "user identities," the core attributes would be their sign-in name, their **User Principal Name** (**UPN**), "password," "location," "assigned roles," "group membership," "devices," "licenses," and "authentication methods."

The **directory service** is the foundation of granting access to resources through **Identity and Access Management (IAM)** for cloud and hybrid environments. It provides authentication and authorization for users, apps, machines, and devices.

*Figure 5.2* visualizes Microsoft Entra ID as the centralized **cloud IDP**:

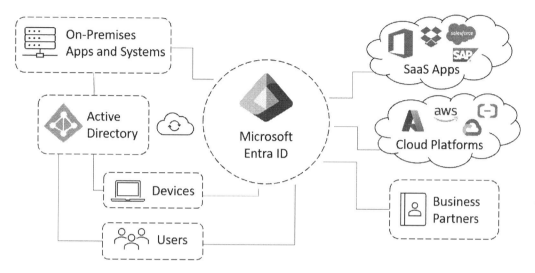

Figure 5.2 – Microsoft Entra ID as a centralized cloud IDP

In addition to an organization's user management, Microsoft Entra ID provides the following:

- Device management
- Application management
- External identity services
- Multi-factor authentication and conditional access
- Integration with Active Directory Federation Services
- Kerberos support
- Microsoft Entra Domain Services

Unlike Active Directory, **Microsoft Entra ID** is a "multi-tenant" **Software-as-a-Service (SaaS)** service. An instance of Microsoft Entra ID—a **directory**—is implemented for each Microsoft **tenant** that is created; each <tenant>.onmicrosoft.com domain represents an instance of Microsoft Entra ID.

You will only have "one" directory per Microsoft tenant domain, and by creating a "new" <tenant>. onmicrosoft.com domain, you will create a "new directory". You can create "multiple" tenant domains (and, therefore, "directories") to meet your needs.

There are four key editions of Microsoft Entra ID is as follows:

- **Microsoft Entra ID Free**: This edition is included when you create a new tenant and is created with the provisioning of a Microsoft online service such as Microsoft 365, Dynamics 365, and Azure.

- **Office 365**: This edition is included with Microsoft 365. It includes an SLA of 99.9% availability and additional functionality such as organization branding and two-way synchronization of objects between AD and Microsoft Entra ID.

- **Microsoft Entra ID P1**: This edition provides additional identity protection and identity governance functionality on top of the basic functionality.

- **Microsoft Entra ID P2**: This edition provides further identity protection and identity governance functionality on top of the Microsoft Entra ID Premium P1 functionality.

Microsoft Entra ID has objects referred to as **security principals** that provide the basis for identities. They can be one of the following types:

- **User**: This is an entity Microsoft Entra ID can manage. This user referred to here can be a member of the "organization's tenancy" or a "guest user" who does not belong to your organization.

  - Microsoft Entra ID supports guest users through a feature called **Business-to-Business (B2B)**. B2B allows access to resources in your organization's tenancy for users not part of your organization, such as business partners.

  - Microsoft Entra ID also supports **Business-to-Consumer (B2C)**, allowing access to Microsoft Entra ID resources via an external IDP account such as Facebook or Google.

- **Application service principal**: This is an entity that represents the identity of a service or application in Azure.

- **Managed identity service principal**: This is an entity representing a special kind of service principal identity for a service or application to use in place of a user identity. There are system- and user-assigned managed identities.

- **Device**: It is a physical entity, such as a laptop, tablet, phone, virtual machine, or a similar device.

This section introduced Microsoft Entra ID. The following section will look at the differences between **Active Directory** (**AD**) and Microsoft Entra ID.

## Comparing Active Directory (AD) and Microsoft Entra ID

**AD** and Microsoft Entra ID are both classed as IDPs; however, they function very differently.

**AD** was introduced in Windows 2000 as Microsoft's "directory service." **AD** is a role installed as part of **Windows Server**, and servers running this role are called **Domain Controllers (DCs)**. It allows access to multiple resources stored as **computer objects** within the directory service, with **identities** stored as **user objects**.

AD is not a single function and has several services that can be provided. The "core" services are as follows:

- AD Domain Services

- AD Certificate Services

- AD Federation Services

Moving to "modern authentication" and "identity services" can transform your IAM strategy and approach, so these legacy services can be replaced and retired by phasing out. However, many of these services are still required and will be around for years. It should be noted that Microsoft Entra ID cannot be considered a "100% replacement" for AD.

*Figure 5.3* visualizes the relationship between these two **IDPs** and **directory services**:

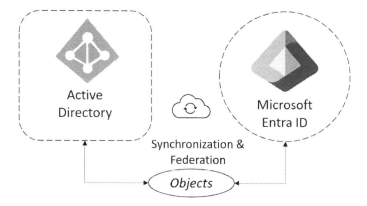

Figure 5.3 – Connection between AD and Microsoft Entra ID

There is a misconception that Microsoft Entra ID is the cloud equivalent of the traditional Windows Server-based AD. However, this is not the case. It is important to know that Microsoft Entra ID is **not a cloud DC** and, at present "cannot replace 100%" of the functionality provided by traditional implementations of **Windows Server AD**.

Unlike AD, there is nothing to install for Microsoft Entra ID. No DCs as **Virtual Machines** (**VMs**) are required. Despite the lack of installation and VMs, Microsoft Entra ID still offers the same functionality of allowing users and computers to appear as objects in the directory. Microsoft provides Microsoft Entra ID as a fully managed IDP platform provided as SaaS.

**AD** can be connected to **Microsoft Entra ID** using **Microsoft Entra Connect**, which is a free download tool with which an organization can establish a **hybrid identity**. This tool synchronizes "user identities," "attributes," and "objects" between both **IDPs**.

A **hybrid identity** provides users with a "common identity" and an approach that allows them to access resources in **Microsoft Entra ID** using their **AD identity**. The "same" username and password are used to access resources accessed in "both" IDP environments.

This section highlighted the distinction between Microsoft Entra ID and AD. The following section looks at Microsoft Entra Domain Services.

## Microsoft Entra Domain Services

To set some context for this section, **Active Directory Domain Services** (**AD DS**), which is included as part of Windows Server, is a directory service and an IDP. Its primary function is to manage access to domain resources—sometimes referred to as network resources—through **authentication** and **authorization**.

Now that you have grasped some context, turn your attention to the focus of this section. **Microsoft Entra Domain Services** (**Microsoft Entra DS**) is a "managed" **Azure Identity Service** provided as **Platform-as-a-Service** (**PaaS**). In simple terms, it provides **Domain Services as a Service**.

When you implement Microsoft Entra DS, you create a **Microsoft-managed domain**. This domain is a Microsoft-managed implementation of AD DS. This provides the functions of **Kerberos/NTLM** authentication, **LDAP**, **domain join**, and **group policy**.

The use case for Microsoft Entra DS is where workloads running in Azure depend on **Domain Services** functions and apps or services that cannot be modified or rewritten to utilize native Microsoft Entra ID and modern authentication such as **OAuth**, **Security Assertion Markup Language** (**SAML**), **REST**, and so on.

You may also wish to integrate your Azure resources into an existing instance of Windows Server AD or perform a lift-and-shift style move of resources that will still depend on **Domain Services** functionality but without wanting to run and manage your own **Domain Controller** virtual machines.

*Figure 5.4* shows how to provide the same on-premises domain functions for workloads once they are moved into Azure:

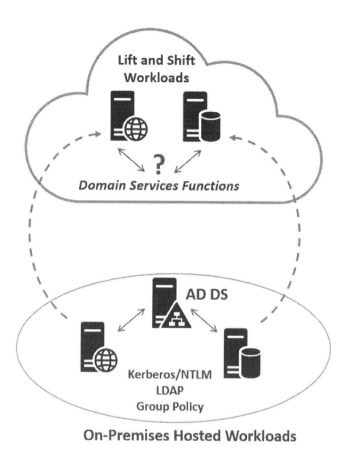

Figure 5.4 – Providing AD Domain Services functions for Azure workloads

For the scenario in *Figure 5.4*, the solution could be one of the following options:

- Implement a VPN so that Azure workloads can authenticate to on-premises DCs.
- Deploy AD domain controller virtual machines in Azure.
- Implement Microsoft Entra Domain Services, that is, Microsoft-managed AD DCs in Azure.

The advantage of providing Microsoft-managed DCs as a PaaS is that you do not need to consider the virtual machine overhead, the physical infrastructure components, or the logical components such as the data store, schema, trusts, partitions, availability, and protection.

The Microsoft Entra DS **managed domain** instance is created by Microsoft with two DCs for high availability, with additional region redundancy across two availability zones, if available in that region. Microsoft will automatically configure the distribution of DCs across the zones.

The following are some characteristics of a managed domain:

- It is Microsoft-managed, not self-managed.

- It is a standalone domain. So, extensions and joining the managed domain to an existing AD DS forest are not possible.

- Trusts are **one-way**—outbound forest trusts only.

- There are **no** domain or enterprise administrator privileges.

- It supports domain join, LDAP, and Kerberos/NTLM.

- Two built-in **Organizational Unit (OU)** containers for computers and users are provided, with an associated built-in **Group Policy Object (GPO)**.

- It supports a custom OU structure and group policy via a flat structure.

- It has no schema extensions.

- DCs are provided as a service and managed by Microsoft.

- Microsoft Entra DS is integrated into the Microsoft Entra ID tenant for cloud-only identity scenarios and can be combined with AD DS for hybrid identity scenarios.

- Microsoft Entra DS can be managed similarly to AD DS through the RSAT tools.

- Object sync occurs in only one direction—from Microsoft Entra ID to Microsoft Entra DS. Any changes made directly to Microsoft Entra DS will be overwritten at the next sync. These should be considered read-only DCs with no direct creation of or changes to objects with DCs.

Passwords cannot be reset in the managed domain; they must be reset in AD or Microsoft Entra ID and synchronized into the managed domain. In the **cloud-only identity** scenario, "users," "passwords," and "groups" are created and managed in the Microsoft Entra ID tenant.

A Microsoft Entra ID tenant acts as the "authoritative" Directory Service and IDP. These "directory objects" are synced to the Microsoft Entra DS **managed domain**. There are **no** direct changes to objects in the managed domain. Any changes should be made in the **authoritative IDP**, which is Microsoft Entra ID in this scenario, and those changes must then be "synchronized" to the **managed domain** to become effective.

*Figure 5.5* shows the relationship between Microsoft Entra ID and the Microsoft Entra DS managed domain in the **cloud-only identity** scenario:

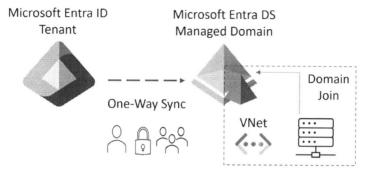

Figure 5.5 – Making changes effective by synchronizing Microsoft Entra ID to the managed domain

In *Figure 5.5*, you can see that objects from the Microsoft Entra ID tenant directory are synchronized one way to the Microsoft Entra DS managed domain directory. Azure VMs will **domain join** to the Microsoft Entra DS managed domain.

If a user's password needs to be reset, the user's password is reset in Microsoft Entra ID. This change is then synchronized to the "DCs" of the **managed domain**. Enabling **Self-Service Password Reset (SSPR)** in the AD tenant is recommended.

*Figure 5.6* shows the relationship between AD, Microsoft Entra ID, and the Microsoft Entra DS managed domain in the **hybrid identity** scenario:

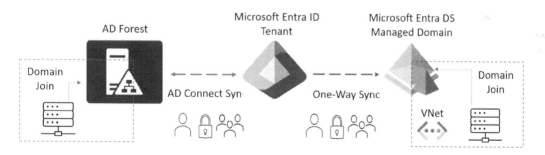

Figure 5.6 – Hybrid identity scenario showing the connection between AD,
Microsoft Entra ID, and the Microsoft Entra DS managed domain

In the hybrid identity scenario, "users," "passwords," and "groups" are created and managed in the **AD forest**, which acts as the "authoritative" Directory Service and IDP. These **directory objects** are then synchronized "two-way" into the Microsoft Entra ID tenant using **Microsoft Entra Connect**, and then the "objects" are synchronized "one-way" to the Microsoft Entra DS managed domain.

There are no direct changes to objects to be made in the managed domain. Changes should be made in the "authoritative" IDP. In this case, it is the AD forest. These changes must then be synchronized to the Microsoft Entra ID tenant using Microsoft Entra Connect and then synchronized from the Microsoft Entra ID tenant to the managed domain to become effective.

To summarize, **no** changes will be made in the Microsoft Entra AD DS managed domain for the previous "cloud-only" and "hybrid identity scenarios." All objects are synchronized from the Microsoft Entra ID tenant, so the only thing left to figure out is how the objects get created in the Microsoft Entra ID in the first instance. This will be done by creating objects directly in the Microsoft Entra ID tenant in the case of cloud-only accounts or allowing these objects to be created in the Microsoft Entra ID tenant from the Microsoft Entra Connect sync from the AD DCs.

## Single Sign-On (SSO)

With **Single Sign-On** (**SSO**), you only need to enter a set of credentials once to access all resources that are enabled to use SSO in your organization. In SSO, you are not prompted to sign in again to access each needed resource.

In addition, user provisioning to apps is accelerated with **Just-In-Time** (**JIT**) access for new hires and temporary staff. It allows a governed leavers process when users no longer need access to an app.

You can configure Microsoft Entra ID as the **trusted IDP** for each app you wish to enable SSO through a centralized portal. These apps can be "cloud apps," "public cloud provider platforms," and "on-premises apps." You can enforce secure access with identity protection through **Multi-Factor Authentication** (**MFA**), "conditional access," and "risk-based access policies."

In this section, you learned about SSO. The following section looks at MFA and conditional access.

## Multi-Factor Authentication (MFA) and Conditional Access

MFA, which includes **Two-Factor Authentication** (**2FA**), provides an additional layer of security for identifying a user. It does this by necessitating the user to submit "two or more" elements for **authentication**.

MFA is based on the following principles:

- **Knowledge**: This is something that only the user knows, such as a "password" or "PIN."
- **Possession**: This is something that only the user has, such as a "code sent to a phone," a "token," or a "key."
- **Inherent**: This is something that only the user is, such as "biometrics."
- **Conditional Access**: This works alongside MFA to provide more granular levels of access control.

For conditional access, **information** is collected from the **sign-in process** (signals). Then decisions are made based upon that information to determine whether access to the requested resource will be granted or denied and whether the user will require additional factors of authentication or require taking other action, such as resetting their password.

Conditional access works as an IF-Then model that is visualized in *Figure 5.7*:

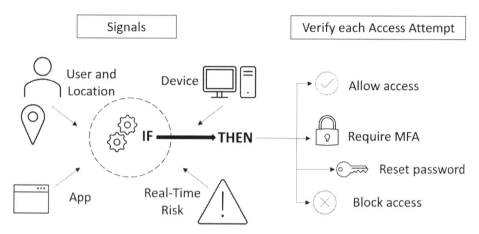

Figure 5.7 – Granting access using conditional access based on
the information collected from the sign-in process

In *Figure 5.7*, the User signal information could be the app trying to get access, the Device or Location it is being accessed from, or the status of any security updates.

This could mean that if the user is trying to access the resource from a location that is unknown, a non-managed/personal Device, or a device that does not have the latest security updates, then the User will be required to authenticate with a second factor of authentication or even be denied access to the resource.

**Conditional access** is a licensed function that requires a **Microsoft Entra ID P1 license** or **Microsoft Entra ID P2 license**. This functionality is also included in some other Microsoft 365 license types.

With the knowledge of MFA and conditional access, it is time to look at the following section that talks about passwordless authentication.

## Passwordless Authentication

**Passwordless authentication** provides users with a more hassle-free user authentication process while still providing the same level of security compared to traditional password-based methods. MFA is still used; however, users now authenticate using "something they have" such as a security key or device, combined with a biometric of "something they are." The passwordless authentication options are as follows:

- Windows Hello for Business

- Microsoft Authenticator

- FIDO2 security keys

> **Note**
> You can find more information on these passwordless authentication options at
> `https://packt.link/Q7rRk`.

This concludes this section on Microsoft Entra ID, Microsoft's multi-tenant cloud-based identity and access management solution. You learned about licensing, security principals, comparison with AD, Entra Domain Services, SSO, MFA with conditional access, and passwordless authentication. You will now explore identity and access management in the next section.

# Identity and Access Management (IAM)

This section will look at aspects of implementing, managing, and controlling IAM; you will cover role-based access control, Azure subscription access control, Azure roles, and external identity access.

## Role-Based Access Control (RBAC)

RBAC is a concept that refers to authorized user access based on defined roles that have been assigned. It allows you to create "granular access control" to Azure resources through "defined roles" and "custom roles." You can segregate duties by granting only the access required to perform the required tasks.

It is an effective practice for governance "only to allow the minimum access" required to complete a task. This is the basis for the principle of **least privilege** and should always be adopted. So, users are only given access through a role(s) that is the most appropriate for the tasks they need to carry out.

This **least privilege** approach enhances governance and control of user access management as the permissions are not given directly to individuals or groups but to roles. Each role has a set of associated permissions. When a user or group is assigned that role, they receive the role's associated permissions.

It is a sound practice not to assign individual users to RBAC but to add users to groups and then assign RBAC to the groups for easier governance and control group membership.

Roles are specified at what level users apply and are inherited from the parent level. So, RBAC roles at the subscription level are inherited by resource groups and subsequently, RBAC roles at the resource group level are inherited by resources.

RBAC assignment is managed via the **Access Control (IAM)** blade in the portal for each resource you wish to control access over. RBAC is based on four elements, and these are as follows:

- **Security principal**: This represents an **identity** that can be "user," "group," "service principal," or "managed identity."

- **Role** (definition): This represents a collection of permissions the security principal will receive and the actions they can take on the resource, such as delete, write, and so on. There are several built-in roles, and you can also create custom roles.

- **Scope**: This represents the resource level that this access will apply to. The scopes are structured in a parent-child relationship from the broadest to narrowest—"management group," "subscription," "resource group," and "resource." A recommended practice is not to set the scope too wide but only at the lowest level needed.

- **Role assignments**: This represents the process of attaching a role definition to a security principal to provide access, creating a role assignment to grant access, and removing a role assignment to revoke access.

The following are the three core RBAC roles for controlling access to Azure resources:

- **Owner**: This role has **full access** to resources. In addition, it can assign access to others.

- **Contributor**: This role is the same as the Owner role; apart from that, it **cannot** assign access to others.

- **Reader**: This role can **only view** resources. It cannot create, edit, delete, or manage any resources.

If you feel that the default permissions of a built-in role may provide too much control or be too restrictive, then a more granular **custom role** can be created with only the permission associated with your required role. These custom roles can then be assigned to "users," "groups," and "service principals" at the "management group," "subscription," and "resource group" scope, the same as for the built-in roles.

So far, you have looked at granting the least privileged access to resources through the RBAC functionality for all Azure resources. The following section will look at Azure subscription access control.

## Azure Subscription Access Control

It is essential to control access to subscriptions to ensure governance of creating resources within a subscription; this utilizes RBAC.

As you learned in the *Role-Based Access Control (RBAC)* section, RBAC allows multiple accounts with different access levels to a subscription as needed by an organization. There can be multiple owners for a subscription, although the number of owners should be limited to a maximum of **three** for "best operational security best practices" defined in **Defender for Cloud**. Microsoft Entra ID accounts are primarily used to assign access to Azure subscriptions through role assignments.

As discussed, there are two levels of access control—**AuthN** and **AuthZ**. Their details are as follows:

- **Authentication** means proving "who you say you are".

- **Authorization** refers to "what actions you are allowed to take" as that identity, such as "read data", "modify data", "delete data", or "give others access to data".

In managing access to an Azure subscription, **authentication** comes from Microsoft Entra ID, and **authorization** comes from Azure RBAC roles. *Figure 5.8* shows the relationship between roles:

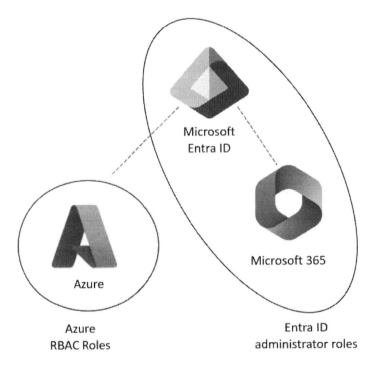

Figure 5.8 – Managing access with authentication from Microsoft Entra ID, and authorization from Azure RBAC

The following should be noted from *Figure 5.8*:

- By default, the Azure roles and Microsoft Entra ID are isolated and do not overlap Microsoft Entra ID; a similar separation or isolation is maintained in Microsoft 365 roles.

- Being assigned a Microsoft Entra ID role gives no assignment of any Azure roles.

- By default, there is no access to Azure resources with an account with the Global Administrator role.

- Access to Azure resources must be explicitly allowed and can only be granted with an account that has the Owner role for a subscription.

This section introduced the concepts of access control to Azure subscriptions. You will now learn about the Azure roles.

## Azure Roles

You will explore the fine-grain roles in this section from the **Azure Resource Manager** (**ARM**) deployment model that replaced the "legacy" **Azure Service Manager** (**ASM**), now referred to as the **classic model**. In addition, custom roles can now be defined within the ARM model.

The four core "ARM roles" are as follows:

- **Owner**: This role has **full access** to all resources and can delegate access to others.

- **Contributor**: This role has full access to all resources but **cannot** "delegate access to others."

- **Reader**: This role has only **read access** to all resources.

- **User Access Administrator**: This role can only manage **user access** to all resources.

The other 70+ roles are specific to individual Azure resources and give granular resource context-specific allow actions, as follows:

- **Backup Operator**: This role allows management of backup services but does not allow the creation of vaults, removing backups, or giving access to others.

- **Storage Account Contributor**: This role allows management of storage accounts; and provides access to the account key.

- **Virtual Machine Administrator Login**: This role allows viewing virtual machines in the portal and logging in as the administrator but does not allow virtual machine creation or disk and network management.

These roles can be further customized to any individual permission required, combining a few of the 1,000 possible roles. The roles and their assignments are managed via the Access Control (IAM) page for the subscription within the Azure portal.

Now you know the Azure roles for access management. Next, you will learn about user access when a user is not part of the tenant's Microsoft Entra ID.

## External Identity Access

As well as internal tenant users, B2B and invited guest user can be invited to access a Microsoft Entra ID tenant through the external identity access capability of **Microsoft Entra B2B**. A Microsoft Entra ID account from another tenancy can be given access to the subscription within a different tenancy.

**Azure Lighthouse** can also be used for "managed security service providers." Although this is not within the scope of the exam objective, this is mentioned here for completeness. Azure Lighthouse provides "delegated admin" access at the "subscription" or "resource group" level to an organization's tenant from an MSP's managing tenant.

In this section, you learned about IAM functionality, the principle of RBAC, Azure subscription access control, Azure roles, and finished with external identity access. This concludes the content for this chapter.

# Summary

This chapter included identity and access content for coverage of the following AZ-900 Azure Fundamentals exam skills area: **Describe Azure identity, access, and security**.

In this chapter, you learned how to describe directory services in Azure including Microsoft Entra ID (previously named Azure AD) and Microsoft Entra Domain Services (previously named Azure AD Domain Services), describe authentication methods in Azure (including SSO, multi-factor authentication, and passwordless), external identities and guest access in Azure, conditional access, and Azure RBAC.

The next chapter looks at **Azure Security**. You will learn the concept of Zero Trust, the purpose of the defense-in-depth model, and Microsoft Defender for Cloud.

# Exam Readiness Drill – Chapter Review Questions

Apart from a solid understanding of key concepts, being able to think quickly under time pressure is a skill that will help you ace your certification exam. That is why working on these skills early on in your learning journey is key.

Chapter review questions are designed to improve your test-taking skills progressively with each chapter you learn and review your understanding of key concepts in the chapter at the same time. You'll find these at the end of each chapter.

> **How To Access These Resources**
>
> To learn how to access these resources, head over to the chapter titled *Chapter 11, Accessing the Online Practice Resources*.

To open the Chapter Review Questions for this chapter, perform the following steps:

1.  Click the link – `https://packt.link/AZ900E2_CH05`.

    Alternatively, you can scan the following **QR code** (*Figure 5.9*):

Figure 5.9 – QR code that opens Chapter Review Questions for logged-in users

2.  Once you log in, you'll see a page similar to the one shown in *Figure 5.10*:

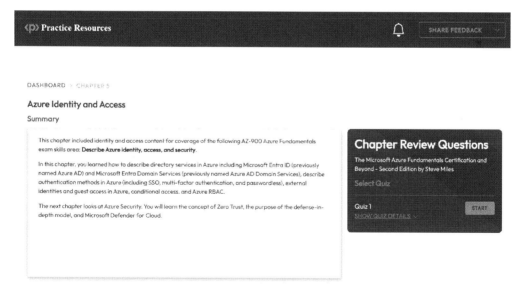

Figure 5.10 – Chapter Review Questions for Chapter 5

3.   Once ready, start the following practice drills, re-attempting the quiz multiple times.

## Exam Readiness Drill

For the first three attempts, don't worry about the time limit.

### ATTEMPT 1

The first time, aim for at least **40%**. Look at the answers you got wrong and read the relevant sections in the chapter again to fix your learning gaps.

### ATTEMPT 2

The second time, aim for at least **60%**. Look at the answers you got wrong and read the relevant sections in the chapter again to fix any remaining learning gaps.

### ATTEMPT 3

The third time, aim for at least **75%**. Once you score 75% or more, you start working on your timing.

> **Tip**
> You may take more than **three** attempts to reach 75%. That's okay. Just review the relevant sections in the chapter till you get there.

## Working On Timing

**Target**: Your aim is to keep the score the same while trying to answer these questions as quickly as possible. Here's an example of how your next attempts should look like:

| Attempt | Score | Time Taken |
|---------|-------|------------|
| Attempt 5 | 77% | 21 mins 30 seconds |
| Attempt 6 | 78% | 18 mins 34 seconds |
| Attempt 7 | 76% | 14 mins 44 seconds |

Table 5.1 – Sample timing practice drills on the online platform

> **Note**
> The time limits shown in the above table are just examples. Set your own time limits with each attempt based on the time limit of the quiz on the website.

With each new attempt, your score should stay above **75%** while your "time taken" to complete should "decrease". Repeat as many attempts as you want till you feel confident dealing with the time pressure.

# Online Hands-On Activities

Once you complete this book, complete the hands-on activities that align with this chapter. These are available on the accompanying online platform. Perform the following steps to open hands-on activities:

1.  Navigate to the `Dashboard`.

2.  Click the `Hands-On Activities` menu.

3.  Select the activity you want to attempt.

4.  The following activities align with this chapter:

    I.   Set 1 – Microsoft Entra ID Users and Groups (Accessible at `https://packt.link/activity2`)

    II.  Set 1 – Tenant Global Administrators (Accessible at `https://packt.link/activity3`)

Each activity will have a set of tasks. Complete all the tasks to shore up your practical knowledge. For example, *Figure 5.11* shows the tasks aligned with the activity *Microsoft Entra ID Users and Groups*:

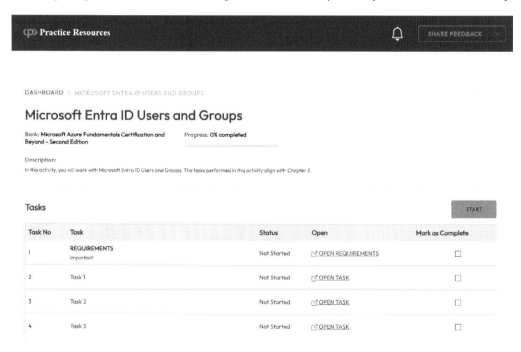

Figure 5.11 – Tasks in Microsoft Entra ID Users and Groups activity

# Additional Information and Study References

This section provides links to additional exam information and study references.

- **Microsoft Learn certification further information**:

  - AZ-900 - Microsoft Azure Fundamentals exam guide: `https://packt.link/on7uD`

  - AZ-900 - Microsoft Azure Fundamentals study guide: `https://packt.link/eCIsf`

- **Microsoft Learn training further information**:

  - AZ-900 - Microsoft Azure Fundamentals course: `https://packt.link/XFHsP`

**6**

# Azure Security

In *Chapter 3, Azure Core Architectural Components*, you learned how to describe identities, directory services, authentication methods, Conditional Access, and role-based access control.

This chapter will outline the services available to protect your Azure resources and operations. The chapter primarily focuses on the **Describe Azure architecture and services** module from the *Skills Measured* section of the AZ-900 Azure Fundamentals exam.

> **Note**
>
> You can find a detailed AZ-900 Azure Fundamentals exam skills area in the *Appendix, Assessing AZ-900 Exam Skills* of this book.

By the end of this chapter, you will be able to answer questions on the following confidently:

- Security posture
- Zero Trust
- The Defense-in-Depth (DiD) model
- Microsoft Defender for the Cloud

In addition, this chapter's goal is to take your knowledge beyond the exam content to prepare you for a real-world, day-to-day Azure-focused role.

## Threat Landscape

The profile of attackers is ever-changing. Threats may come in the form of attacks from "foreign nations," "competitors," "criminal hackers," "hacktivists," "script kiddies," and "opportunists." Usually, the internal threat in an organization or environment is hardest to detect, guard against, and often forgotten. **Attackers** are not always strangers; they could be insiders or disgruntled ex-employees, and they can have the greatest impact due to their insights into the systems and data.

To not become an easy target for opportunists and crafted attacks, you must put in **measures** that aim to raise the attacker's costs significantly. This forces them to divert their resources and activities to an easier attack target with a higher return on their attack investment.

> **Note**
>
> To learn about the reality of insider threats, enter `Sly Dog gang` into your search engine to learn about the threat of a real espionage attack on one of the highest-profile manufacturers of electric vehicles.

The aim of an attack may be specific to an organization, which might be to "steal data," "deface a website," alter the integrity of an app or a service, or extort money through ransom. Usually, there are two motivations of attackers: money or a mission.

*Figure 6.1* aims to visualize these motivations:

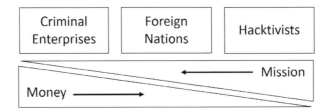

Figure 6.1 – Attack motivations

The motivation is more apparent in "money-driven attacks" involving a calculated assessment by the attacker on their **Return On Investment** (**ROI**) before deciding to give up on the current target and move on to another one. However, a "mission-driven attack" is often more of a **moral standard** and a matter of "ethics," "principles," "politics," and control than money. Thus, the attacks may be more sustained, and the attackers may be determined to succeed at any cost because the reward may not have a price that can be attached.

## Common Threats

Some of the most common threats to protect against are as follows:

- **Ransomware**: This is malware that will encrypt files and folders in an attempt to extort money.
- **Data breach**: This includes **phishing**, **spear phishing**, **Structured Query Language** (**SQL**) injection, "stealing" passwords/bank details/other sensitive information, luring somebody to click a link, and opening a file.

- **Dictionary attack**: This is an **identity theft attack**, also known as a **brute-force attack**. In this attack, "known passwords" are used against an account to steal an identity.

- **Disruptive attack**: This is a **network and workload attack**. A **Distributed Denial of Service (DDoS)** attack is disruptive as it attempts to make a network or workload (such as an application or service) unavailable by "flooding" it with requests and attempting to exhaust its resources.

Attackers plan and structure their attacks to stay undetected on the network and in the user's systems without the victim being alerted. Attacks follow a sequence or chain of events, known as an **attack chain** or **kill chain**. A common chain is represented in *Figure 6.2*:

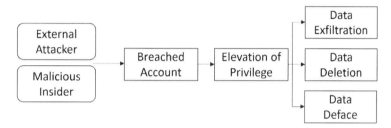

Figure 6.2 – An attack chain showing the sequence of an attack

When a user account is compromised, it can access the network and then work to elevate privileges to an admin account that can move laterally within the network. This access can then be used to access systems and execute activities, such as stealing, deleting, corrupting, and encrypting data. It can also manipulate a service, such as by adding/editing **Domain Name Service (DNS)** records and **Active Directory (AD)** objects, installing software, enabling service credits, and purchasing goods/services.

So, how do you disrupt this chain of events and save an organization's data and resources? This can be done through a Zero Trust and **Defense-in-Depth (DiD)** approach to prevent and disrupt this chain of events. You need to put multiple obstacles in the attacker's way and increase their attack costs so that they will move on to launching an easier attack elsewhere that offers less resistance. This will be discussed later in this chapter in more detail.

Security must be in place before a single line of code is written, a system is created, or data is stored; however, this can often be seen as the "anti-pattern" of operations, availability, and productivity. You may have encountered overzealous security teams referred to as "business prevention teams."

A culture akin to **Development-Operations (DevOps)** that fosters trust between all teams and security teams must exist, and leaders must introduce the concept and culture of **Security-Development-Operations (SecDevOps)** to an organization.

The bottom line is that security is not just somebody else's problem but everybody's responsibility. The popular adage goes as follows:

*If you are not part of the solution, you are part of the problem.*

## What Can Be Done to Prevent Threats?

The approach that should be taken is to adopt a **threat priority model**. To determine the risk priority, you must determine the impact and probability. A risk solution can be derived from the risk classification given from the risk analysis. The visualization of the threat priority model is represented in *Figure 6.3*:

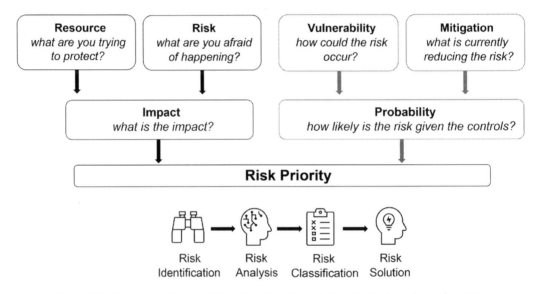

Figure 6.3 – Threat priority model showing the adopted risk solution based on risk priority

The threat priority model can aid in identifying your risk priorities, as well as where security investments should be made to reduce your security operations costs and increase your attacker's kill-chain costs. The next section will focus on the security posture from an organization's perspective.

## Security Posture

A **security posture** is an organization's "threat-protection" and "response capabilities." This ensures that the organization has the ability for systems, data, and identities to be recoverable and operational should an attack be successful.

Any security approach must start from an inward look at the current security position. Secure Score can be thought of as a "credit-rating" score you receive to see how likely you are to be accepted for a finance agreement. In other words, Secure Score will indicate your security posture. However, in security terms, it looks at where you are on the attack vulnerability scale of 1 to 10.

It is critical to know that you cannot prevent or eliminate threats and attacks. An attacker only must be successful once, while you must protect everything all the time. A security posture's goal should be to reduce exposure to threats, shrinking attack surface areas and vectors while building resilience to attacks, as attacks cannot be eliminated.

A security strategy and security posture should use the guiding principles of **Confidentiality, Integrity, and Availability (CIA)**. This is also referred to as the **CIA triangle**, which is a common industry model used by security professionals.

There is no perfect threat prevention or security solution; there will always be a trade-off, and the CIA model is a way to consider that. The CIA triangle model can be visualized as represented in *Figure 6.4*:

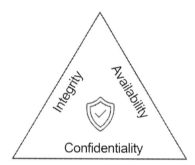

Figure 6.4 – A security posture CIA triangle

The following are the guiding principles in more detail:

- **Confidentiality**: This is a requirement that sensitive data be kept protected and can only be accessed by those who should have access through the principle of least privilege. This is the confidence that the data cannot be accessed, read, or interpreted by anybody other than those intended to read and access this data; this can be achieved by encrypting the data. The encryption keys also need to be made confidential and available to those who need access to the data.

- **Integrity**: This means that the data transferred is the same as the data received; the bytes sent are the same bytes received. This is the confidence that the data has not been altered from its original form or tampered with; this can be achieved by hashing the data. Malware can threaten the integrity of systems and data.

- **Availability**: This means that data and systems are available to those who need them, including access to encryption keys, but in a secure and governed manner. This is a trade-off between the triangle's three sides and a balance between being locked down for security but accessible for operational needs and productivity. A DDoS attack will threaten the availability of systems, data, and encryption keys.

This section introduced the concept of security posture with the knowledge of the principles of the "CIA triangle" as well as the concept of "Secure Score." Now, learn more about Zero Trust in the following section.

## Zero Trust

You need to think beyond traditional network perimeter-based security and adopt a holistic approach to security. An important concept to consider in a security strategy is Zero Trust, which uses the approach of never trust and always verify.

**Zero Trust** is not a product, service, or solution but a wider-thinking security strategy and framework to be adopted. It works on the notion of ensuring compliance and securing access to the resource and no longer the location or network the resource is on. You must not assume trust because of the resource's network or location.

The Zero Trust framework is built upon the following foundational principles:

- **Assume breach**: This principle assumes that systems have already been compromised and infiltrated by an attacker; they are already inside your systems. The impact can be mitigated by requiring the use of DiD measures with segmented access to prevent lateral movement.

- **Verify explicitly**: Regardless of the scenario, all data points should be used to ensure authentication and authorization are always performed and never skipped, due to implicit data signals. This requires the use of multiple factors or authentication, such as combining biometric or authenticator codes with usernames and passwords with Conditional Access controls.

- **Use least privilege**: Access is limited to those only required to perform specific tasks or activities. This requires the use of the **Just in Time (JIT)** and **Just Enough Access (JEA)** principles.

In this new world of hybrid work, where organizations' traditional firewalls and security service-controlled network perimeters have vanished, you must now consider identity as the new perimeter and control pane. The Zero Trust framework encompasses identities as one of its six foundational elements.

The following are the Zero Trust framework's six foundational elements:

- **Identities**: This represents users, services, and devices; each represents an element to be compromised

- **Devices**: This represents an attack surface and threat vector for data flows

- **Applications**: This represents the consumer of the data flows

- **Data**: This represents the data stored that is to be protected

- **Infrastructure**: This represents an attack surface and threat vector, whether locally on-premises or remotely hosted by a cloud provider

- **Network**: This represents an attack surface and threat vector and should be segmented

With the concept of the Zero Trust framework, you have now learned about the three foundational principles and the six foundational elements. You will learn about the concept of DiD next.

# Defense-in-Depth (DiD)

**DiD** is a security strategy that places multiple layers of different forms of defense between attackers and the resources that need to be protected. Adopting a DiD strategy allows an organization to adopt a strong security posture and helps ensure that all systems, data, and users are better protected from threats and compromise.

A DiD strategy means no "single layer" of protection or security service is solely responsible for protecting resources. Multiple layers of protection in a DiD strategy can slow down an attack path by implementing several types of defenses at individual layers. Attackers may successfully breach one defensive layer but will be halted by subsequent protection layers, preventing the protected resource from being exposed.

*Figure 6.5* shows DiD as a concept and that it is nothing new as a strategy, as it can be considered the medieval castle approach to protecting resources:

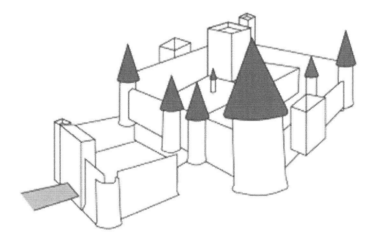

Figure 6.5 – The medieval castle defense approach

The medieval castle approach should be part of your strategy for building your resources in Azure. This approach defines multiple layers that can be protected by different security services as most appropriate at each layer.

In the medieval castle analogy, each layer from the center to the outside and back to the center provides its own independent protection service, tailored to protect the characteristics of that layer best.

The DiD approach layers, from the outside layer to the inside layer, can be represented as follows:

- Application
- Compute
- Network
- Perimeter
- Identity and access
- Physical security
- Data

*Figure 6.6* helps to visualize the layered security approach that defines a DiD strategy for a protected resource:

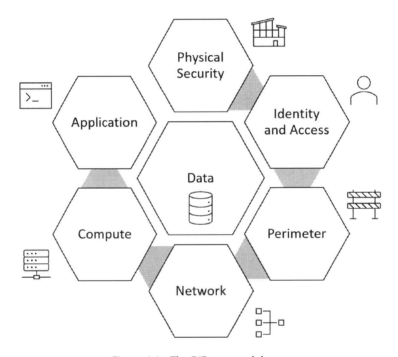

Figure 6.6 – The DiD approach layers

As no "one-size-fits-all" security service can protect all the layers, you must have security services at each layer that work in conjunction and complement the outside and inside layers. There must be a unified view so that telemetry and threat intelligence can be passed between each layer and enhance protection at each layer. Microsoft uses **Artificial Intelligence** (**AI**), threat intelligence, and analytics to enhance these capabilities.

You have now learned about the DiD strategy and explored the seven defense layers of the approach. In the next section, you will learn about Microsoft Defender for Cloud.

# Microsoft Defender for Cloud

**Microsoft Defender for Cloud** is a cloud-native security solution that is used by an organization to improve its **security posture** and **workload protection**. It is automatically enabled at no cost for all subscriptions; however, only basic **Cloud Security Posture Management (CSPM)** functionality is provided to ensure a security posture management capability is available as default.

The Secure Score function of the CSPM capability in Defender for Cloud measures an organization's **security posture**. The security posture and Secure Score are determined by the number of "security recommendations" and controls met. This Secure Score function provides information on the current and maximum scores available and the potential increase by implementing the recommendations provided. **Microsoft Defender for Cloud** will also compare an environment with industry standards and regulatory compliance that may need to be conformed to, such as the **International Organization for Standardization (ISO)** 27001 or the **Payment Card Industry (PCI)**; these reports can also be exported.

The **continuous assessments**, **security recommendations**, and **Secure Score** are part of the included capabilities enabled by default within Defender for Cloud. However, to take full advantage of the **Cloud Workload Protection (CWP)** capabilities provided by Defender for Cloud, you need to enable the enhanced features. Once enabled, these extended security posture, detection, and response features are available to improve your security posture and workload protection. These features can be enabled for subscriptions via the paid-for Defender plans.

Defender for Cloud can also be integrated with Microsoft Sentinel as the **Security Information and Event Management (SIEM)** solution, providing seamless integration and sharing threat intelligence and resources' signal data.

The following are some capabilities and terminology used with Defender for Cloud:

- **Security operations**: The **Security Operations (SecOps)** function deals with managing the inclusion of the day-to-day security monitoring needs of an organization in IT operations.

- **Security posture**: This is the status of an organization's cybersecurity measures and its ability to detect and react to security threats.

- **Secure Score**: This is a percentage-based score based on Microsoft's best practice security recommendations. It measures your security posture; the higher your score, the greater your security positioning.

- **Cloud Security Posture Management**: CSPM is the means to measure an organization's security posture—a proactive security service that provides a Secure Score to measure your security protection levels. It provides actionable recommendations and insights for the remediation of identified threat vectors and vulnerabilities.

- **Cloud Workload Protection**: These are reactive security measure tools that can be implemented to protect workloads identified as potentially at risk from the CSPM insights.

Both Defender for Cloud and Sentinel go beyond the scope of Azure. They also allow agent-based hybrid **Virtual Machine** (**VM**) scenarios from on-premises, as well as integrating AWS and GCP cloud security information to get a single source of truth.

In this section, you explored how adopting Defender for Cloud improves an organization's security posture and workload protection capabilities. In the following section, you will learn more about security operations using Microsoft Sentinel.

## Microsoft Sentinel

**Microsoft Sentinel** is Microsoft's cloud-based SIEM and **Security Orchestration, Automation, and Response** (**SOAR**) tool. It provides security data aggregation, threat analysis, and response across public cloud and on-premises environments. This service is your bird's-eye view of centralized security data and events across an organization, using integrated AI for large-scale threat analysis and response.

A SIEM solution collects "security log data"—**security signalling**—and examines it for patterns that could indicate an attack. Then, it correlates event information to identify potentially abnormal activity. Finally, any issues are alerted, and this automates responses and remediation. *Figure 6.7* illustrates this relationship between the security analytics of Microsoft Sentinel and the security signalling collected from the security tooling of the security data sources:

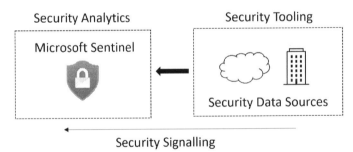

Figure 6.7 – The relationship between the security analytics of
Microsoft Sentinel and the security signalling

Microsoft Sentinel provides the following core capabilities:

- It collects security data across an organization
- It detects threats through AI-powered threat intelligence
- It investigates threat-generated critical incidents
- It responds through automated reactions and remediations

Microsoft Sentinel is more than a regular SIEM tool whose core focus is only to provide visibility of threats by collecting security data. The collected data's value is only as effective as the analysis of that data in finding threat and attack patterns.

Microsoft Sentinel's remits go beyond traditional SIEM solutions. It provides integrated SOAR capabilities that allow you to orchestrate and automate responses once critical incidents occur, with unlimited speed and scale that only a public cloud platform such as Azure can provide. *Figure 6.8* outlines these capabilities of SIEM and SOAR for an end-to-end security operations solution:

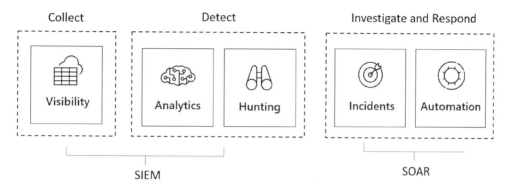

Figure 6.8 – A Sentinel security operations proposition

The additional benefits of Microsoft Sentinel from an organization's perspective are as follows:

- Microsoft Sentinel is a Microsoft-provided and managed SaaS solution and, thus, does not require an infrastructure setup or maintenance

- It can unburden teams from non-intelligent, manual SecOps tasks so the team can be re-tasked on higher-value initiatives and activities

- Implementing Sentinel will increase an attacker's attack costs while reducing a defender's operational protection costs from these threats and attacks

Some may question the affordability of these security solutions, but can your organization afford not to implement these measures?

Sentinel supports several different ways to collect data, such as connecting to Microsoft solutions natively (for example, Microsoft 365 sources and Azure Active Directory), as well as from non-Microsoft security data sources, along with any source at another cloud provider or on-premises location that uses the **System Logging Protocol** (**Syslog**) or **Common Event Format** (**CEF**) or has a **Representational State Transfer** (**REST**) API. After connecting the security data sources to Sentinel, the Azure Log Analytics service is used. The Log Analytics workspaces act as the data store for collecting and retaining logs.

With a grip on security operations using Microsoft Sentinel, you have learned about the core capabilities, benefits, and the way security signal data can be collected, stored, analyzed, and responded to in an automated way. This concludes the learning content for this chapter.

# Summary

This chapter included complete coverage of the AZ-900 Azure Fundamentals exam skills area: **Describe Azure identity, access, and security**.

In this chapter, you explored the threat landscape and the common threats. You then learned about the concept of Zero Trust and the purpose of the DiD model, and you looked at the security solutions of Microsoft Defender for Cloud and Microsoft Sentinel.

The key takeaway from this chapter is that security is not somebody else's problem but everybody's responsibility. Further knowledge beyond the required exam content was provided to prepare you for a real-world, day-to-day Azure-focused role.

In the next chapter, you will look at **Azure Cost Management**. You will learn about the factors that affect costs by looking at the Azure Pricing Calculator, the Total Cost of Ownership (TCO) calculator, Cost Management, and the Billing tool, as well as the purpose of resource tags.

# Exam Readiness Drill – Chapter Review Questions

Apart from a solid understanding of key concepts, being able to think quickly under time pressure is a skill that will help you ace your certification exam. That is why working on these skills early on in your learning journey is key.

Chapter review questions are designed to improve your test-taking skills progressively with each chapter you learn and review your understanding of key concepts in the chapter at the same time. You'll find these at the end of each chapter.

> **How To Access These Resources**
> To learn how to access these resources, head over to the chapter titled *Chapter 11, Accessing the Online Practice Resources*.

To open the Chapter Review Questions for this chapter, perform the following steps:

1.  Click the link – `https://packt.link/AZ900E2_CH06`.

    Alternatively, you can scan the following **QR code** (*Figure 6.9*):

Figure 6.9 – QR code that opens Chapter Review Questions for logged-in users

2.  Once you log in, you'll see a page similar to the one shown in *Figure 6.10*:

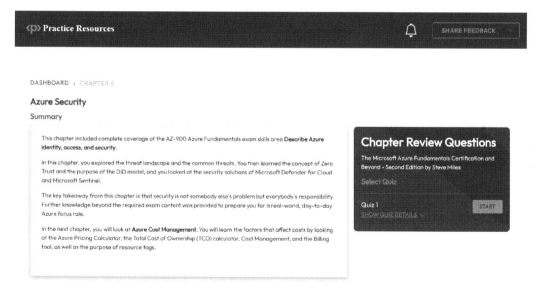

Figure 6.10 – Chapter Review Questions for Chapter 6

3.  Once ready, start the following practice drills, re-attempting the quiz multiple times.

## Exam Readiness Drill

For the first three attempts, don't worry about the time limit.

### ATTEMPT 1

The first time, aim for at least **40%**. Look at the answers you got wrong and read the relevant sections in the chapter again to fix your learning gaps.

### ATTEMPT 2

The second time, aim for at least **60%**. Look at the answers you got wrong and read the relevant sections in the chapter again to fix any remaining learning gaps.

### ATTEMPT 3

The third time, aim for at least **75%**. Once you score 75% or more, you start working on your timing.

> **Tip**
> You may take more than **three** attempts to reach 75%. That's okay. Just review the relevant sections in the chapter till you get there.

## Working On Timing

**Target**: Your aim is to keep the score the same while trying to answer these questions as quickly as possible. Here's an example of how your next attempts should look like:

| Attempt | Score | Time Taken |
|---------|-------|------------|
| Attempt 5 | 77% | 21 mins 30 seconds |
| Attempt 6 | 78% | 18 mins 34 seconds |
| Attempt 7 | 76% | 14 mins 44 seconds |

Table 6.1 – Sample timing practice drills on the online platform

> **Note**
> The time limits shown in the above table are just examples. Set your own time limits with each attempt based on the time limit of the quiz on the website.

With each new attempt, your score should stay above **75%** while your "time taken" to complete should "decrease". Repeat as many attempts as you want till you feel confident dealing with the time pressure.

# Online Hands-On Activities

Once you complete this book, complete the hands-on activities that align with this chapter. These are available on the accompanying online platform. Perform the following steps to open hands-on activities:

1. Navigate to the `Dashboard`.

2. Click the `Hands-On Activities` menu.

3. Select the activity you want to attempt.

4. The following activity aligns with this chapter:

     I.   Set 1 – Security Defaults (Accessible at `https://packt.link/activity1`)

Each activity will have a set of tasks. Complete all the tasks to shore up your practical knowledge. For example, *Figure 6.11* shows the tasks aligned with the activity *Security Defaults*:

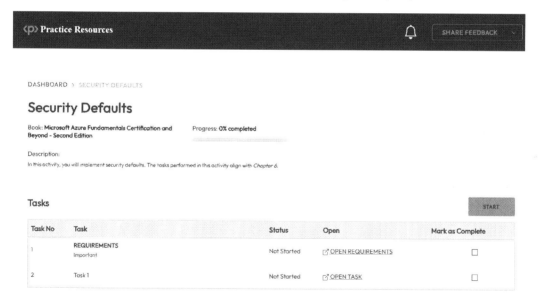

Figure 6.11 – Tasks in Security Defaults activity

# Additional Information and Study References

This section provides links to additional exam information and study references:

- **Microsoft Learn certification further information**:

  - AZ-900 - Microsoft Azure Fundamentals exam guide: `https://packt.link/grmSI`

  - AZ-900 - Microsoft Azure Fundamentals study guide: `https://packt.link/YnUY5`

- **Microsoft Learn training further information**:

  - AZ-900 - Microsoft Azure Fundamentals course: `https://packt.link/SoMX0`

# 7
# Azure Cost Management

In *Chapter 6, Azure Security*, you learned how to describe the concepts of Zero Trust and the **Defense-in-Depth (DiD)** model as well as looking at security posture management, the purpose of Microsoft Defender for Cloud, and Microsoft Sentinel, which is Microsoft's cloud-native **Security Information and Event Management (SIEM)** service.

This chapter will cover the methods for planning and managing costs in Azure. You will learn about the available tools, services, resources, and approaches. The chapter primarily focuses on the **Describe Azure management and governance** module from the *Skills Measured* section of the AZ-900 Azure Fundamentals exam.

> **Note**
>
> You can find a detailed AZ-900 Azure Fundamentals exam skills area in the *Appendix, Assessing AZ-900 Exam Skills* of this book.

By the end of this chapter, you will be able to answer questions on the following confidently:

- Azure cost factors
- Azure Cost Management
- The Azure Pricing calculator
- The **Total Cost of Ownership (TCO)** calculator

In addition, this chapter's goal is to take your knowledge beyond the exam content, so you are prepared to perform a role that includes a focus on Azure.

# Factors Influencing Costs in Azure

Each Azure consumption-based (usage) service has one or more usage meters that define the price rate and unit of cost. The "service" type determines the different units of cost.

Billing is performed monthly for each subscription based on the resource consumption collected from individual meters for that subscription. This means that you may receive a different invoice every month based on a different set of costs incurred; maybe you consumed more on one resource meter and less on another and created new resources that created costs against another meter.

The following are the primary factors that can affect costs:

- **Purchasing model**: The costs for resources may differ, depending on your purchase model. You can purchase Azure either directly from Microsoft or through a **Cloud Solution Provider (CSP)**.

> **Note**
> You can find the Azure purchase options at `https://packt.link/f4zDa`.

- **Resource type**: The costs are specific to your resources; each resource has a **billing meter** and **costs unit**.

  For example, data storage and data transfer will have a unit of billing of GB/month, a **Virtual Machine ( VM)** or Azure SQL database will have a unit of billing of one hour, and a Premium SSD-managed disk will have a unit of billing of one month.

  Storage accounts can charge for any read-and-write operations unless you're using Premium, in which case these charges are not applicable. It is important to know about the billing units for each resource you create.

- **Location**: The resource costs will vary between the defined Azure regions; you should not choose a location based solely on costs, as you may have more data transfer charges if the resources are located in different regions.

- **Usage period**: Some resources, such as VMs, can be shut down (**deallocated**) to prevent running costs. This is because two identical VMs running for different running hours will have different costs. You would continue to pay for storage costs but would not pay for data transfer costs when the VM is not passing network traffic. It is also worth noting that services (Azure AD Domain Services, Azure Bastion, App Service plans, and the Azure VPN Gateway service), once created, will still be billed even if they are not used. The only way to prevent costs for these services is to delete them.

- **Network traffic**: Ingress data transfer—data entering or **incoming**—for an Azure region or between resources within the same region is always free. However, egress data transfer—data leaving or **outgoing**—from a region is billed at a per-GB unit, irrespective of the fact that this is internet traffic or that the region is using a VPN or ExpressRoute circuit.

Remember that some resource types are free and have no billing meter or cost implications. The following are examples of resources that can be created or enabled at no cost:

- User accounts or groups

- Resource groups

- Virtual networks

- Virtual network peering

- Network interfaces

- **Network Security Groups (NSGs)**

- Availability sets and availability zones

> **Note**
>
> Removing any of these will not reduce your costs or the amount on the invoice you receive.

Thus, knowing which resources incur costs and which ones do not is crucial.

By now you have grasped the factors that affect costs, in addition to learning about some resource types that are free and have no billing meter or cost implications. In the next section, you'll look at ways to reduce costs.

## Reducing and Controlling Costs

The **Cloud Adoption Framework (CAF)** governance model defines five disciplines of cloud governance, with the "Cost Management" discipline being one.

> **Note**
>
> You can find more information on this discipline at `https://packt.link/xRsdy`.

The following are some of the ways you can reduce and control costs:

- **Optimize resources**: This is an operational activity. It has the following purposes:

    I.   Identifying any resources that are not being used and deleting them.

    II.  Recognizing resources that can be right-sized to more cost-optimal resource types or sizes.

    III. Identifying resources that do not need to be running 24/7 and that could be shut down or paused to avoid costs.

IV.   Evaluating resources running on IaaS to see whether they can be moved to PaaS, serverless, or SaaS. Azure Advisor is an essential tool for this activity.

V.    Tags should also be used to identify cost owners.

- **Azure Hybrid Benefit**: This is a licensing benefit and allows an organization to maximize any investment in existing on-premises **Software Assurance** (**SA**)-enabled Windows Server or SQL licenses (or eligible subscription-based licenses). This removes the need to license and pay with the **Pay-as-You-Go** (**PAYG**) consumption model.

    For a VM, this does not discount or remove the compute costs or any storage or networking costs; you are still liable for those and need to factor this into the total operating costs of a VM.

- **Azure reservations**: This is a resource benefit and acts as a billing discount mechanism to reduce PAYG consumption charges. It does this by allowing you to commit to paying for an amount of capacity for a fixed term at a discounted rate than you would pay on the PAYG consumption rate.

    Reservations are available for a range of resources. For example, VMs make the most sense and are best used where the workloads must run for long periods of time or 24/7. Though compute costs are usually reduced by shutting down the VMs to save costs, this is no longer possible with reservations and has no cost-saving benefit. In addition, for VMs, the reservations do not remove the software license costs or any storage or networking costs; you are still liable for those and need to factor this into the total operating costs of a VM.

- **Spot pricing**: This is a resource benefit and allows an organization to make considerable savings by taking advantage of the unused capacity. Spot pricing is best used for workloads such as test/dev, analytics, machine learning, batch processes, and rendering that do not need a specific period in which they must run. An analogy can be used for travel. If, for example, you plan to travel to a location and stay overnight at any time over the next week but are not sure which specific day or time to arrive, then you can take advantage of what days the travel and accommodation will be the cheapest. You may have decided to take a vacation in the first week of a month, but if that is not a specific requirement, then you may be able to take advantage of cheaper pricing if you take your vacation in the last week of the month instead, or midweek instead of a weekend or public holiday. There is a risk, however, that those spot VMs can be evicted at any time, when Azure compute demand goes up. Therefore, while bringing in a big cost benefit (up to 90% discount), it should be used for workloads that can handle interruptions.

In this section, you looked at the factors influencing costs in Azure and learned about the purchasing model, the resource type, the location, the usage period, and the network traffic. You also looked at how to reduce and control costs as part of the cost governance discipline. The next section will deal with Azure Cost Management, which provides core cost functionalities.

# Azure Cost Management

**Azure Cost Management** is provided through a **Cost Management + Billing** dashboard functionality in the Azure portal. This interface provides core functionality such as "cost visibility," "optimizations," and "accountability." *Figure 7.1* shows the cost analysis screen in the Azure portal:

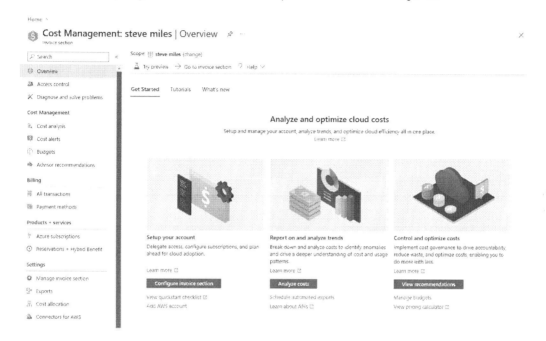

Figure 7.1 – Managing costs associated with Azure services using Azure Cost Management

The two most important capabilities provided within the Cost Management + Billing function in the Azure portal are as follows:

- **Cost Management**: You can perform cost analysis, set cost alerts, and create budgets.
- **Billing**: You can view and download invoices, view payment methods, and make payments.

This section looked at Azure Cost Management to monitor and analyze costs, set budgets, generate invoices and reports, and other tasks related to the financial aspects of using Azure resources.

In the next section, you will look at the Azure pricing calculator.

# The Azure Pricing Calculator

The **Azure pricing calculator** is a publicly accessible browser-based tool to estimate the cost of services that can be created in Azure. An Azure pricing calculator looks like the one shown in *Figure 7.2*:

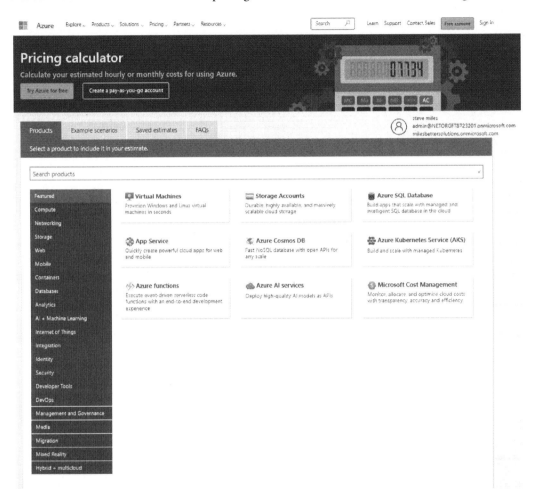

Figure 7.2 – Azure pricing calculator showing categorized resources

All Azure resources that can be purchased are organized into categories and you can browse through to view all resources.

The calculator has a search function that allows you to search for specific resources. When you add a resource to the estimate by using the calculator, a hyperlink is displayed beside it. Clicking the hyperlink shows the product details for each resource and its pricing page. This hyperlink is useful if you need to know the pricing structure for each resource and any factors that may impact costs.

To make the calculator provide cost estimations for your chosen resources, you must add the required resources to the estimate. You will then see the total estimate and breakdown. From here, you can set the currency and then export (download), save, or share the cost estimate.

Remember that the estimates are not intended to be used as final quotes. This is because the resource's availability, pricing structure, and costs may vary from the time of estimation to resource creation.

> **Note**
>
> You can access the Azure pricing calculator at `https://packt.link/t0XPq`.

Now that you have grasped the functions of the Azure pricing calculator, it is time to look at the TCO calculator.

## The Azure TCO Calculator

The Azure **TCO** calculator can be accessed as a browser-based tool to estimate cost savings by moving workloads to Azure. The TCO calculator allows you to enter details for the on-premises workloads. It will then provide some assumptions based on industry average operational costs, including data center facility costs, electricity, labor, hardware, software, and networking costs. It then provides potential cost savings by moving those workloads to Azure. These reports can be saved, downloaded (exported), or shared. *Figure 7.3* shows the TCO calculator:

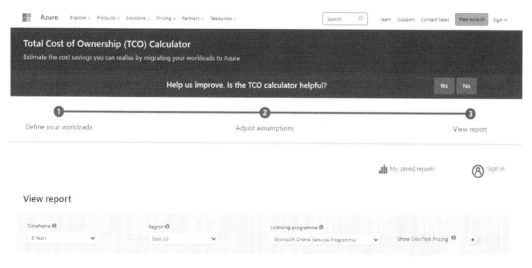

Figure 7.3 – Azure TCO calculator providing estimates using industry-average operational costs

To work with the tool, perform the following steps:

1.  Visit the URL with a browser.

2.  When the tool loads, from the **Define your workloads** page, add information as required with the details for your on-premises servers, databases, storage, and networking.

3.  Then click Next to move to the next page in the tool.

4.  From the **Adjust Assumptions** page, adjust the default entries as required.

5.  Click Next to move to the next page in the tool.

6.  From the **View report** page, a report will be generated that compares the costs of workloads running in on-premises environments with those running in Azure.

    The provided report will display summary statements, graphs, and charts to show comparative total cost breakdowns for on-premises and Azure over a selected timeframe, region, and licensing program. You may go back and adjust your workloads and assumptions to see how they impact changes in those costs.

> **Note**
> You can access the TCO calculator at `https://packt.link/1Tnaq`.

In this section, you looked at the browser-based, publicly accessible Azure pricing calculator and the TCO calculator. This concludes the learning content for this chapter.

## Summary

This chapter included complete coverage of the AZ-900 Azure Fundamentals exam skills area: **Describe cost management in Azure**.

In this chapter, you learned about the factors that can affect costs in Azure and about the Azure Cost Management and Billing tool, as well as comparing the pricing calculator and the TCO calculator.

Further knowledge beyond the required exam content was provided to prepare you for a real-world, day-to-day Azure-focused role.

In the next chapter, you will look at **Azure Governance and Compliance**.

# Exam Readiness Drill – Chapter Review Questions

Apart from a solid understanding of key concepts, being able to think quickly under time pressure is a skill that will help you ace your certification exam. That is why working on these skills early on in your learning journey is key.

Chapter review questions are designed to improve your test-taking skills progressively with each chapter you learn and review your understanding of key concepts in the chapter at the same time. You'll find these at the end of each chapter.

> **How To Access These Resources**
>
> To learn how to access these resources, head over to the chapter titled *Chapter 11, Accessing the Online Practice Resources*.

To open the Chapter Review Questions for this chapter, perform the following steps:

1.  Click the link – `https://packt.link/AZ900E2_CH07`.

    Alternatively, you can scan the following **QR code** (*Figure 7.4*):

Figure 7.4 – QR code that opens Chapter Review Questions for logged-in users

2.  Once you log in, you'll see a page similar to the one shown in *Figure 7.5*:

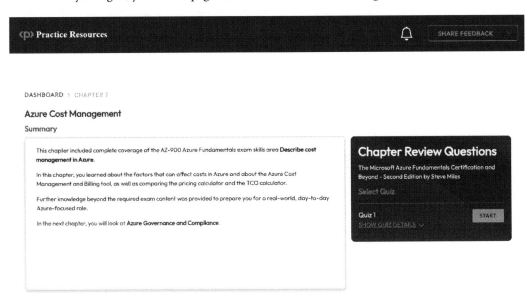

Figure 7.5 – Chapter Review Questions for Chapter 7

3.  Once ready, start the following practice drills, re-attempting the quiz multiple times.

## Exam Readiness Drill

For the first three attempts, don't worry about the time limit.

### *ATTEMPT 1*

The first time, aim for at least **40%**. Look at the answers you got wrong and read the relevant sections in the chapter again to fix your learning gaps.

### *ATTEMPT 2*

The second time, aim for at least **60%**. Look at the answers you got wrong and read the relevant sections in the chapter again to fix any remaining learning gaps.

### ATTEMPT 3

The third time, aim for at least **75%**. Once you score 75% or more, you start working on your timing.

> **Tip**
>
> You may take more than **three** attempts to reach 75%. That's okay. Just review the relevant sections in the chapter till you get there.

## Working On Timing

**Target**: Your aim is to keep the score the same while trying to answer these questions as quickly as possible. Here's an example of how your next attempts should look like:

| Attempt | Score | Time Taken |
|---------|-------|------------|
| Attempt 5 | 77% | 21 mins 30 seconds |
| Attempt 6 | 78% | 18 mins 34 seconds |
| Attempt 7 | 76% | 14 mins 44 seconds |

Table 7.1 – Sample timing practice drills on the online platform

> **Note**
>
> The time limits shown in the above table are just examples. Set your own time limits with each attempt based on the time limit of the quiz on the website.

With each new attempt, your score should stay above **75%** while your "time taken" to complete should "decrease". Repeat as many attempts as you want till you feel confident dealing with the time pressure.

## Additional Information and Study References

This section provides links to additional exam information and study references:

- **Microsoft Learn certification further information**:

  - AZ-900 - Microsoft Azure Fundamentals exam guide: `https://packt.link/isK8X`

  - AZ-900 - Microsoft Azure Fundamentals study guide: `https://packt.link/EjoYh`

- **Microsoft Learn training further information**:

  - AZ-900 - Microsoft Azure Fundamentals course: `https://packt.link/WdHIM`

# 8
# Azure Governance and Compliance

In *Chapter 7, Azure Cost Management*, you looked at cost management, the factors that can affect costs in Azure, and the tools and resources available, such as the Azure pricing calculator, and the **Total Cost of Ownership** (TCO) calculator.

This chapter will cover the methods of adopting governance and implementing compliance for Azure environments. The chapter primarily focuses on the **Describe Azure management and governance** module from the *Skills Measured* section of the AZ-900 Azure Fundamentals exam.

> **Note**
>
> You can find a detailed AZ-900 Azure Fundamentals exam skills area in the *Appendix, Assessing AZ-900 Exam Skills* of this book.

By the end of this chapter, you will be able to answer questions on the following confidently:

- Purpose of Microsoft Purview in Azure
- Purpose of Azure Policy
- Purpose of resource locks
- Purpose of tags
- The Azure service lifecycle
- Microsoft trusted cloud principles
- The Microsoft Trust Center

In addition, this chapter's goal is to take your knowledge beyond the exam content so that you are prepared to perform a role that includes a focus on Azure.

# Microsoft Purview in Azure

**Microsoft Purview** in Azure (previously called **Azure Purview**) is a unified data governance solution that can be used across **Software-as-a-Service (SaaS)** applications, multi-clouds, and on-premises data locations.

Microsoft Purview in Azure enables you to gain insights and stay informed on your distributed data landscape through the following features:

- Data discovery automation
- Mapping of an entire data estate
- Classification of sensitive data
- Lineage of data end to end
- Data storage and usage insights
- Data access management at scale
- Data security environment

The target audience is data producers, data consumers, and data officers.

> **Note**
>
> You can find more information on data governance solutions at
> `https://packt.link/TmZbd`.

You learned in this section how Microsoft Purview relates to Azure through its data governance solution capabilities. Next, you will look at Azure Policy.

# Azure Policy

**Azure Policy** is a set of resource creation and management rules that apply across multiple subscriptions. It provides the following functions and capabilities:

- Defines what actions are allowed within a subscription

- Assesses resources to ensure that compliance standards are met

- Enforces organization mandates

- Automates the remediation process addressing drift or non-compliance

One typical example use case of Azure Policy is to limit what regions can be accessed for resources to be created so that data sovereignty can be complied with. You can even limit **Virtual Machine (VM)** types or storage types so that expensive or operationally inefficient resources are not created.

*Table 8.1* lists the key differences to comprehend between Azure Policy and Azure **Role-Based Access Control** (**RBAC**):

| **Azure Policy** | **Azure RBAC** |
|---|---|
| Controls what can be done (regardless of the user) | Controls who can do what (specific to each user) |
| Focuses on resource properties | Focuses on user actions |
| Applied during the creation or change of Azure resources | Applied to each action—create, read, update, and delete |
| No specific roles model in place | Built-in and custom roles |
| Supports different "effects": `deny`, `audit`, `deployifnotexist` as the most common | Default `Deny`, explicit `Allow` |
| An example would be that you are the contributor of a resource group, but a policy blocks you from deploying a VM in `WestUS`. Another example would be that you cannot deploy an older generation type but can deploy `D4s_v5` v. | An example would be having contributor rights on a resource group in a dev/test subscription but only VM admin rights in a production subscription. |

Table 8.1 – Distinguishing factors between Azure Policy and RBAC

> **Note**
>
> You can read *Chapter 5, Azure Identity and Access*, to learn more about RBAC.

Policies are described in **JSON** format via **policy definitions**—that is, the **business rules** to be applied to the policy. These policy definitions (rules) can be grouped to form a **policy initiative** (or policy set). The policy definition is assigned to a **resource-level scope** and applied by **policy assignments**. The policy will then evaluate all resources in the **level assigned**. *Figure 8.1* shows that policies are scoped at the subscription, resource group, and resource levels:

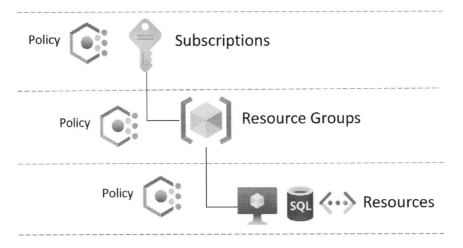

Figure 8.1 – Azure Policy scope level

> **Note**
>
> Management groups, while not referenced directly in this context, can be learned about in *Chapter 3, Azure Core Architectural Components*.

With the knowledge of Azure Policy and its difference from RBAC, read on about resource locks.

## Resource Locks

**Resource locks** are used to prevent resources from being modified. More importantly, they are used to prevent resources from being accidentally deleted, as locks override any permissions that have been set through RBAC.

Resource locks are managed at the subscription, resource group, and resource level and can be one of the following types:

- **Read-only lock**: Admins cannot delete or update a resource
- **CanNotDelete lock**: Admins can update but cannot delete a resource

Unlike **resource tags**, resource locks are "inherited" by child resources. This means that all the resources in that scope will inherit a parent scope lock. You can add both **Read-only** and **Cannotdelete** lock types to resources; multiple locks could be applied to a resource, with the most restrictive inherited lock applying and taking precedence. *Figure 8.2* aims to visualize the levels at which locks can be applied and inherited:

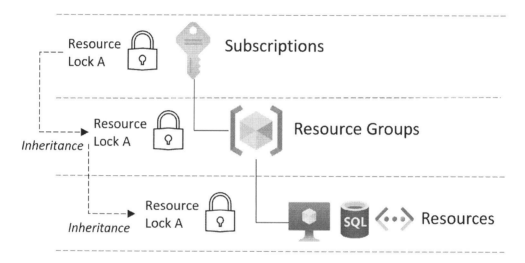

Figure 8.2 – Azure resource locks preventing accidental deletion of resources

Resource locks are applied through the Azure portal, Azure PowerShell, the Azure CLI, ARM templates, or the REST API. You must be an **owner** of a resource or have the **User Access Administrator** role to create a resource lock. Alternatively, a "custom" role can be used that grants the right to create or delete locks.

This section looked at resource locks and the levels at which the locks can be applied. Next, you will learn about tags.

# Tags

Tags provide metadata or descriptive information for Azure resources; metadata is a way to describe data. Think of it like a sticky note, comments in a document, or a tooltip—a sticky label that provides further information on the object it is describing. This is why it is called a tag.

Tags can be created via the Azure portal, PowerShell, the Azure CLI, ARM templates, or the REST API; they can also be managed via Azure Policy.

Up to 15 tags for each resource can be created, and there is no automatic inheritance by resources; if a tag is set at the resource group level, the tag only applies to the resource it is attached to. This may be useful if you want to group things logically by a resource group but have a way to independently label the resource with metadata that is not tied to a resource group or subscription.

Each tag consists of a tag name and tag value, which forms a key-value pair; you can define the name and value as you wish. This can be seen in *Figure 8.3*:

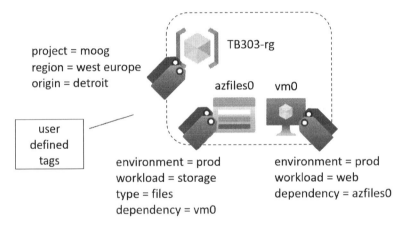

Figure 8.3 – Tags used for resource metadata

This data can then be used to logically organize all the resources that share the same values. Tags can be used to take action or enforce a policy on all resources that share the same tags or are flagged with the same values. The following are some common use cases for tags:

- **Billing information**: Cost center, billing ID, project ID, team, business unit, region, and so on

- **Ownership information**: Department or team, named point of contact, stakeholder, and so on

- **Purpose information**: Environment (dev, test, stage, or prod), application name, and so on

- **Classification and compliance information**: SLA, confidentiality marking, region, compliance standard, and so on

One of the most common use cases for tags will be to capture billing information for cost management purposes. A cost center/project/team tag could be used where you wish to use a show-back or charge-back for granular cost reporting for resources consumed within a subscription.

Tags appear in the **CSV export** of an Azure bill so that the **resource tag** column can be filtered and used with automation.

In this section, you looked at tagging Azure resources to create a taxonomy for governance. Next, you will learn about the Azure service lifecycle.

# Azure Service Lifecycle

New Azure services are introduced through preview services. The **service lifecycle** defines how each service introduced is made available and released for general use, known as **general availability**. Services are (unless an explicit service exception) not provided with an SLA or support during the preview.

The service lifecycle and access to services are as follows:

- **Development**: Not available to the public

- **Private preview**: Available only to a selected audience

- **Public preview**: Available to all customers

- **General availability** (**GA**): Available to all customers

Preview services are accessed from the Azure portal.

> **Note**
>
> You can get the latest updates on services and their statuses at
> `https://packt.link/BpH8z`.

The section discussed the service lifecycle in Azure. You will learn of Microsoft's trusted cloud principles in the next section.

## Core Security, Privacy, and Security Tenets

As you learned in *Chapter 1*, *Introduction to Cloud Computing*, security is a **shared responsibility model**. This means that while certain responsibilities transfer to the cloud provider in a cloud environment operating model, the customer retains other responsibilities. You should be aware of when it is your responsibility to provide the appropriate level of security and control. Conversely, you must know where it is not your responsibility—that is, you must know the responsibilities of the cloud services provider in terms of ensuring that their platform is kept compliant and your data is kept private.

Security, compliance, privacy, and transparency are fundamental for a trust model and are core tenets of Microsoft's Online Services. *Figure 8.4* highlights the trust principles:

Figure 8.4 – Microsoft trusted cloud principles

*Figure 8.4* shows that while it is your data and your control, Microsoft is responsible for delivering and operating a cloud services platform that will provide the data residency that an organization needs and ensure it will keep that data secure, private, and compliant with recognized compliance and regulatory standards. These, however, are not just principles but contractual guarantees.

With the knowledge about Microsoft's trusted cloud principles, you will now look at how Microsoft delivers on these core tenets with the Trust Center.

## Trust Center

The **Trust Center** is a website that acts as a single point of focus for an organization that needs resources and in-depth information regarding the Microsoft principles of security, privacy, and compliance.

> **Note**
> You can access the Trust Center at `https://packt.link/htsy3`.

Microsoft's Trust Center is a centralized portal for any organization that needs information or resources on security, privacy, and compliance regarding Microsoft Online Services, not just Azure. This concludes the learning content for this chapter.

# Summary

This chapter included complete coverage of the following AZ-900 Azure Fundamentals exam skills area: **Describe Azure management and governance**.

In this chapter, you learned about the purpose of Microsoft Purview in Azure, the purpose of Azure Policy, resource locks, and tags, the Azure service lifecycle, Microsoft trusted cloud principles, and the Trust Center.

Further knowledge beyond required exam content was provided to prepare for a real-world, day-to-day Azure-focused role.

The next chapter will look at **Azure Resource Deployment and Management**.

# Exam Readiness Drill – Chapter Review Questions

Apart from a solid understanding of key concepts, being able to think quickly under time pressure is a skill that will help you ace your certification exam. That is why working on these skills early on in your learning journey is key.

Chapter review questions are designed to improve your test-taking skills progressively with each chapter you learn and review your understanding of key concepts in the chapter at the same time. You'll find these at the end of each chapter.

> **How To Access These Resources**
>
> To learn how to access these resources, head over to the chapter titled *Chapter 11, Accessing the Online Practice Resources*.

To open the Chapter Review Questions for this chapter, perform the following steps:

1. Click the link – `https://packt.link/AZ900E2_CH08`.

    Alternatively, you can scan the following **QR code** (*Figure 8.5*):

Figure 8.5 – QR code that opens Chapter Review Questions for logged-in users

2.    Once you log in, you'll see a page similar to the one shown in *Figure 8.6*:

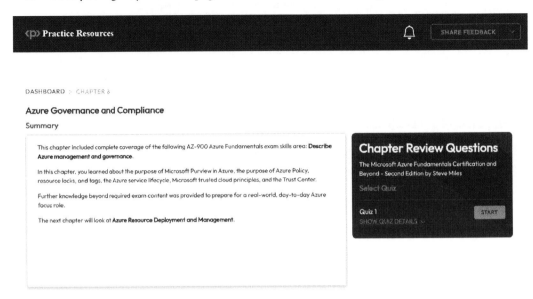

Figure 8.6 – Chapter Review Questions for Chapter 8

3.    Once ready, start the following practice drills, re-attempting the quiz multiple times.

## Exam Readiness Drill

For the first three attempts, don't worry about the time limit.

### *ATTEMPT 1*

The first time, aim for at least **40%**. Look at the answers you got wrong and read the relevant sections in the chapter again to fix your learning gaps.

### *ATTEMPT 2*

The second time, aim for at least **60%**. Look at the answers you got wrong and read the relevant sections in the chapter again to fix any remaining learning gaps.

*ATTEMPT 3*

The third time, aim for at least **75%**. Once you score 75% or more, you start working on your timing.

> **Tip**
>
> You may take more than **three** attempts to reach 75%. That's okay. Just review the relevant sections in the chapter till you get there.

# Working On Timing

**Target**: Your aim is to keep the score the same while trying to answer these questions as quickly as possible. Here's an example of how your next attempts should look like:

| Attempt | Score | Time Taken |
|---------|-------|------------|
| Attempt 5 | 77% | 21 mins 30 seconds |
| Attempt 6 | 78% | 18 mins 34 seconds |
| Attempt 7 | 76% | 14 mins 44 seconds |

Table 8.2 – Sample timing practice drills on the online platform

> **Note**
>
> The time limits shown in the above table are just examples. Set your own time limits with each attempt based on the time limit of the quiz on the website.

With each new attempt, your score should stay above **75%** while your "time taken" to complete should "decrease". Repeat as many attempts as you want till you feel confident dealing with the time pressure.

# Online Hands-On Activities

Once you complete this book, complete the hands-on activities that align with this chapter. These are available on the accompanying online platform. Perform the following steps to open hands-on activities:

1.   Navigate to the `Dashboard`.

2.   Click the `Hands-On Activities` menu.

3.   Select the activity you want to attempt.

4.   The following activities align with this chapter:

     I.   Set 3 – Azure Policy (Accessible at `https://packt.link/activity11`)

Each activity will have a set of tasks. Complete all the tasks to shore up your practical knowledge. For example, *Figure 8.7* shows the tasks aligned with the activity *Azure Policy*:

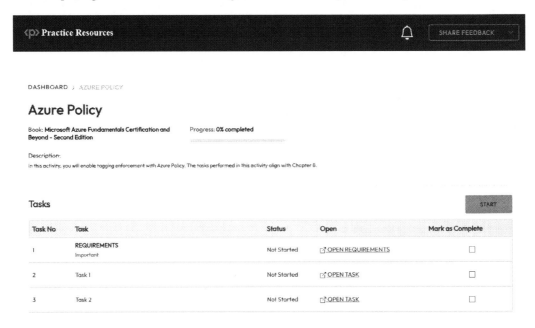

Figure 8.7 – Tasks in Azure Policy activity.

# Additional Information and Study References

This section provides links to additional exam information and study references:

- **Microsoft Learn certification further information**:

  - AZ-900 - Microsoft Azure Fundamentals exam guide: `https://packt.link/yD42x`

  - AZ-900 - Microsoft Azure Fundamentals study guide: `https://packt.link/CyoaP`

- **Microsoft Learn training further information**:

  - AZ-900 - Microsoft Azure Fundamentals course: `https://packt.link/zZqEd`

# 9
# Azure Resource Deployment and Management

In *Chapter 8, Azure Governance and Compliance*, you were introduced to Microsoft Purview in Azure, Azure Policy, resource locks, and tags. This chapter will outline resource deployment, management capabilities, and tooling in Azure.

This chapter primarily focuses on the **Describe Azure management and governance** module from the *Skills Measured* section of the AZ-900 Azure Fundamentals exam.

> **Note**
>
> You can find a detailed AZ-900 Azure Fundamentals exam skills area in the *Appendix, Assessing AZ-900 Exam Skills* of this book.

By the end of this chapter, you will be able to answer questions on the following confidently:

- The Azure portal
- Azure Cloud Shell, including the Azure CLI and Azure PowerShell
- Azure Arc
- Azure Resource Manager (ARM) templates

In this chapter, you will learn how to use each of these to interact with your Azure resources. In addition, this chapter's goal is to take your knowledge beyond the exam content, so you are prepared to perform a role that includes a focus on Azure.

# Azure Portal

The **Azure portal** is a browser-based **Graphical User Interface (GUI)** console for interacting with Azure resources. The Azure portal is public-facing and can be accessed at `https://packt.link/y8dms`.

The portal is designed for self-service and is the most common method for creating and managing your Azure environments. It is the quickest way for anybody new to Azure to get started and carry out simple tasks.

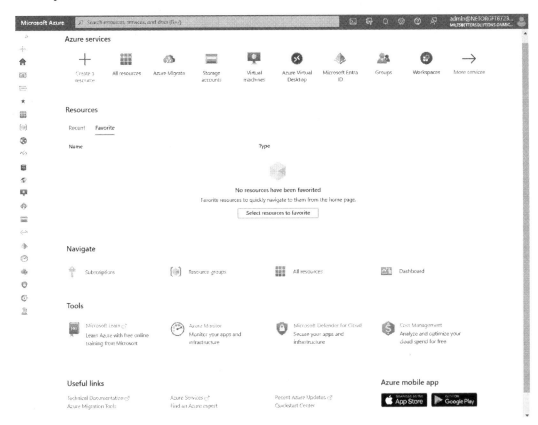

Figure 9.1 – The Azure portal

The Azure portal provides users with a quick and straightforward way to access Azure resources, often through dashboard views or high-level overview visualizations. These can also be exported in various formats, such as reports and Excel, based on the resource type. The Azure portal allows users to create, change, and delete resources directly within the portal as a seamless single-user-interface experience.

Being a web-based console, the portal can be accessed from anywhere with an internet connection and from all modern desktops, laptops, and tablet devices (running Windows, Android, and so on). The only limitation is that your browser must have JavaScript enabled, and your OS must be capable of running one of the following supported browsers:

- Microsoft Edge (latest version)
- Safari (latest version, Mac only)
- Chrome (latest version)
- Firefox (latest version)

The portal user experience can be customized through personal settings. These settings can be accessed by clicking **Settings** (the gears icon) on the top right of the portal toolbar. Once clicked, the following settings are displayed:

- Directories + subscriptions
- Appearance + Startup views
- Language + region
- My information
- Signing out + notifications

In addition to the preceding settings, customized dashboards can be created.

Finally, there are other ways to interact with Azure services and resources; if you want to create and manage more complex resources or perform automation tasks, you can use a **Command-Line Interface (CLI)** such as **PowerShell** or **Bourne Again Shell (Bash)**.

All tasks carried out in the portal use the underlying **Azure Resource Manager (ARM)** API. The **ARM API** performs all the activities in the background and will "notify" you of the progress and whether any tasks have been completed or failed.

Full deployment and activity logging is provided, which details all the activities/tasks initiated by users and the Azure platform; this can be helpful for troubleshooting issues and audit and compliance purposes.

Governance can also be put in place through **Azure Policy**, and access controls can be put in place through **RBAC**. **Access controls** can prevent users from adding, changing, or deleting resources, and locks can also be added to resources to prevent accidental deletion.

This section looked at the Azure portal and covered some of its functionalities. The following section will look at Azure PowerShell.

# Azure PowerShell

**PowerShell** is a "cross-platform CLI management tool" for interacting with Azure resources. This tool can be used instead of the GUI of the Azure portal or desktop/mobile apps for creating and managing your Azure environments.

**Azure PowerShell** is a module installed as part of **Windows PowerShell**. The **AzPowerShell** module contains a set of **cmdlets** (pronounced as commandlets) for PowerShell that allows you to manage resources from within PowerShell directly at the CLI "without the need to access the portal."

**PowerShell** is a popular management tool where the focus is on **Windows** systems and is designed for complex automation tasks. It can be used interactively, meaning commands can be entered manually by typing them directly into the shell command prompt. Its cross-platform support—from PowerShell Core 6.x and PowerShell 7.x—means that you can install and use the Az PowerShell module on **Windows**, **Linux**, or **macOS** to interact with your Azure environments. The **Az module** provides a set of "cmdlets" for resource management and is based on the .NET Standard library. The Az module for PowerShell replaces **AzureRM** for Azure interaction as it now has the full capabilities of AzureRM, plus more.

> **Note**
> The AzureRM PowerShell modules are set to be retired on 29 February 2024.

You can also access the CLI through the portal using **Cloud Shell**, which provides access to the Az PowerShell module cmdlets. You will cover more on Cloud Shell in the *Azure Cloud Shell* section.

**PowerShell 7** is the recommended version of PowerShell to use with Az PowerShell on all platforms, that is, Windows, macOS, and Linux. **PowerShell 7.0.6** or 7.1.3 or later is required for **Az module 6.0.0** and later; however, PowerShell 5.1 is still supported.

To use the **Az PowerShell module**, you must **install** it (it is pre-installed in Azure Cloud Shell). The preferred installation method for the Az module is to use the **Install-Module** cmdlet, and the recommended installation scope is for the current user only.

The "syntax" of PowerShell commands uses the "verb-noun" pair format, and the **data** (response or answer to your question) that is returned is called an **object**. These verb-noun pairs work as follows:

- The "verb (first part)" of the pair refers to the "action that the cmdlet must perform". The following are the actions:

  - Get
  - Set
  - Show
  - Find

- New

- Resize

- The "noun" (second part) of the pair refers to the "entity that the action is performed against"— that is, "do this" or "to that."

A simple example of this is Get-<Verb>, which can be used to get the following approved PowerShell command verbs:

- Connect-AzAccount: This command can be used to log in to Azure.

- Get-AzResourceGroup: This command will list all resource groups.

- New-AzResourceGroup: This command will create a new resource group.

- New-AzVM: This command will create a new VM.

You can also check the PowerShell version by running the following command from within PowerShell:

```
$PSVersionTable.PSVersion
```

These are just a few PowerShell examples.

PowerShell can also run **PowerShell scripts**. These scripts contain **PowerShell cmdlets** and code and can only be **run** (executed) from within PowerShell. Scripts automate "repetitive" or complex tasks that have many steps and actions to be performed against many different entities. In this case, a series of commands can be assembled in the syntax format of the shell being used, and the script can then be executed by issuing a single command at the PowerShell prompt.

With this knowledge of the PowerShell CLI as an Azure management tool under your belt, next you shall learn about the Azure CLI.

## Azure CLI

The Azure CLI is a "cross-platform CLI management tool" for interacting with Azure resources. It is written in **Python**. The CLI can be used instead of the GUI for creating and managing your Azure environments.

The Azure CLI provides **cross-platform** support, meaning you can install and use it on **Windows**, **Linux**, or **macOS**. It draws parallels to **Bash** scripting and is a popular management tool choice when the focus is on Linux systems and is designed for complex and automation tasks.

Much like the **Az PowerShell module**, commands can be executed using interactive commands. You can use commands directly from the shell prompt or scripts to automate repetitive or complex tasks that have many steps and require actions to be performed against many different entities.

In this case, a series of commands are assembled in the syntax format of the shell being used, and the script is then executed by issuing a single command at the shell prompt. This is done within the shell of the OS you have installed the Azure CLI on, for example, `cmd.exe` for **Windows** or `Bash` for **Linux** and **Mac**.

> **Note**
>
> Cloud Shell is a Microsoft-provided shell environment "hosted" for you on **Ubuntu Linux** containers (which Microsoft manages and maintains, and you do not pay for). You can think of this as a **Shell Environment as a Service (SEaaS)**. The quickest way to start using the Azure CLI is by running it in Azure Cloud Shell instead of a local shell environment hosted on Windows, Linux, or macOS machines.

You can start using the **Azure CLI** to perform creation and management tasks as you would do in the portal or via the Az PowerShell module (Azure PowerShell). So, first sign in by using the following command:

```
az login
```

This command will load an Azure sign-in page; this sign-in method is referred to as an interactive sign-in.

The syntax of the Azure CLI follows a similar (but still different) pattern to PowerShell; it uses the following format:

```
az <command group> <parameters>
```

The following are the same example tasks you looked at in the *Azure PowerShell* section, but this time using the Azure CLI syntax:

- `az login`: This command can be used to log in to Azure.
- `az group`: This command list will list all resource groups.
- `az group`: This command will create a new resource group.
- `az vm`: This command will create a new VM.

These are just a few Azure CLI examples. After installing the Azure CLI, you can check its version by running the following command from either **Windows Command Prompt** or **PowerShell**:

```
az version
```

The following screenshot shows the command output for Windows PowerShell:

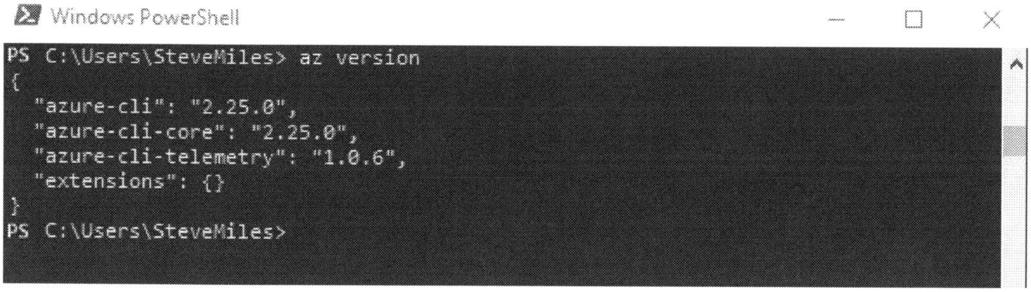

Figure 9.2 – The azure-cli version command in PowerShell

The following screenshot shows the command output for Windows Command Prompt:

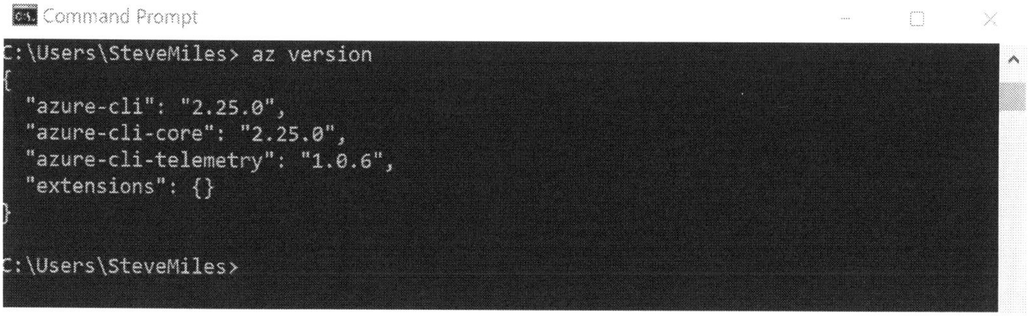

Figure 9.3 – The azure-cli version command in Windows Command Prompt

Now that you are familiar with the Azure CLI as an Azure management tool, it is time to look at Azure Cloud Shell as a browser-based alternative to a shell environment on a physical or virtual machine.

# Azure Cloud Shell

**Azure Cloud Shell** is a cross-platform, interactive, hosted shell and scripting environment that Microsoft provides, hosted on Ubuntu containers. As stated previously, you can think of this as a **SEaaS**.

Cloud Shell enables a browser-based CLI. The benefit of using Cloud Shell is that you do not need to download, install, or update any CLI management tools in a local shell environment on a device or machine. Being a cross-platform management tool, all you need is a browser to run shell commands and the Az PowerShell module.

Imagine that you were to move between devices; you might not have access to the necessary CLI tools, and you may not have the PowerShell modules or updates. This means that your scripts may fail to run or your interactive commands error as they are intended for a different version than you have installed locally. However, with **Cloud Shell**, wherever you have access to a browser, you have access to a CLI; you will always have a consistent and up-to-date experience. You can also use Cloud Shell from a **browser** to have a shell environment from anywhere, anytime.

Cloud Shell provides two shell environments so that you can choose the one that best suits your requirements. The two shell environments are as follows:

- **Bash**: This comes with the Azure CLI installed.

- **PowerShell**: This comes with the Azure PowerShell module installed.

Cloud Shell can be accessed directly within the Azure portal via the code icon at the top of the portal toolbar, as shown in *Figure 9.4*:

Figure 9.4 – Azure Cloud Shell with the PowerShell interface via the Azure portal

You can select your required shell environment from a dropdown, depending on whether you wish to run **Bash** or **PowerShell** commands. You can drag the Cloud Shell pane up and down to resize it and have a split view, as shown in *Figure 9.5*:

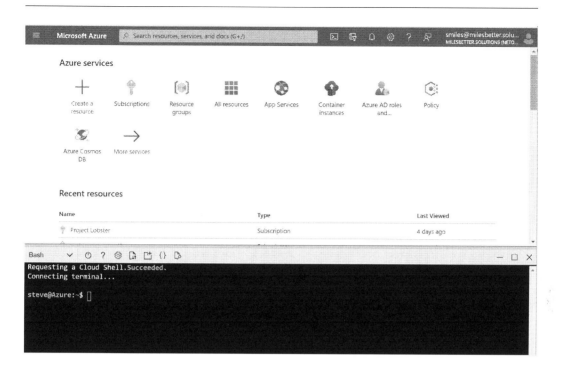

Figure 9.5 – Azure Cloud Shell with the Bash interface via the Azure portal

Cloud Shell is also available via a standalone browser-based shell without the need to access it via the Azure portal. You can access this standalone browser-based shell experience at `https://packt.link/QDoci`.

As mentioned in the *Azure CLI* section of this chapter, the Azure CLI can be accessed either via the PowerShell or Bash shell environment within Cloud Shell. This is pre-installed, and unlike running it on your device it is always available wherever you have access to a browser. This feature makes it portable by nature, unlike an installation that needs to be carried out on every device that you may access.

You learned that Cloud Shell as an Azure management tool is utilized for writing scripts and automating various tasks. The next section will look at ARM templates, which are integrated within these scripts to automate the deployment of Azure resources.

## Azure Resource Manager (ARM) Templates

ARM templates are an **Infrastructure as Code** (**IAC**) approach to resource deployment. This approach allows the repeatable and reliable deployment of multiple dependent resources into an Azure subscription in an automated and governed manner.

ARM templates are **JSON** files—a minimal, readable format for structuring data as an alternative to **Extensible Markup Language** (**XML**)—that define the configuration to be used for resource deployment.

With ARM templates, you define your desired deployment outcome with all resources you want to be created and any properties you wish to be specified in a single request; this is achieved by utilizing a **declarative** syntax (as opposed to an imperative syntax) in the templates.

*Figure 9.6* shows this approach of **ARM** versus **non-ARM IAC**:

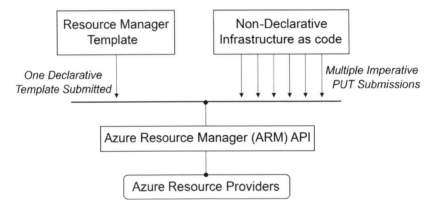

Figure 9.6 – ARM template declarative approach

Instead of issuing multiple commands at each stage of the process to create each resource individually with no orchestration, you must also consider dependencies and the order in which the commands are processed.

You have now learned that ARM templates are JSON files that define the configuration to be used for resource deployment. The next section will detail a tool that supports physical and virtual machines—Azure ARC.

## Azure Arc

**Azure Arc** is a "hybrid management and governance tool" that supports physical and virtual machines. These hybrid servers can be on-premises, in provider edge locations, or hosted on other cloud providers' platforms. This is represented in *Figure 9.7*:

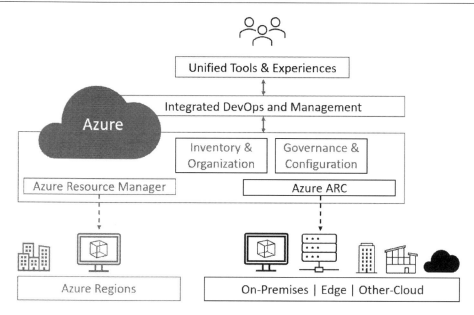

Figure 9.7 – Azure Arc for servers

When connected in this way, a hybrid server becomes an **Azure resource** that can be "controlled," "secured," and "managed" the same as an Azure native VM.

Each hybrid machine is given an **Azure resource ID** allowing the machine to be added to a resource group and be managed by **ARM**; these Azure Arc-managed servers are classed as **Arc-enabled servers**.

To connect a Windows server to Azure Arc, an **Azure Connected Machine agent** is deployed and configured on the server. It should be noted that this does not replace the **Azure Monitor agent** for Windows servers; "both agents" are required for "Arc-enabled servers."

The following "hybrid functionality" and cloud operations can be performed when a hybrid server is Azure Arc enabled:

- **Configure**: **Azure Automation** can be used to speed up routine management tasks. "Change Tracking and Inventory capabilities" are used for configuration changes, software installation, services, and registry updates.

- **Govern**: Azure Policy "guest configurations" can be assigned to perform machine settings audits.

- **Monitor**: **VM Insights** is used to monitor the OS, components, processes, services, and software applications. Log data can be collected and analyzed through Log Analytics.

- **Protect**: **Microsoft Defender for Cloud** provides endpoint protection through Microsoft Defender for Endpoint. Microsoft Sentinel can provide **Security Information and Event Management** (**SIEM**) and orchestrated and automated responses.

Azure Arc can be enabled manually on servers or automated through the **Windows Admin Center (WAC)**. This can be used to deploy the **Connected Machine agent** and perform the **Azure registration** in a single place.

In this section, you looked at Azure Arc for servers. This concludes the learning content for this chapter.

# Summary

This chapter covered the AZ-900 Azure Fundamentals exam skills area: **Describe features and tools for managing and deploying Azure resources**.

In this chapter, you learned how to describe the Azure portal and Azure Cloud Shell, including the Azure CLI and Azure PowerShell, Azure Arc's purpose, and ARM and its templates.

Knowledge beyond the level required for the exam content was provided to prepare you for a real-world, day-to-day Azure-focused role.

In the next chapter, you will look at **Azure Monitoring and Tools**.

# Exam Readiness Drill – Chapter Review Questions

Apart from a solid understanding of key concepts, being able to think quickly under time pressure is a skill that will help you ace your certification exam. That is why working on these skills early on in your learning journey is key.

Chapter review questions are designed to improve your test-taking skills progressively with each chapter you learn and review your understanding of key concepts in the chapter at the same time. You'll find these at the end of each chapter.

> **How To Access These Resources**
>
> To learn how to access these resources, head over to the chapter titled *Chapter 11, Accessing the Online Practice Resources*.

To open the Chapter Review Questions for this chapter, perform the following steps:

1. Click the link – `https://packt.link/AZ900E2_CH09`.

   Alternatively, you can scan the following **QR code** (*Figure 9.8*):

Figure 9.8 – QR code that opens Chapter Review Questions for logged-in users

2. Once you log in, you'll see a page similar to the one shown in *Figure 9.9*:

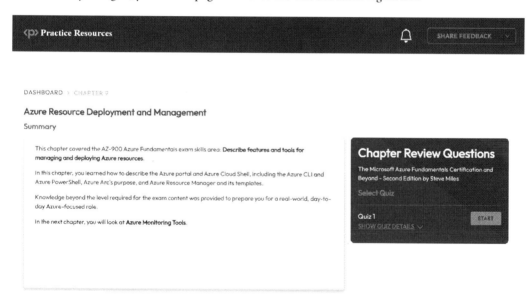

Figure 9.9 – Chapter Review Questions for Chapter 9

3. Once ready, start the following practice drills, re-attempting the quiz multiple times.

## Exam Readiness Drill

For the first three attempts, don't worry about the time limit.

### ATTEMPT 1

The first time, aim for at least **40%**. Look at the answers you got wrong and read the relevant sections in the chapter again to fix your learning gaps.

### ATTEMPT 2

The second time, aim for at least **60%**. Look at the answers you got wrong and read the relevant sections in the chapter again to fix any remaining learning gaps.

### ATTEMPT 3

The third time, aim for at least **75%**. Once you score 75% or more, you start working on your timing.

> Tip
>
> You may take more than **three** attempts to reach 75%. That's okay. Just review the relevant sections in the chapter till you get there.

# Working On Timing

**Target**: Your aim is to keep the score the same while trying to answer these questions as quickly as possible. Here's an example of how your next attempts should look like:

| Attempt | Score | Time Taken |
|---|---|---|
| Attempt 5 | 77% | 21 mins 30 seconds |
| Attempt 6 | 78% | 18 mins 34 seconds |
| Attempt 7 | 76% | 14 mins 44 seconds |

Table 9.1 – Sample timing practice drills on the online platform

> Note
>
> The time limits shown in the above table are just examples. Set your own time limits with each attempt based on the time limit of the quiz on the website.

With each new attempt, your score should stay above **75%** while your "time taken" to complete should "decrease". Repeat as many attempts as you want till you feel confident dealing with the time pressure.

## Additional Information and Study References

This section provides links to additional exam information and study references:

- **Microsoft Certification Exam further information**:

  - Exam AZ-900: Microsoft Azure Fundamentals: `https://packt.link/I4zTI`

- **Microsoft Learn further study references**:

  - Azure Fundamentals: Describe Azure management and governance: `https://packt.link/Ag3Ow`

# 10

# Azure Monitoring and Tools

In *Chapter 9, Azure Resource Deployment and Management*, you learned how to describe the Azure portal and Azure Cloud Shell, including the Azure CLI and Azure PowerShell, and you learned about Azure Arc's purpose, and Azure Resource Manager and Azure Resource Manager templates.

This chapter will outline the monitoring capabilities and tooling available in Azure and will primarily focus on the **Describe Azure management and governance** module from the *Skills Measured* section of the AZ-900 Azure Fundamentals exam.

> **Note**
>
> You can find the detailed AZ-900 Azure Fundamentals exam skills area in the *Appendix, Assessing AZ-900 Exam Skills* of this book.

By the end of this chapter, you will be able to answer questions on the following confidently:

- Azure Advisor

- Azure Monitor, including Log Analytics, Azure Monitor alerts, and Application Insights

- Azure Service Health

In addition, this chapter's goal is to take your knowledge beyond the exam content, so you are prepared to perform a role that includes a focus on Azure.

# Azure Advisor

Azure Advisor is an included, no-cost service that provides advice on optimizing your Azure resources. It provides personalized and actionable best practice recommendations based on usage analysis and can be accessed directly within the portal. It is recommended to use Azure Advisor and take action based on the recommendations. To view Azure Advisor, as shown in *Figure 10.1*, log in to the Azure portal:

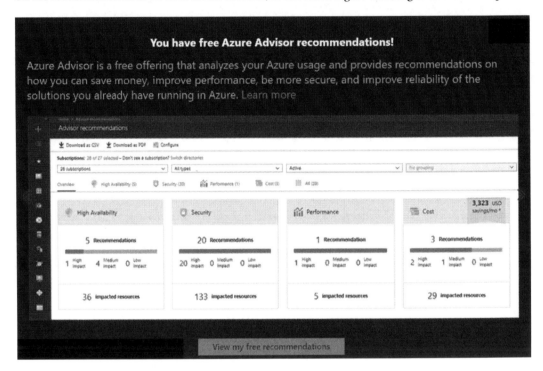

Figure 10.1 – Azure Advisor recommendations prompt screen

Azure Advisor recommendations are available across the following categories, and the URLs point to the complete list of recommendations available for each category (*Table 10.1*):

| Category | Recommendation | URL |
|---|---|---|
| Cost | Provided for optimizing and reducing Azure subscription spend | https://packt.link/Hz5fc |
| Operational Excellence | Provided for process and workflow efficiency, resource manageability, and deployment best practices | https://packt.link/n8qLD |

| Category | Recommendation | URL |
|---|---|---|
| Performance | Provided for optimizing a workload's speed and responsiveness to demand | `https://packt.link/29JO6` |
| Reliability (formerly High Availability) | Provided to ensure and improve the continuity of your workloads | `https://packt.link/835SR` |
| Security | Provided to protect against vulnerabilities and threats | `https://packt.link/Z96m8` |

Table 10.1 – Advisor recommendations for each category along with URL

*Figure 10.2* shows the `Azure Advisor | Overview` blade displaying these recommendations in a dashboard view:

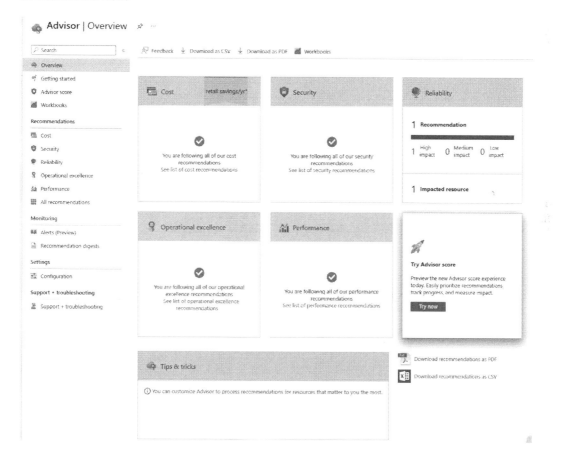

Figure 10.2 – Azure Advisor recommendations being displayed on the dashboard

You can also download the recommendations in PDF and Excel format. A `Tips & tricks` section at the bottom of the overview blade is provided; Microsoft will use this "information pane" to provide useful hints for you to get the most out of Azure Advisor.

Azure Advisor recommendations are based on the approach of notifying users of aspects that are "not implemented" rather than things that "are implemented;" for example, Azure Advisor will generate the following list:

- VMs that are not protected by a network security group

- VMs that do not have backup enabled, updates applied, a premium SSD when capable, and so on

- Storage accounts that do not have soft delete enabled, and so on

You can click on each recommendation category to get more information on the recommendations and the actions that can be taken.

Once security recommendations are implemented, you will see the organization's Secure Score increase. However, there is no requirement for any recommendations to be implemented to be supported by Microsoft. You can decide whether to implement these recommendations or not; they can be dismissed or postponed.

This section looked at Azure Advisor as a recommendation engine to aid in optimizing your Azure environments. The following section will explore Azure Monitor, which can help you gain visibility and insights into all the resources created in your Azure environments.

## Azure Monitor

Azure Monitor is an included service that provides actionable insights into the health, availability, and performance of Azure and on-premises environments by collecting and analyzing **logs** and **metrics** ("telemetry"). It allows you to find and fix problems faster, optimize your workload's performance, and then provide actions to remediate and alert; it provides all these insights from within the portal.

Azure Monitor collects resources and platform data from the following data sources:

- PaaS resources such as applications and databases

- IaaS resources, including VMs, containers, virtual desktops, databases, and storage

- On-premises resources via Azure Monitor, agent-based, or Syslog-based for appliances

With Azure Monitor, you can create alerts to notify individuals, such as an administrator or resource owner, when certain conditions are triggered. This could be when a resource exceeds a set threshold, when a resource is stopped (such as a VM), or when a resource is deleted (such as a storage account). There are cost implications with using Azure Monitor, especially Log Analytics, depending on the data stream and retention.

*Figure 10.3* visualizes the Azure Monitor service and its three core elements—that is, data sources, data stores, and data functions:

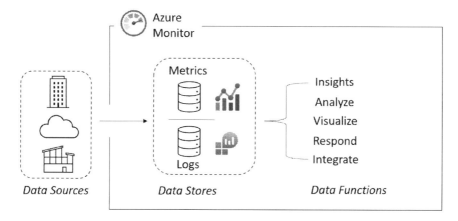

Figure 10.3 – Azure Monitor components architecture

The Azure Monitor service uses two fundamental data types: logs and metrics data. The monitoring **Data Sources** "populate" these two data stores. The **Data Functions** then "consume" these **Data Stores**. The data stores support near-real-time events.

The differences between logs and metrics are as follows:

- **Logs**: These record the activities of a data source representing some "action taken against the resources." This could include the following:

  - Capturing a login

  - A create/delete/update action

  - Listing storage account keys

  - Whether a policy was run

  - Whether an automation job started

This data is presented in column format and utilizes Log Analytics (*Figure 10.4*):

Figure 10.4 – Azure Monitor log analytics showing ingested log data

- **Metrics**: These record the "performance and consumption" of a data source and represent the meters and counters being triggered. Metrics can capture the following:

  - Utilization of CPU

  - Memory

  - Network bandwidth

  - Disk throughput

  The data is presented in chart format and using service metrics (*Figure 10.5*):

Figure 10.5 – Azure Monitor service metrics showing ingested metrics data

Application Insights is a feature of Azure Monitor for monitoring your applications. It can be used for monitoring and health diagnostics for applications whether they are located in Azure, another cloud provider platform, or on-premises.

Applications can be monitored by installing a **Software Development Kit** (**SDK**) or the "Application Insights agent" that supports .NET, Node.js, Python, and Java.

The following are the different types of information that can be collected once Application Insights is set up with your application:

- CPU, memory, and network usage through Windows and Linux machines' performance counters

- Counts for sessions and users

- Browser load performance and page views

- Response times, failure rates, response rates, request rates, and dependency rates

- Web pages from AJAX

In addition, during low-activity periods, it provides periodic synthetic application request configuration. *Figure 10.6* shows the Application Insights dashboard:

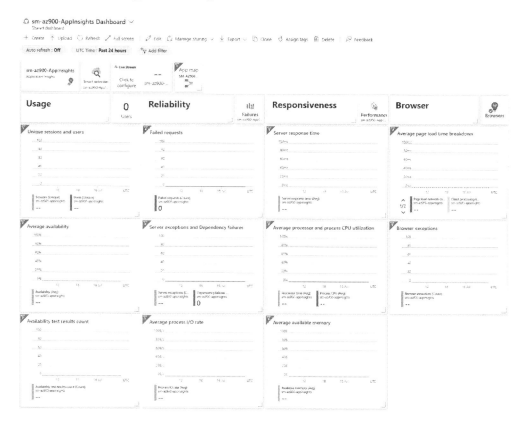

Figure 10.6 – Application Insights dashboard showing application performance and health at a glance

You looked at Azure Monitor in this section and learned about the three core elements of the service – data sources, data stores, and data functions – and the fundamental data types – logs and metrics. You then looked at Application Insights for monitoring applications. Azure Monitor is better when used with Azure Service Health. So, the next section will cover how to provide a personalized view of health with actionable insights for all your Azure resources, in addition to the differences between the personalized view and the Azure status page.

# Azure Service Health

Azure Service Health is an included, no-cost service that provides a personalized view of the health of all your Azure resources. It provides guidance and notifications, such as planned maintenance and other advisories, on the resource health that are specific to you.

These actionable insights are provided directly within the portal as a subset of the Azure Monitor service. These insights allow you to be alerted to notifications or a health status change so that you can evaluate the situation and take any actions you deem necessary. In addition, you can download reports and **Root Cause Analyses (RCAs)**.

The difference between **Azure Service Health** and the **Azure status** page is that the status page is a public-facing website that requires "no login." It has a global view of all the services across all regions and is useful to get a quicker and bigger picture of incidents that have a widespread impact.

> **Note**
>
> You can access the Azure status page at `https://packt.link/4af6w`.

*Figure 10.7* shows the **Azure status** page, which links **Azure Service Health** to display issues specific to your resources that may be impacted.

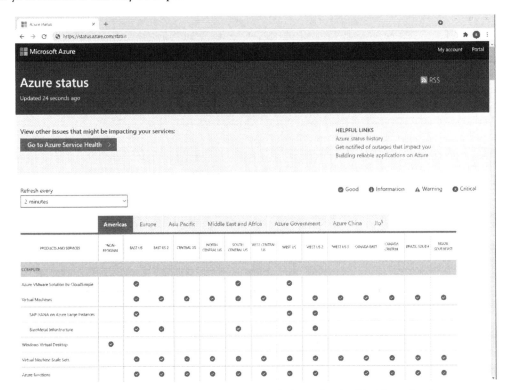

Figure 10.7 – Linking the Azure status page with Azure Service Health to view issues

Upon clicking **Go to Azure Service Health**, you will be redirected to sign in to the Azure portal.

In this section, you looked at Azure Service Health, which offers a customized view of the well-being of your Azure resources by providing a health status change so that you can evaluate the situation and take any actions you deem necessary. This section was completed with a look at the individual Azure management tools that can be utilized.

This concludes the learning content for this chapter.

## Summary

This chapter included complete coverage of the AZ-900 Azure Fundamentals exam skills area: **Describe monitoring tools in Azure**.

In this chapter, you learned how to describe the purpose of Azure Advisor, Azure Service Health, and Azure Monitor, including Log Analytics, Azure Monitor alerts, and Application Insights.

Further knowledge beyond the required exam content was provided to prepare for a real-world, day-to-day Azure-focused role.

In the next chapter, the *Appendix, Assessing AZ-900 Exam Skills*, you will find an overview of the "skills measured" by the certification and potential topics the exam may cover.

## Exam Readiness Drill – Chapter Review Questions

Apart from a solid understanding of key concepts, being able to think quickly under time pressure is a skill that will help you ace your certification exam. That is why working on these skills early on in your learning journey is key.

Chapter review questions are designed to improve your test-taking skills progressively with each chapter you learn and review your understanding of key concepts in the chapter at the same time. You'll find these at the end of each chapter.

> **How To Access These Resources**
>
> To learn how to access these resources, head over to the chapter titled *Chapter 11, Accessing the Online Practice Resources*.

To open the Chapter Review Questions for this chapter, perform the following steps:

1.  Click the link – `https://packt.link/AZ900E2_CH10`.

    Alternatively, you can scan the following **QR code** (*Figure 10.8*):

Figure 10.8 – QR code that opens Chapter Review Questions for logged-in users

2.  Once you log in, you'll see a page similar to the one shown in *Figure 10.9*:

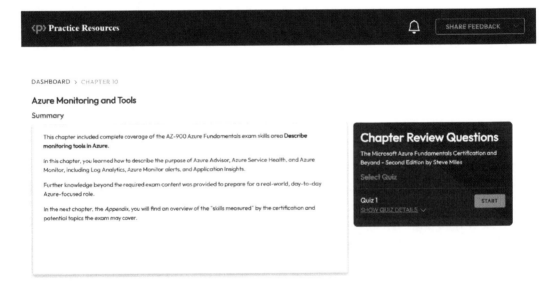

Figure 10.9 – Chapter Review Questions for Chapter 10

3.  Once ready, start the following practice drills, re-attempting the quiz multiple times.

## Exam Readiness Drill

For the first three attempts, don't worry about the time limit.

### *ATTEMPT 1*

The first time, aim for at least **40%**. Look at the answers you got wrong and read the relevant sections in the chapter again to fix your learning gaps.

### *ATTEMPT 2*

The second time, aim for at least **60%**. Look at the answers you got wrong and read the relevant sections in the chapter again to fix any remaining learning gaps.

### *ATTEMPT 3*

The third time, aim for at least **75%**. Once you score 75% or more, you start working on your timing.

> Tip
>
> You may take more than **three** attempts to reach 75%. That's okay. Just review the relevant sections in the chapter till you get there.

# Working On Timing

**Target**: Your aim is to keep the score the same while trying to answer these questions as quickly as possible. Here's an example of how your next attempts should look like:

| Attempt | Score | Time Taken |
|---|---|---|
| Attempt 5 | 77% | 21 mins 30 seconds |
| Attempt 6 | 78% | 18 mins 34 seconds |
| Attempt 7 | 76% | 14 mins 44 seconds |

Table 10.2 – Sample timing practice drills on the online platform

> Note
>
> The time limits shown in the above table are just examples. Set your own time limits with each attempt based on the time limit of the quiz on the website.

With each new attempt, your score should stay above **75%** while your "time taken" to complete should "decrease". Repeat as many attempts as you want till you feel confident dealing with the time pressure.

# Additional Information and Study References

This section provides links to additional exam information and study references.

- **Microsoft Learn certification further information**:

  - AZ-900 - Microsoft Azure Fundamentals exam guide: `https://packt.link/ya9p0`

  - AZ-900 - Microsoft Azure Fundamentals study guide: `https://packt.link/SGRsg`

- **Microsoft Learn training further information**:

  - AZ-900 - Microsoft Azure Fundamentals course: `https://packt.link/DCNfg`

# 11
# Accessing the Online Practice Resources

Your copy of *Microsoft Azure Fundamentals Certification and Beyond, Second Edition* comes with free online practice resources. Use these to hone your exam readiness even further by attempting practice questions on the companion website. The website is user-friendly and can be accessed from mobile, desktop, and tablet devices. It also includes interactive timers for an exam-like experience.

## How to Access These Resources

Here's how you can start accessing these resources depending on your source of purchase.

## Purchased from Packt Store (packtpub.com)

If you've bought the book from the Packt store (`packtpub.com`) eBook or Print, head to `https://packt.link/az900practice`. There, log in using the same Packt account you created or used to purchase the book.

## Packt+ Subscription

If you're a *Packt+ subscriber*, you can head over to the same link (`https://packt.link/az900practice`), log in with your `Packt ID`, and start using the resources. You will have access to them as long as your subscription is active.

If you face any issues accessing your free resources, contact us at `customercare@packt.com`.

## Purchased from Amazon and Other Sources

If you've purchased from sources other than the ones mentioned above (like *Amazon*), you'll need to unlock the resources first by entering your unique sign-up code provided in this section. **Unlocking takes less than 10 minutes, can be done from any device, and needs to be done only once**. Follow these five easy steps to complete the process:

### *STEP 1*

Open the link `https://packt.link/az900unlock` OR scan the following **QR code** (*Figure 11.1*):

Figure 11.1 – QR code for the page that lets you unlock this book's free online content.

Either of those links will lead to the following page as shown in *Figure 11.2*:

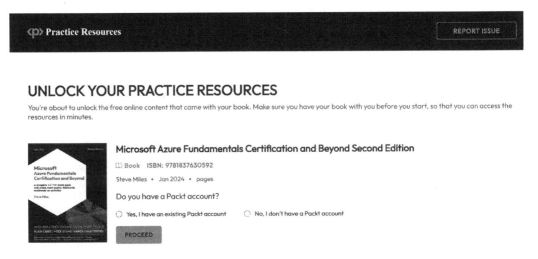

Figure 11.2 – Unlock page for the online practice resources

## STEP 2

If you already have a Packt account, select the option `Yes, I have an existing Packt account`. If not, select the option `No, I don't have a Packt account`.

If you don't have a Packt account, you'll be prompted to create a new account on the next page. It's free and only takes a minute to create.

Click `Proceed` after selecting one of those options.

## STEP 3

After you've created your account or logged in to an existing one, you'll be directed to the following page as shown in *Figure 11.3*:

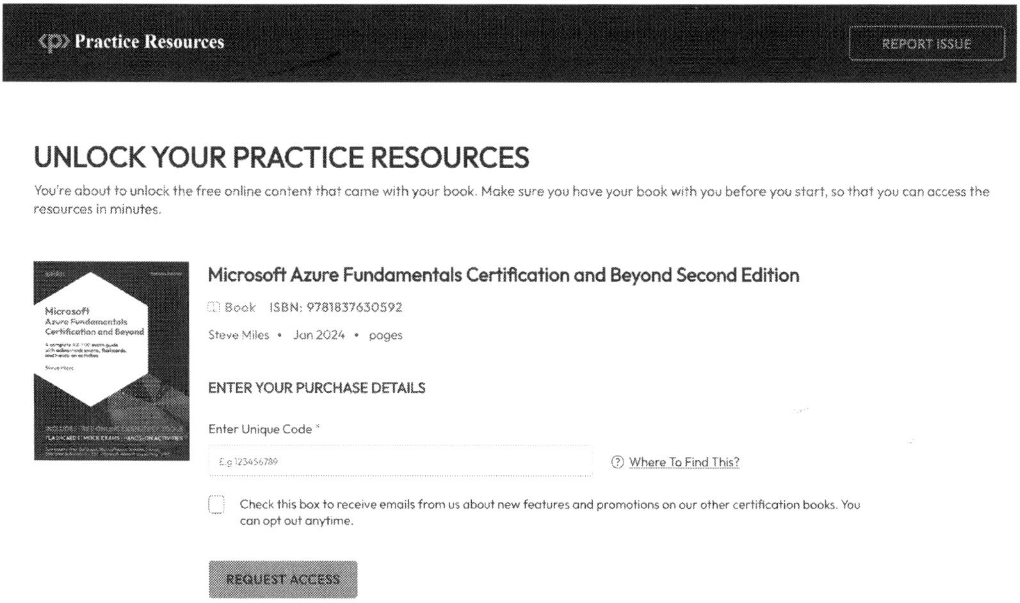

Figure 11.3 – Enter your unique sign-up code to unlock the resources

> **Troubleshooting Tip**
>
> After creating an account, if your connection drops off or you accidentally close the page, you can reopen the page shown in *Figure 11.2* and select `Yes, I have an existing account`. Then, sign in with the account you had created before you closed the page. You'll be redirected to the screen shown in *Figure 11.3*.

## *STEP 4*

Enter the following unique code:

HMB9268

> **Note**
> You may choose to opt into emails regarding new feature updates. We don't spam, and it's easy to opt out at any time.

Click Request Access.

## *STEP 5*

If the code you entered is correct, you'll see a button that says, OPEN PRACTICE RESOURCES, as shown in *Figure 11.4*:

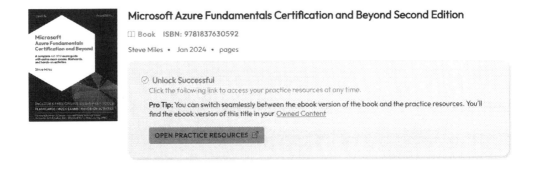

Figure 11.4 – Page that shows up after a successful unlock

Click the OPEN PRACTICE RESOURCES link to start using your free online content. You'll be redirected to the Dashboard shown in *Figure 11.5*:

Figure 11.5 – Dashboard page for AZ-900 practice resources

> **Bookmark this link**
>
> Now that you've unlocked the resources, you can come back to them anytime by visiting https://packt.link/az900practice or scanning the following QR code provided in *Figure 11.6*:

Figure 11.6 – QR code to bookmark practice resources website

## Troubleshooting Tips

If you're facing issues unlocking, here are three things you can do:

- Double-check your unique code. All unique codes in our books are case-sensitive and your code needs to match exactly as it is shown in *STEP 4*.

- If that doesn't work, use the `Report Issue` button located at the top-right corner of the page.

- If you're not able to open the unlock page at all, write to `customercare@packt.com` and mention the name of the book.

## Practice Resources – A Quick Tour

This book will equip you with all the knowledge necessary to clear the exam. As important as learning the key concepts is, your chances of passing the exam are much higher if you apply and practice what you learn in the book. This is where the online practice resources come in. With interactive mock exams, flashcards, hands-on activities, and exam tips, you can practice everything you learned in the book on the go. Here's a quick walkthrough of what you get.

### A Clean, Simple Cert Practice Experience

You get a clean, simple user interface that works on all modern devices, including your phone and tablet. All the features work on all devices, provided you have a working internet connection. From the Dashboard (*Figure 11.7*), you can access all the practice resources that come with this book with just a click. If you want to jump back to the book, you can do that from *Figure 11.7* as well:

Figure 11.7 – Dashboard interface on a desktop device

## Practice Questions

The **Quiz Interface** (*Figure 11.8*) is designed to help you focus on the question without any clutter.

You can navigate between multiple questions quickly and skip a question if you don't know the answer. The interface also includes a live timer that auto-submits your quiz if you run out of time.

Click End Quiz if you want to jump straight to the results page to reveal all the solutions.

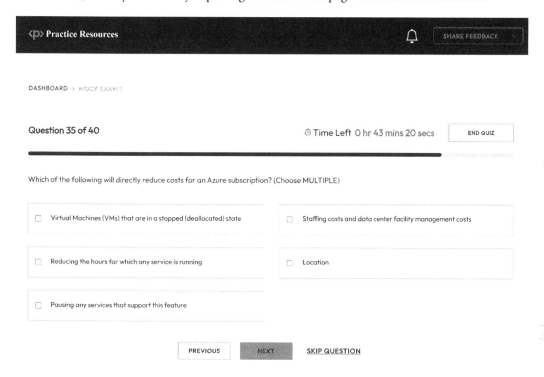

Figure 11.8 – Practice Questions Interface on a desktop device

Be it a long train ride to work with just your phone or a lazy Sunday afternoon on the couch with your tablet, the quiz interface works just as well on all your devices as long as they're connected to the internet.

*Figure 11.9* shows a screenshot of how the interface looks on mobile devices:

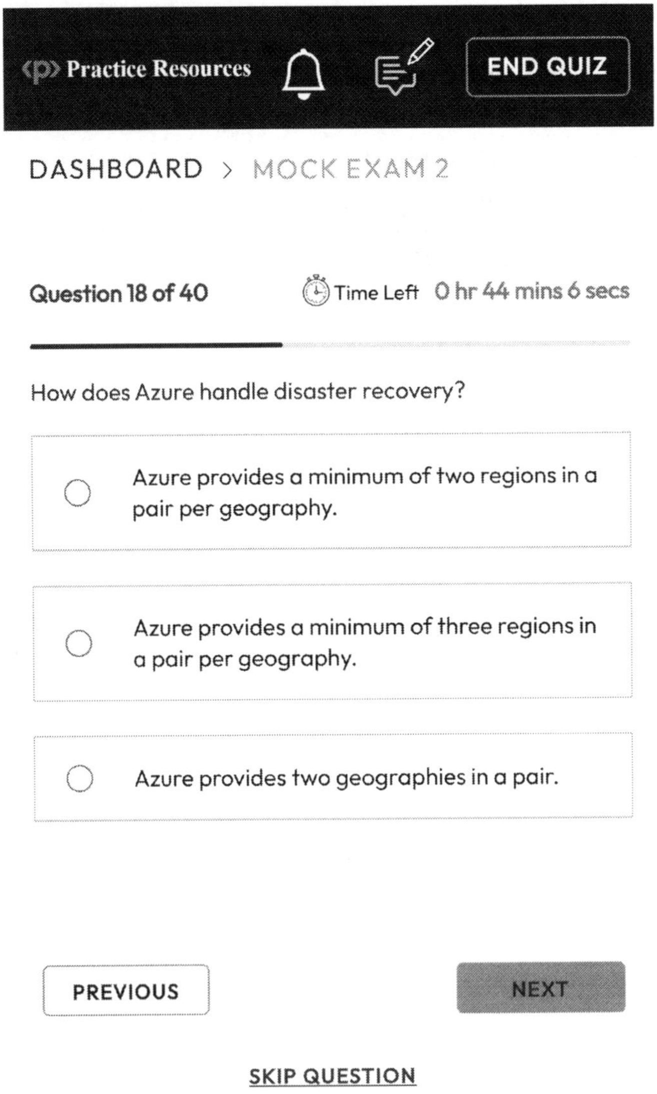

Figure 11.9 – Quiz interface on a mobile device

## Flashcards

**Flashcards** are designed to help you memorize key concepts. Here's how to make the most of them:

- We've organized all the flashcards into stacks. Think of these like an actual stack of cards in your hand.

- You start with a full stack of cards.

- When you open a card, take a few minutes to recall the answer.

- Click anywhere on the card to reveal the answer (*Figure 11.10*).

- Flip the card back and forth multiple times and memorize the card completely.

- Once you feel you've memorized it, click the `Mark as memorized` button on the top-right corner of the card. Move on to the next card by clicking Next.

- Repeat this process as you move to other cards in the stack.

You may not be able to memorize all the cards in one go. That's why, when you open the stack the next time, you'll only see the cards you're yet to memorize.

Your goal is to get to an empty stack, having memorized each flashcards in that stack.

Figure 11.10 – Flashcards interface

## Exam Tips

**Exam Tips** (see *Figure 11.11*) are designed to help you get exam-ready. From the start of your preparation journey to your exam day, these tips are organized such that you can review all of them in one go. If an exam tip comes in handy in your preparation, make sure to mark it as helpful so that other readers can benefit from your insights and experiences.

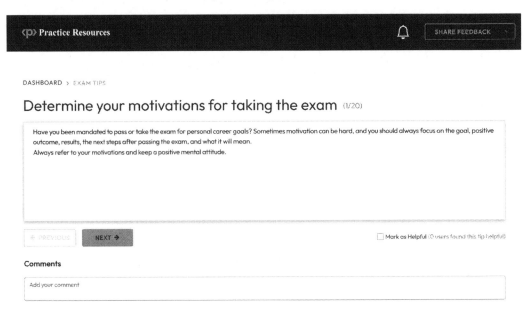

Figure 11.11 – Exam Tips Interface

# Chapter Review Questions

You'll find a link to **Chapter Review Questions** at the end of each chapter, just after the *Summary* section. These are designed to help you consolidate your learning from a chapter before moving on to the next one. Each chapter will have a benchmark score. Aim to match that score or beat it before picking up the next chapter. On the *Chapter Review Questions* page, you'll find a summary of the chapter for quick reference, as shown in *Figure 11.12*:

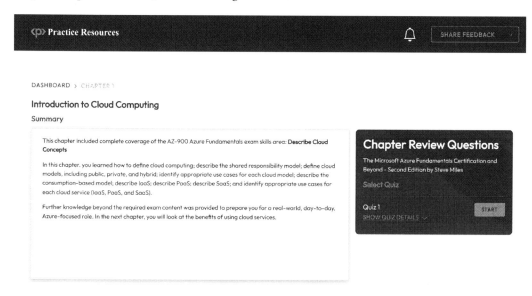

Figure 11.12 – Chapter Review Questions Page

## Hands-On Activities

To support your learning with some practical skills, you can try out the Hands-on Activities provided on the platform (*Figure 11.13*) shows a hands-on activity from the platform). Complete all tasks in each activity so that you can create and configure some of the resources and services covered in this book.

The activities should be followed in sequence so that you can get the most out of this book.

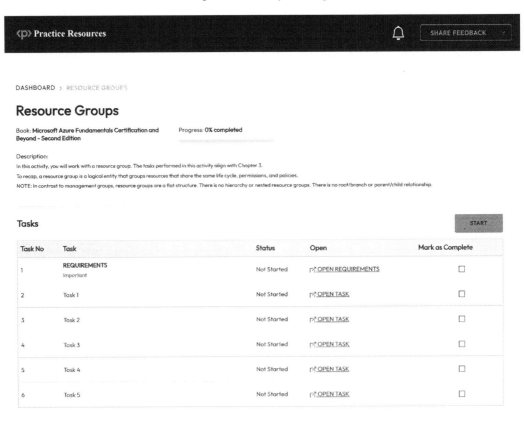

Figure 11.13 – Example of a hands-on activity

## Share Feedback

If you find any issues with the platform, the book, or any of the practice materials, you can click the Share Feedback button from any page and reach out to us. If you have any suggestions for improvement, you can share those as well.

## Back to the Book

To make switching between the book and practice resources easy, we've added a link that takes you back to the book (*Figure 11.14*). Click it to open your book in Packt's online reader. Your reading position is synced so you can jump right back to where you left off when you last opened the book.

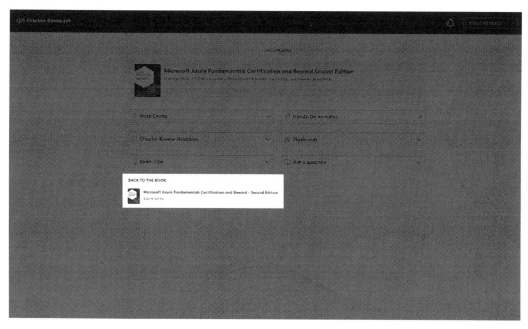

Figure 11.14 – Jump back to the book from the dashboard

> **Note**
> Certain elements of the website might change over time and thus may end up looking different from how they are represented in the screenshots of this book.

# Appendix
## Assessing AZ-900 Exam Skills

You have covered several topics throughout this book and learned the skills to prepare for the Microsoft certification exam AZ-900: **Microsoft Azure Fundamentals**.

This **Appendix** will provide an overview of the "skills measured" by the certification and the potential topics the exam may cover. This may help you track and record your progress as you become competent in each skill area.

## Skills Measured

The three skills' measured areas of coverage are listed as follows:

1. Describe cloud concepts (25–30%)
2. Describe Azure architecture and services (35–40%)
3. Describe Azure management and governance (30–35%)

Each area is broken down into individual skills measured topics, as shown in *Table App.1*:

| Module | Topics | Concepts | Concept Reference Number |
|---|---|---|---|
| 1. Describe cloud concepts (25–30%) | 1. Describe cloud computing | 1. Define cloud computing | 1.1.1 |
| | | 2. Describe the shared responsibility model | 1.1.2 |
| | | 3. Define cloud models, including public, private, and hybrid | 1.1.3 |
| | | 4. Identify appropriate use cases for each cloud model | 1.1.4 |
| | | 5. Describe the consumption-based model | 1.1.5 |
| | | 6. Compare cloud pricing models | 1.1.6 |
| | | 7. Describe serverless | 1.1.7 |
| | 2. Describe the benefits of using cloud services | 1. Describe the benefits of high availability and scalability in the cloud | 1.2.1 |
| | | 2. Describe the benefits of reliability and predictability in the cloud | 1.2.2 |
| | | 3. Describe the benefits of security and governance in the cloud | 1.2.3 |
| | | 4. Describe the benefits of manageability in the cloud | 1.2.4 |
| | 3. Describe cloud service types | 1. Describe Infrastructure-as-a-Service (IaaS) | 1.3.1 |
| | | 2. Describe Platform-as-a-Service (PaaS) | 1.3.2 |
| | | 3. Describe Software-as-a-Service (SaaS) | 1.3.3 |
| | | 4. Identify appropriate use cases for each cloud service (IaaS, PaaS, and SaaS) | 1.3.4 |

| Module | Topics | Concepts | Concept Reference Number |
|---|---|---|---|
| 2. Describe Azure architecture and services (35–40%) | 1. Describe the core architectural components of Azure | 1. Describe Azure regions, region pairs, and sovereign regions | 2.1.1 |
| | | 2. Describe availability zones | 2.1.2 |
| | | 3. Describe Azure data centers | 2.1.3 |
| | | 4. Describe Azure resources and resource groups | 2.1.4 |
| | | 5. Describe subscriptions | 2.1.5 |
| | | 6. Describe management groups | 2.1.6 |
| | | 7. Describe the hierarchy of resource groups, subscriptions, and management groups | 2.1.7 |
| | 2. Describe Azure compute and networking services | 1. Compare compute types, including containers, virtual machines, and functions | 2.2.1 |
| | | 2. Describe virtual machine options, including Azure Virtual Machines (VMs), Azure Virtual Machine Scale Sets, availability sets, and Azure Virtual Desktop | 2.2.2 |
| | | 3. Describe the resources required for virtual machines | 2.2.3 |
| | | 4. Describe application hosting options, including web apps, containers, and virtual machines | 2.2.4 |
| | | 5. Describe virtual networking, including the purpose of Azure virtual networks, Azure virtual subnets, peering, Azure DNS, Azure VPN Gateway, and ExpressRoute | 2.2.5 |
| | | 6. Define public and private endpoints | 2.2.6 |
| | 3. Describe Azure storage services | 1. Compare Azure storage services | 2.3.1 |
| | | 2. Describe storage tiers | 2.3.2 |
| | | 3. Describe redundancy options | 2.3.3 |
| | | 4. Describe storage account options and storage types | 2.3.4 |
| | | 5. Identify options for moving files, including AzCopy, Azure Storage Explorer, and Azure File Sync | 2.3.5 |
| | | 6. Describe migration options, including Azure Migrate and Azure Data Box | 2.3.6 |
| | 4. Describe Azure identity, access, and security | 1. Describe directory services in Azure, including Azure Active Directory (Azure AD), part of Microsoft Entra, and Azure Active Directory Domain Services (Azure AD DS) | 2.4.1 |
| | | 2. Describe authentication methods in Azure, including Single Sign-On (SSO), Multi-Factor Authentication (MFA), and passwordless | 2.4.2 |
| | | 3. Describe external identities in Azure, including Business-to-Business (B2B) and Business-to-Customer (B2C) | 2.4.3 |
| | | 4. Describe Conditional Access in Azure AD | 2.4.4 |
| | | 5. Describe Azure Role-Based Access Control (RBAC) | 2.4.5 |
| | | 6. Describe the concept of Zero Trust | 2.4.6 |
| | | 7. Describe the purpose of the Defense-in-Depth (DiD) model | 2.4.7 |
| | | 8. Describe the purpose of Microsoft Defender for Cloud | 2.4.8 |

| Module | Topics | Concepts | Concept Reference Number |
|---|---|---|---|
| 3. Describe Azure management and governance (30–35%) | 1. Describe cost management in Azure | 1. Describe factors that can affect costs in Azure | 3.1.1 |
| | | 2. Compare the pricing calculator and the Total Cost of Ownership (TCO) Calculator | 3.1.2 |
| | | 3. Describe cost management capabilities in Azure | 3.1.3 |
| | | 4. Describe the purpose of tags | 3.1.4 |
| | 2. Describe features and tools in Azure for governance and compliance | 1. Describe the purpose of Microsoft Purview in Azure | 3.2.1 |
| | | 2. Describe the purpose of Azure Policy | 3.2.2 |
| | | 3. Describe the purpose of resource locks | 3.2.3 |
| | 3. Describe features and tools for managing and deploying Azure resources | 1. Describe the Azure portal | 3.3.1 |
| | | 2. Describe Azure Cloud Shell, including the Azure Command-Line Interface (CLI) and Azure PowerShell | 3.3.2 |
| | | 3. Describe the purpose of Azure Arc | 3.3.3 |
| | | 4. Describe Infrastructure as Code (IaC) | 3.3.4 |
| | | 5. Describe Azure Resource Manager (ARM) and ARM templates | 3.3.5 |
| | 4. Describe monitoring tools in Azure | 1. Describe the purpose of Azure Advisor | 3.4.1 |
| | | 2. Describe Azure Service Health | 3.4.2 |
| | | 3. Describe Azure Monitor, including Log Analytics, Azure Monitor alerts, and Application Insights | 3.4.3 |

Table App.1 – AZ-900 modules, topics, and their concepts

You can find information about these "skills measured" areas in Microsoft's online study guide for AZ-900. This official study guide also includes any information regarding updates or changes to the exam.

> **Note**
>
> You can find Microsoft's online study guide at `https://packt.link/oghxc`.

You are now closer than ever to becoming **Microsoft Certified for Azure Fundamentals and Beyond**. Keep up the good spirit, continue with passion, and carry on with the next step toward honing your skills and achieving your career goals.

# Index

## A

# T

www.packtpub.com

Subscribe to our online digital library for full access to over 7,000 books and videos, as well as industry leading tools to help you plan your personal development and advance your career. For more information, please visit our website.

## Why subscribe?

- Spend less time learning and more time coding with practical eBooks and Videos from over 4,000 industry professionals

- Improve your learning with Skill Plans built especially for you

- Get a free eBook or video every month

- Fully searchable for easy access to vital information

- Copy and paste, print, and bookmark content

At www.packtpub.com, you can also read a collection of free technical articles, sign up for a range of free newsletters, and receive exclusive discounts and offers on Packt books and eBooks.

# Other Books You May Enjoy

If you enjoyed this book, you may be interested in these other books by Packt:

**Microsoft 365 Certified Fundamentals MS-900 Exam Guide, Third Edition**

Aaron Guilmette, Yura Lee, and Marcos Zanre

ISBN: 978-1-83763-679-2

- Gain insight into the exam objectives and knowledge needed to take the MS-900 exam
- Discover and implement best practices for licensing options available in Microsoft 365
- Understand the different Microsoft 365 Defender services
- Prepare to address the most common types of threats against an environment
- Identify and unblock the most common cloud adoption challenges
- Articulate key productivity, collaboration, security, and compliance selling points of M365
- Explore licensing and payment models available for M365

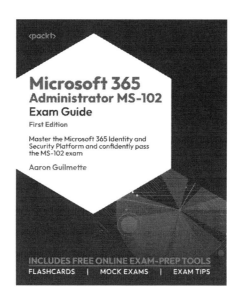

**Microsoft 365 Administrator MS-102 Exam Guide**

Aaron Guilmette

ISBN: 978-1-83508-396-3

- Implement and manage Microsoft 365 tenants

- Administer users, groups, and contacts in Entra ID

- Configure and manage roles across Microsoft 365 services

- Troubleshoot identity synchronization issues

- Deploy modern authentication methods to enhance security

- Analyze and respond to security incidents using Microsoft 365 Defender

- Implement retention policies and sensitivity labels

- Establish data loss prevention for enhanced information protection

## Share Your Thoughts

Now you've finished *Microsoft Azure Fundamentals Certification and Beyond, Second Edition*, we'd love to hear your thoughts! Scan the QR code below to go straight to the Amazon review page for this book and share your feedback or leave a review on the site that you purchased it from.

https://packt.link/r/1837630593

Your review is important to us and the tech community and will help us make sure we're delivering excellent quality content.

# Download a Free PDF Copy of This Book

Thanks for purchasing this book!

Do you like to read on the go but are unable to carry your print books everywhere?

Is your eBook purchase not compatible with the device of your choice?

Don't worry, now with every Packt book you get a DRM-free PDF version of that book at no cost.

Read anywhere, any place, on any device. Search, copy, and paste code from your favorite technical books directly into your application.

The perks don't stop there, you can get exclusive access to discounts, newsletters, and great free content in your inbox daily.

Follow these simple steps to get the benefits:

1. Scan the QR code or visit the link below:

https://packt.link/free-ebook/9781837630592

2. Submit your proof of purchase.

3. That's it! We'll send your free PDF and other benefits to your email directly.

Printed in Great Britain
by Amazon

46973055R00159